SOVIET ANIMATION and the Thaw of the 1960s

Not Only for Children

To my girls Nicole and Natalie

Front cover: Stills from *There Once Lived Koziavin*; *Film, Film, Film*; *The Glass Harmonica*; *Great Troubles*, *The Man in the Frame*, and *Story of a Crime*.

SOVIET ANIMATION and the Thaw of the 1960s

Not Only for Children

Laura Pontieri

SOVIET ANIMATION and the Thaw of the 1960s

British Library Cataloguing in Publication Data

SOVIET ANIMATION and the Thaw of the 1960s:
Not Only for Children

A catalogue entry for this book is available from the British Library

ISBN: 9780 86196 705 6 (Paperback)

Published by
John Libbey Publishing Ltd, 205 Crescent Road, New Barnet, Herts EN4 8SB, United Kingdom   e-mail: libbeyj@truemail.co.th; web site: www.johnlibbey.com

Distributed Worldwide by
Indiana University Press, Herman B Wells Library—350, 1320 E. 10th St., Bloomington, IN 47405, USA. www.iupress.indiana.edu

Reprinted 2021

© 2012 Copyright John Libbey Publishing Ltd. All rights reserved.
Unauthorized duplication contravenes applicable laws.

Printed and bound in the USA.

Contents

	Acknowledgements	vii
	Note on Transliteration and Translations	viii
	Introduction	**1**
Chapter 1	**From Propaganda to Children's Films: The Earliest Beginnings and the Stalin Era of Soviet Animation**	**5**
	Insects in motion: the first Russian animated films	6
	Moving caricatures and propaganda posters: the beginning of Soviet drawn animation	6
	Enlightening the masses: educational and scientific films	14
	Entertaining and educating: the first animated films for children	15
	Waiting for cel animation: drawings and flat marionettes	18
	Puppet and stop-motion animation	19
	The Leningrad experience: book illustrations meet avant-garde works in Mikhail Tsekhanovskii's films	22
	The advent of sound: Tsekhanovskii's experiments	29
	The 1930s: the last satirical animated films	36
	A change of direction: animation for children only, the Disney influence	38
	The animation of World War II and the restrained reawakening of political films	42
	Animation after World War II: fables and folk art	44
Chapter 2	**Russian Animation of the Thaw in its Socio-Political and Cultural Context**	**51**
	Khrushchev's Thaw: innovations and restrictions	51
	Animation shifts in new directions: from the Stalin Era to the Thaw	55
	Space flights, sport, and the "Scientific-Technological Revolution"	57
	Propaganda and social criticism: new agitational films on the problem of alcoholism	61
	Satire in Soviet animation	65
	Popular culture and western influence	69
	From thematic to stylistic changes	75
	Foreign influence on stylistic choices	78
	General characteristics of the new stylistic tendencies	81

Chapter 3	**Case Studies: Early 1960s**	83
	Introduction	83
	Great Troubles (*Bol'shie nepriiatnosti*, Valentina and Zinaida Brumberg, 1961)	85
	Narration and self-reflexivity	86
	Satire of contemporary society: *stiliagi*, parasitism, and corruption	87
	Style and language: children's language interprets the Soviet reality	89
	Spatial choices: unstable ground	96
	Story of a Crime (*Istoriia odnogo prestupleniia*, Fedor Khitruk, 1962)	99
	Violation of norms: crime and *Kul'turnost'*	99
	New themes bring a new graphic style	105
	The Soviet Union of the 1960s appears on the screen: references and concretizations	108
	Lack of boundaries in the relationship between private and public: a semiotic reading	112
	Play with different artistic languages results in a comic effect	115
Chapter 4	**Russian Animation in the Second Half of the 1960s: Between the Khrushchev Thaw and the Brezhnev Stagnation**	121
	Context	121
	Attacks on the bureaucrat: *The Man in the Frame* (*Chelovek v ramke*, Fedor Khitruk, 1966)	124
	Bureaucratic world once more under attack: *There Once Lived Koziavin* (*Zhil-byl Koziavin*, Andrei Khrzhanovskii, 1966)	139
	Animation as a means for political criticism: *The Glass Harmonica* (*Stekliannaia garmonika*, Andrei Khrzhanovskii, 1968)	147
Chapter 5	**Conclusion: The Beginning of New Tendencies**	169
	Bibliography	**183**
	Archival material	183
	Soviet animation bibliography and works cited	184
	Suggested readings on animation art and on critical and historical works	211
	Filmography	**217**
	Soviet animated films 1910–1979	217
	Films and TV programs on Soviet animation	240
	World animated films cited	240
	Index	**241**

Acknowledgements

My first acknowledgement must go to Sveta Kim of the Muzei Kino Animation Fund in Moscow for involving me in the world of Russian animation from the very first day of my research in Russia in 2003. I owe a special debt of gratitude to Georgii Borodin, who constantly shared with me his immeasurable knowledge of Soviet animation and greatly helped me in gathering information and material in Moscow and from Moscow.

I would like to acknowledge Elena Chugunova at the RGALI archive (Russian State Archive of Literature and Art) and Valerii Bosenko at the Gosfil'mofond for easing my days of research; and Anatolii Volkov and Natalia Lukinykh for supplying films and texts, and for allowing me to attend their classes at VGIK (Russian State Institute of Cinematography).

I am also grateful to Iurii Norshtein, Fedor Khitruk, Sergei Alimov, and Andrei Khrzhanovskii for patiently answering all my questions and giving me access to their works.

And thanks to the directors Stanislav Sokolov, Mariia Muat, Ivan Maksimov, Mikhail Aldashin, Mikhail Tumelia, Sergei Seregin, Evgenii Sivokon', and the late Aleksandr Tatarskii for contributing to my research with their expertise in animation.

In addition, I would like to express my gratitude to Giannalberto Bendazzi and Massimo Maisctti, director of the ISCA (Institute for the Study and Diffusion of Animated Cinema), for providing material on Russian animation and for their constant support.

On this side of the world, I would like to thank Katerina Clark for her belief in this project and her continuous assistance. Thanks to John MacKay for having infected me with his enthusiasm for Soviet cinema and film theory in general, and to Charles Musser and Dudley Andrew for introducing me to the extended cinema world. I would also like to acknowledge Yale University whose research grants enabled me to visit Russian archives and conduct my initial research.

I am also grateful to Deborah Perkins-Leitman for her tireless help with this text, and to John Libbey for pursuing this project and approving a rich collection of illustrations.

On a personal note, thanks to my father for his constant encouragement, and to my mother for her loving understanding, I wish she could see the end of this project.

Thanks to my girls for their sweet patience, this book is dedicated to them. Last but not least I want to thank my husband, Daniel Hlavacek, who supported me at every moment, patiently accepting all my long research trips to Moscow, and being next to me whenever I needed it most.

Note on Transliteration

In this book, names from the Russian have been transliterated using the Library of Congress System. When names of well-known figures appear in the text, they are rendered in a standard anglicized spelling (for example Mayakovsky, Tschaikovsky, Meyerhold, Maxim Gorky, Joseph Brodsky, Sergei Eisenstein, El Lissitzky, Marc Chagall and Tsar Nicholas II), but all names in the Bibliography appear as they are cited in the source in question, using Library of Congress transliteration where applicable.

Note on Translations

Unless otherwise noted, all translations are my own.

Introduction

Animation is an independent and vital branch of film art with its own peculiarities, codes, and conventions. It is worth studying as a form of art in itself, and as an original means for looking at cultural and social phenomena. This is even more appropriate in the case of Soviet animation in that films were inextricably linked to the all-embracing Soviet system.

Unlike American animation, the earliest Soviet films did not have an entertainment purpose, but were used as propaganda tools to promote the newborn Soviet society. Adopting the caricature and poster-like style in vogue in these years, or referring to contemporary avant-garde tendencies, these first films addressed a predominantly adult public. After the imposition of socialist realism between 1932 and 1934, animators were gradually forced to abandon all experimentation and to turn exclusively to young audiences. Only with the Khrushchev Thaw did animation seem to take a different path.

The Thaw's relatively liberal atmosphere, although intermittent and contradictory, allowed new themes to be discussed in the arts and favored a zealous search for creative stylistic choices. In this innovative climate, spectators underwent a change of expectations, while, in turn, animation was proposing a fresh reading of reality, questioning the conception and perception of animated films as solely children's entertainment. A group of animators began to reject the fantastic worlds of the mainstream films produced for young spectators during Stalin's time and called for topics drawn from contemporary life. Following the example of their predecessors in the 1920s, animators of the Thaw sought to give their first films a civic role, that is, to use them as a didactic tool in order to correct the societal ills that could finally be discussed in these years of relative *détente*. Animation of the early 1960s performed this task with wit and humor, rather than by being dogmatic, and attacked Soviet weaknesses through caricature and satire. The first films for an adult audience tended to air the same concerns as those expressed by the authorities. Only gradually did directors push the limits of the permissible and start to attack the system more openly. Eventually, towards the end of the 1960s, animation developed a lyric genre, a pure manifestation of the artists' subjective vision.

The desire for innovation in animated films seems to have originally focused on thematic content, and only subsequently on stylistic choices. Initially, animators adopted a satirical mode, still using anthropomorphized characters in the traditional style. Later they would resist the officially accepted canon, which, paradoxically in this Cold War era, was greatly influenced by the American Disney style and method of production. Directors refused to adhere to a standardized manner of artistic expression; they searched for more personal forms and aimed to engage with topical issues in the most effective way. While seeking simplified forms and concise language, artists contemplated modern art and design now accessible in the Soviet Union, as well as the laconic language and minimalist style that characterized the fervid animation world of the mid-to-late 1950s.

The core of this book spans the years of Khrushchev's Thaw and a little beyond. The Thaw is usually seen as coinciding with the years of Khrushchev's rule, from 1953 to 1964, with peaks during the years 1953–54, 1956, and 1962. Yet my study interprets this chronology somewhat liberally. My interest lies in the particular wave of Soviet animation that began in the more liberal climate of Khrushchev's reforms, in the late 1950s, and that crested between 1962 and 1968, the latter being the year when the most subversive films started to be shelved.

First, this book outlines a brief panoramic view of the development of Soviet animation, from its origins in the 1920s up to the late 1950s, in order to provide the context within which the innovations of the 1960s took place. This introductory part is followed by a discussion of the Thaw era, in particular of the political circumstances, the cultural framework, and the complex interconnections between animation and the broader artistic system in these years. Throughout the book, detailed analyses of key films focus on formal choices used to convey direct or subtle meanings, on references and borrowings from traditional forms of art, and on influences from foreign styles. The films are also discussed in terms of the role they have played within the political sphere, the conditions that permitted such films to be made, and the audience's reception, whenever that information is available. Films of this peculiar time in Soviet history adhered strictly to specific socio-political phenomena, which determined the topics allowed or promulgated, the method of production, and the techniques used.

My research is based on a close inspection of numerous films that were made in these years, including several that are only available at the Gosfil'mofond archive in Moscow. Although the majority of works produced at Soiuzmul'tfil'm continued to be addressed to children, this study discusses mainly that type of animation directed at adults. The reason is twofold: first, films for adults gave animation an important new role in Soviet culture and society; second, the stylistic innovations that characterized films for adults would later be adopted by filmmakers for children's cartoons.

A large body of written archival material was also crucial to the writing of this book, as it offered insights into the atmosphere of the time. Of particular interest were the minutes of the artists' formal meetings at the Soiuzmul'tfil'm studio. These documents, preserved in the Soiuzmul'tfil'm files at the Russian State Archive of Literature and Art (RGALI), have proved invaluable in reconstructing Soviet animation of the Thaw, from the dynamics of interaction within the studio, to relationships between the animators and the political establishment.

My study concentrates on Soiuzmul'tfil'm, the most important, and for many years the only centralized animation studio in the Soviet Union. Animated films made in other republics were mainly influenced by what was being done in Moscow, but at the same time maintained some traits typical of their ethnic traditions. Thus, while I may refer to works made in other studios, I do not discuss them in detail, since to do so would require a separate study of their regional peculiarities.

SOVIET ANIMATION and the Thaw of the 1960s

This book attempts to make up for a dearth of studies on Soviet animation, especially in the English-speaking world. It does not claim to provide a comprehensive survey of Russian animation, but focuses on the 1960s, and in particular on animation tailored to adult audiences. By analyzing films and tendencies that developed in these years, this study aims to shed light on the important function of animation in a period that could be considered a high point not only in the history of Soviet animation, but also in the general history of that complex socio-cultural system that was the Soviet Union.

Chapter 1

From Propaganda to Children's Films: The Earliest Beginnings and the Stalinist Era of Soviet Animation

Insects in motion: the first Russian animated films

The very first animated films in Russia were the last vestiges of a pre-Revolutionary world, an isolated episode that began in 1910 and ended outside of the Soviet Union, when their director, Vladislav Starevich,[1] emigrated to France.[2] Initially, his peculiar characters – dead insects – were moved by wires,[3] but soon this gave way to plasticine models animated by stop-motion. This technique, which consists of taking a series of pictures of objects that are moved in small increments for each frame, was already used in trick film sequences, but it was rarely employed for an entire film. In Great Britain, Arthur Melbourne Cooper employed the stop-motion technique as early as 1899 to animate matches in a short advertisement film (*Matches: An Appeal*), and used it again with toys in *Dreams of Toyland* (1908);[4] while in America, the technique was adopted only a few years later, in the mid-1910s, by Willis O'Brien. But Starevich developed an expressive and sophisticated form of puppet animation independently. His films had mainly an entertainment purpose and were based on original stories, adaptations from literary works, and, most commonly, on fables. The films were quite successful among audiences that were not accustomed to seeing puppets move onscreen, least of all insects. They were also appreciated by Tsar Nicholas II himself, who awarded a

---

1 Vladislav Starevich (1882–1965) was born in Russia to a Polish family. His original Polish name was Władysław Starewicz. He is also known as Ladislav Starewich.

2 Recently discovered puppet animation films made by the famous dancer Aleksandr Shiryaev predates Starevich's works, but these films were not produced for the public. See Beumers et al. eds., *Aleksandr Shiryaev*.

3 See Starevich's first films: *Lucanus Cervus*, 1910; *The Beautiful Liukanida, or the Battle Between Stag Beetles and Long-horn Beetles* (*Prekrasnaia Liukanida, ili voina rogachei i usachei*, 1910).

4 Bendazzi, *Cartoons*, 40.

prize to *The Grasshopper and the Ant* (*Strekoza i muravei*, 1911).[5] Starevich produced most of his films independently – including the well-known *The Cameraman's Revenge* (*Mest' kinooperatora,* 1911) – but he was still able to maintain his connection with the Russian cinema world of the 1910s. In 1911 he joined one of the biggest Russian cinema companies of this period, the Khanzhonkov studio, and the following year he started to employ for the live-action sequences of his films a young actor who would soon become the best-known Soviet cinema star of the silent era, Ivan Mozzhukhin.[6] After the Revolution, Starevich left Russia and moved to Fontenay-sous-Bois, near Paris. Back home, the new, politically engaged Soviet directors began to criticize his work and dismiss him as a "children's entertainer without educational value".[7] A few years passed before other animated films were created in Soviet Russia, and still more years before three-dimensional animated films returned to the screen.

Moving caricatures and propaganda posters: the beginning of Soviet drawn animation

It was drawn animation that instead developed in the fledgling Soviet Union in the 1920s. The particular political and historical situation of Soviet Russia demanded a kind of animation that was mainly propagandistic, thus distinct from the generally entertaining cartoons that formed the mainstream of US animation. While American animation had its roots in comic strips and vaudeville acts, most of the early Soviet animated films came out of political manifestos and satirical vignettes; they were primarily caricatures and propaganda works addressed to an adult audience.

The Revolution brought with it a fervid impetus to any art accessible to the masses. Posters, caricatures, and animation were all able to convey in simple, linear traits and easily understandable conventions a message that could reach the largely uneducated common people. These popular forms of art were geared to serve the new Socialist order, promoting the construction of a new society, as well as clearly defining its enemies. The most famous posters of the period, the *Okna ROSTA* (The Russian Telegraph and Press Agency Windows), have many traits in common with the

5 Martin, *Ladislav Starewitch*, 15.

6 Mozzhukhin starred in *The Terrible Vengeance* (*Strashnaia mest'*, 1912; an adaptation from Gogol''s story), which has not been preserved, and *The Night Before Christmas* (*Noch' pered rozhdestvom*, 1913). Bendazzi, *Cartoons*, 36; Martin, *Ladislav Starewitch*, 15.

7 Bushkin, "Kadro-s"emka", 21.

first Soviet animated films. The *Okna ROSTA* team (some of the main artists being Vladimir Mayakovsky, Mikhail Cheremnykh, and Ivan Maliutin) was charged with translating agitational messages and daily news into eye-catching pictures and brief texts. Some of these pictures represented a specific situation; others formed a succession of framed images, giving the poster a narrative quality in a form similar to comic strips. In Russia, however, the same organization of text and images originates not so much in the comic strip, but in religious icons and in the traditional *lubok*, a popular form of art that presented information or stories through images and straightforward texts, often with wit and humor. A violation of the picture's temporal unity through the depiction of the heroes in several places characterized *lubok* works much in the way that in Russian religious icons, stages in a saint's life are represented in contiguous small frames.

The *Okna ROSTA* utilized similar formal principles with an intent that was neither religious nor entertaining, but strongly political. The spirit that permeated these posters, the linear traits of the drawings, much like caricatures, and the juxtaposition of pictures in frames in order to tell a contemporary story made these posters a prototype storyboard for the Soviet animated films of the 1920s. Soviet cartoons sought to give life to the static pictures of Revolutionary graphics and thus to increase the expressiveness and, consequently, the accessibility of their message. Animation was regarded as a step forward in the search for new means of propaganda, since it successfully combined the immediacy of caricatures and posters with the original Soviet idea of cinema as an educational tool for the illiterate.[8]

The animation of these years had a strong link not only with posters, but also with caricatures of the time, namely those by the famous Viktor Denisov (Deni), Dmitrii Moor, Boris Efimov, Mikhail Cheremnykh, and other masters of poster graphics, who often worked for *Okna ROSTA* as well as satirical journals such as *Bezbozhnik* (later called *Bezbozhnik u stanka*) and *Krokodil*. Not only did the films reflect the style and themes of the caricaturists, but some of their drawings were themselves animated in what went by the name of "animated caricature" (*ozhivshaia karikatura*), such as the film *Political Revues* (*Politicheskie obozreniia*, Fig. 1.1), in which

---

8 For a discussion of Soviet cinema of this time as a didactic tool for illiterate people, see Youngblood, *Movies for the Masses*, and *Soviet Cinema in the Silent Era, 1918–1935*; Lawton, *The Red Screen*; Kenez, *Cinema and Soviet Society*; Taylor and Christie, eds., *The Film Factory*; and Gosudarstvennoe izdatelstvo, *Kinematograf.*

Figure 1.1. *Animated caricatures. Still from* Political Revues.

Iurii Merkulov and Daniil Cherkes brought Deni's caricatures to the screen.

Animated caricatures were a Soviet version of the filming of "lightning sketches" (also called "chalk talks"), vaudeville acts in which the artist would draw quick caricatures while performing a monologue. According to the early animation historian Donald Crafton, American animation stems from this form of popular stage performance – the first attempts to put these vaudeville acts on screen date back to the earliest American films, specifically James Stuart Blackton's *The Enchanted Drawing* (1900), and later, in a pure frame by frame animation, *Humorous Phases of Funny Faces* (1906).[9] Despite early Soviet animation's similarity to the "lightning sketches" technique and graphic caricatures, the Russian version was never meant to be mere entertainment, but had a specific political, ideological, and social goal.[10]

This purpose is already clear in the very first examples of drawn animated sequences that appeared on the Soviet screen, that is, the brief animated passages that Dziga Vertov introduced in his newsreel series *Kino-Pravda (Film Truth*, issued by Goskino from 1922 to 1925). One of the earliest animated clips found in Soviet cinema is in fact a fragment that survived from a lost *Kino-Pravda* film called *Today (Segodnia,* 1923, Goskino [Kul'tkino]). This fragment, called *Live Map (Zhivaia karta),* depicts the international political situation of the time with the help of a map on

[9] Bendazzi, *Cartoons,* 8. For a comprehensive study of early animation, see Crafton, *Before Mickey;* and Crafton, *Emile Cohl, Caricature, and Film.*

[10] Among those films that were preserved, see Merkulov's *kinoplakaty* and political caricatures made in the 1920s (no precise date is known): *Our caricatures (Nashi karikatury), We Are With You, Cuba! (My s toboi, Kuba!), On the Material of Political Caricatures (Po materialam politicheskikh karikatur);* Merkulov's short made in 1927, *Our Answer to Chamberlain (Nash otvet Chamberlenu,* 1927); and Nikolai Khodataev's films *We'll Be Vigilant (Budem zorki,* 1927) and *The Menacing Vavila and Aunt Arina (Groznyi Vavila i tetka Arina,* 1928).

which countries' borders are animated. Segments of animated sequences appeared not only in *Kino-Pravda*, but also in Vertov's weekly newsreel series *Kinonedelia*; their themes ranged from depictions of army movements during World War I to animated leaflets promoting the fight against tuberculosis.

It was the same Vertov, in collaboration with the director Aleksandr Bushkin and animator Ivan Beliakov, who created the first Soviet animated movie, *Soviet Toys* (*Sovetskie igrushki*, Dz. Vertov, 1924, Goskino [Kul'tkino]), a propaganda film based on Deni's drawings published in *Pravda*. The film provided a harsh critique of bourgeois behavior, from excesses in food and alcohol consumption to womanizing; it also satirized the Church and capitalists' faith in redemption granted by corrupt priests. *Soviet Toys* hinted at specific contemporary matters, providing "solutions" to topical problems in a simple and straightforward way, such as the symbolic double figure of a worker-peasant, who fights a NEP (New Economic Policy) bourgeois and directs his money to the Bank of the People ("Narodnyi Bank"); and the film's final image: a pyramid of Bolsheviks, with Red Army soldiers at its base, the peasant and the worker climbing to the top, and all the representatives of the hated enemies hanging from it. It seems that the film was not widely publicized at the time; an article that appeared in the journal *Kinonedelia* in 1924 bemoaned the silence surrounding this film and the general lack of films depicting everyday Soviet life.[11] Other articles published in 1924 lamented the scarcity of animated films released, and stressed the need to take full advantage of this new media. *Soviet Toys* has the quintessential elements of the ideal Soviet animated film of the time; it features topical issues, caricature style, simple traits, communist indoctrination, and, at the end, self-advertising.

It was common practice for Soviet studios to advertise their own films. In the 1920s, most studios had a division dedicated to advertising and frequently used animation not only to promote their own live-action films, but also to advertise commercial products,[12] which constituted the lifeblood of the small private enterprises of the NEP era. The advertising business became an active branch in the cinema industry of the time; as Vertov comments in 1923, it was not only relevant but inevitable.

---

11 Gessen, "Sovetskii sharzh", 3.

12 *Animatsiia ot A do IA*, dir. M.P. Liakhovetskii and I.P. Margolina. RenTV, 1997.

> For five years there was no motion picture production in the Soviet Union. There's none now. There is no money for it. Film advertising is the gateway to work, to production, to prosperity. We must make this "compromise"; we have to.[13]

The quality of directness possessed by animation was indeed functional for both political films and commercial propaganda.

In the meantime, Vertov still considered political animated films to be of extreme importance in these Revolutionary years, and collaborated with Bushkin and Beliakov on other films, such as *Humorous Stories* (*Iumoreski*, 1924), a series of political cartoons concerning topical issues (only a few frames survived), and *Boris Savinkov: Story of a Disappointment* (*Boris Savinkov. Istoriia odnogo razocharovaniia*, 1924). But in reality it was Bushkin who had a bigger role than Vertov in early Soviet animation. Bushkin founded an animation studio at Goskino (Kul'tkino) in 1922,[14] and gave an account of his experiments in animation in a couple of publications: *Frame Shooting* (*Kadro-s"emka*, 1926), and a longer publication, *Trick and Animation* (*Triuk i mul'tiplikatsiia*, 1926), which explained the use and the goal of animation technology at that time. Bushkin's films exemplify the function of animation in these early years. They are all propaganda works that deal with political and social themes: the film *Who Dreams of What* (*Komu chto snitsia*, 1924) endorsed antireligious propaganda; *In the Snout of the Second International* (*V mordu Vtoromu Internatsionalu*, 1924, of which only a fragment survives) presented in a schematic way international relations before World War I, and attacked the socialist grouping of the Second International, who betrayed the socialist cause by joining their respective ruling classes at the beginning of World War I; *What the 13th Party Congress Said About Cooperatives* (*Chto skazal XIII s"ezd partii o kooperatsii*, attributed to A. Bushkin and A. Ivanov, 1924) promoted the organization of peasant labor into cooperatives; *Dem'ian's Fuddle* (*Durman Dem'iana*, A. Bushkin, 1925) attacked alcoholism and encouraged attendance at Party clubs; and *MacDonald's Career* (*Kar'era Makdonal'da*, A. Bushkin, 1925, never released) was an attack on international politics, showing MacDonald, the leader of the English Laborites, as a puppet in the hands of capitalists.[15]

Propaganda films, political satires, and films based on caricatures and political pamphlets characterized most of the

---

13 Vertov, *Kino-eye*, 31.

14 For an account of Bushkin's works, see Elizarov, *Sovetskaia mul'tiplikatsiia*, 137.

15 Fragments of Bushkin's films had been shown in the documentary series *Animatsiia ot A do IA*, dir. Liakhovetskii and Margolina.

Chapter 1   From Propaganda to Children's Films

production of Soviet animation during these early years. The most significant personalities in Soviet animation came out of the prestigious institute VKhUTEMAS (Vysshie Khudozhestvenno-Tekhnicheskie Masterskie – High Art and Technical Studios), namely Zenon Komissarenko, Iurii Merkulov, Nikolai Khodataev, Daniil Cherkes, and later Ivan Ivanov-Vano, the sisters Valentina and Zinaida Brumberg, Ol'ga Khodataeva (sister of Nikolai), and Vladimir Suteev. All of them gathered at the new animation workshop at the studio "Mezhrabpom-Rus'"[16] with the task of creating advertising and agitation reels.

In the titles of the first films made by the group formed by Komissarenko, Merkulov, and Khodataev, one can already sense the political agenda of the artists and their ideological and propagandistic approach: *Interplanetary Revolution* (*Mezhplanetnaia revoliutsiia*, Z. Komisarenko, Iu. Merkulov, N. Khodataev, 1924), *China in Flames* (Kitai v ogne, Z. Komisarenko, Iu. Merkulov, N. Khodataev, 1925), and *How Avdotia Became Literate* (*Kak Avdotia stala gramotnoi*, Z. Komisarenko, Iu. Merkulov, N. Khodataev, 1925), which was not preserved.[17]

Interplanetary Revolution is a political science fiction animated film showing how the Soviet power would conquer the entire universe. It is a parody of *Aelita* (1924), the famous film by Iakov Protazanov, in which Zenon Komissarenko made the animated sequences. *Interplanetary Revolution* was not released, but its creators did not lose their enthusiasm for animation, and after a year they were already undertaking a second film, *China in Flames*.[18] Released in 1924, this was the first feature-length animated film made in the Soviet Union. It allegorically depicts the history of the repression of the poor Chinese population by capitalists and colonizers, and the birth of a national movement of liberation supported by the young Soviet rule. Stylistically, the film lacked unity, mainly because different episodes were assigned to three different artists, who did not have a homogeneous style. In every film created by this team, in fact, each episode bore the specific character of the artist who created it – Khodataev was more inclined towards realistic representation, Merkulov towards grotesque figures, and Komissarenko was closer in style to the caricatures of Moor and Cheremnykh. By the beginning of the 1930s, Komissarenko no longer worked on animation and had returned to draw-

16   The studio Mezhrabpom, which subsumed Rus' in 1924, was financed by International Arbeitershilfe (International Worker's Relief), a socialist organization created in Germany in 1921, whose task was to aid Soviet Russia during the famine time. After the initial emergency the fund was destined to help the nascent Soviet cinema, in particular providing the necessary equipment and film from abroad, and also facilitating circulation of Soviet films in Germany and later in the rest of Europe. Youngblood, *Movies for the Masses*, 14; Kenez, *Cinema and Soviet Society*, 38–39.

17   For an account of the activity of all early animators mentioned here, see Elizarov, *Sovetskaia mul'tplikatsua*. For a description of the films' content see Macheret and Glagoleva, *Sovetskie khudozhestvennye fil'my*.

18   Elizarov, *Sovetskaia mul'tiplikatsiia*, 168; Ginzburg, *Risovannyi i kukol'nyi fil'm*, 81.

ing caricatures and posters; not only most of his films, but also his drawings disappeared.[19] Several films did not survive. Some were destroyed during the war or simply burnt – films were highly flammable and often caught fire – and some were just not preserved often enough; it was not a concern of the directors at that time to keep copies of their films, and no archives existed. Later, as was likely the case with Komissarenko, some films probably disappeared for political reasons. The increasing production of films in the genre of political satire, pamphlet, and drawn animated posters (*kinoplakaty*) can also be linked to the particular historical juncture. In 1921, Lenin launched the New Economic Policy (NEP) in order to recover from the difficult times of the Revolution and the Civil War, and to foster a rebirth of the Soviet economy by allowing a partial return to a market economy with small private enterprise. Though film production and distribution had been nationalized, in this period, private entrepreneurs, cooperatives, and associations financed many theatres.[20] Audiences were reluctant to pay the high ticket prices (especially because of galloping inflation) for the agit-films that had been the staple of production during the Civil War.[21] The market orientation of this period of time led to a diversification of the repertory in live-action films, and in the mid-1920s most of the entertainment-oriented films for the masses were imported from the West. In 1924, approximately 95 per cent of the films in distribution were foreign; most of these were German, but after 1924 American films were also very popular.[22]

The so-created cult of foreign films provoked a vivid discussion in the cinema world, the extreme consequence of which was the accusation of one of the main cinema studios, Sovkino, during the Party Conference on Cinema Affairs on 15 March 1928, and its eventual closing in 1930.[23] This debate over foreign films sheds light on the 1927 film *One Among Many* (*Odna iz mnogikh*, N. Khodataev, Fig. 1.2), which focuses on American cinema stars Mary Pickford and Douglas Fairbanks and also includes some live action footage of Pickford and Fairbanks's recent visit to the USSR. While offering a satire of the American cinema world, this film also provides evidence of the success of American films during the 1920s. *One Among Many* had the twofold goal of attracting the contemporary public and, at the same time,

[19] Elizarov, *Sovetskaia mul'tiplikatsiia*, 168. There is also an issue of the documentary series *Animatsiia ot A do IA* dedicated to Komissarenko.

[20] Youngblood, *Movies for the Masses*, 14.

[21] Youngblood, *Movies for the Masses*, 14.

[22] Youngblood, *Movies for the Masses*, 15.

[23] Youngblood, *Movies for the Masses*, 29.

Chapter 1   From Propaganda to Children's Films

Figure 1.2. *Charlie Chaplin. Still from* One Among Many.

Figure 1.3. *Sequence of* One Among Many *in* The Kiss of Mary Pickford. *Still from* The Kiss of Mary Pickford.

ridiculing their attitude towards foreign films, putting a particular emphasis on the supposedly capitalist, dictatorial world from which these foreign films originated. Incidentally, sequences of this film were shown also in Sergei Komarov's live-action film *The Kiss of Mary Pickford* (*Potselui Meri Pikford,* 1927, Fig. 1.3), creating an instance of film-within-film that accentuates the criticism of the American cinema world.

This change in orientation within live-action cinema might have pushed animation to take up the propagandistic role fulfilled until that point mainly by agitational films. Animation started to develop inside Soviet cinema studios already in 1923, and the number of animated films produced in the Soviet Union rose every year, from one in 1923 to 7 in 1924, 9 in 1925, 22 in 1927, and 24 in 1928.[24] It seems that there is a break in production in 1926, in which only two films were made, maybe due to a fire that forced the animation division of one of the most productive studios, Mezhrabpom-Rus', to look for another location.[25]

By the beginning of the 1930s, there were active sectors of animation in the Soviet cinema studios Mezhrabpomfil'm (closed in 1936), the Moscow and Leningrad studios of Sovkino (abolished in 1930 and replaced by Soiuzkino in 1935), Mosfil'm (founded in 1935), VUFKU (Ukraine), and Goskinprom Gruzii (Georgia). Some animation collectives were also created at the studio in Erevan. The directors of these film studios (*kinofabriki*) usually supported the young animators, but left them free to choose themes and styles for their films.[26] Thus, the animators were more independent and more prone to experimentation. In addition to animated features, animation was employed partially or totally in other sections of the studios, such as in the educational and scientific film divisions, which started to be quite active in the mid-1920s.

Enlightening the masses: educational and scientific films

The Soviet communist ideal of educating the masses was a stimulus to produce not only propaganda but also educational and scientific films. However, the first scientific films in Russia were made not after the Revolution, but already in Tsarist time, between 1911 and 1915. Nikolai Baklin, a physicist and a contributor to these films, recalls in his writings how Khanzhonkov succeeded in establishing in his production company, Aktsionernoe Obshchestvo Khanzhonkov i K°, a division dedicated to educational and scientific films, despite the general difficulty of obtaining funds for such films. Some of the films featured only some animated scenes, but some others were entirely animated. Most of the purely educational and scientific films were hard to show; schools did not have projectors, and films could be screened only during organized lectures, which were quite rare since the Ministry of Education did not express any

24 For details about the films, see Macheret and Glagoleva, *Sovetskie khudozhestvennye fil'my*.

25 The accident is mentioned by Ivanov-Vano in his *Kadr za kadrom*.

26 Ivanov-Vano, *Kadr za kadrom*; Sergei Ginzburg, *Risovannyi i kukol'nyi fil'm*.

interest in them.²⁷ The war put a halt to the production of the Khanzhonkov studio section, and films of this kind did not appear again until a few years after the Revolution. Some films were made at Kul'tkino, a division of Goskino (which in 1925 became Sovkino) where Baklin worked, others in the studio Mezhrabpom-Rus', where, in the 1920s, the now-famous director Ivanov-Vano began his career as an animator. Ivanov-Vano briefly recalls in *Frame by Frame* his first works at the studio in the 1920s: an educational film that explained bottle making, *Glass and China Industry* (*Stekol'no-farforovaia promyshlennost'*, date unknown); and animated sequences of a more detailed scientific film, *Mechanics of the Brain* (*Mekhanika golovnogo mozga*, 1926), made by the renowned live-action director Vsevolod Pudovkin.²⁸

A few articles published in the mid-1920s²⁹ stressed the importance of educational and scientific films in the new Soviet society. Among them, an article that appeared in 1925 in one of the leading cinema journals, *Sovetskoe kino*, provided a lengthy list of the goals of animation in the Soviet Union.³⁰ This list is worth mentioning since it gives a glimpse of the ambitions and concerns of directors and cinema personalities alike. According to the author O. Kuz'ma, animation should deal with an extraordinary variety of issues, from the eradication of illiteracy to the teaching of productive land tenure; it should illustrate social and health problems (such as tuberculosis, syphilis, alcoholism) and provide elementary notions of geography, ethnography, natural science, technology, economics, and politics. Films should also address various contemporary topics, such as plans of electrification in Soviet Russia, introduction of cooperatives in villages, communist education, history of the Revolutionary movement, the Soviet regime's undertakings, the role of farming and industry in the country, and the place of the Soviet Union among bourgeois countries.³¹ Animation was designated as the privileged media for rendering all these themes accessible to the masses. Regrettably, only a small amount of animated films actually came into being.

27 N.V. Baklin and A.G. Kalashnikov, "Pervye shagi nauchnogo kino v Rossii", 184; Baklin, "Vospominaniia o dorevoliutsionnom periode v kinematografii", 171.

28 Ivanov-Vano, *Kadr za kadrom*, 23–25.

29 The most relevant articles being: Bushkin, "Kadro-s"emka"; and O. Kuz'ma, "Zadachi mul'tiplikatsii v kino".

30 Kuz'ma, "Zadachi mul'tiplikatsii v kino", 56–60.

31 Kuz'ma, "Zadachi mul'tiplikatsii v kino", 56–60.

Entertaining and educating: the first animated films for children

If most of the first Soviet drawn animated films were tar-

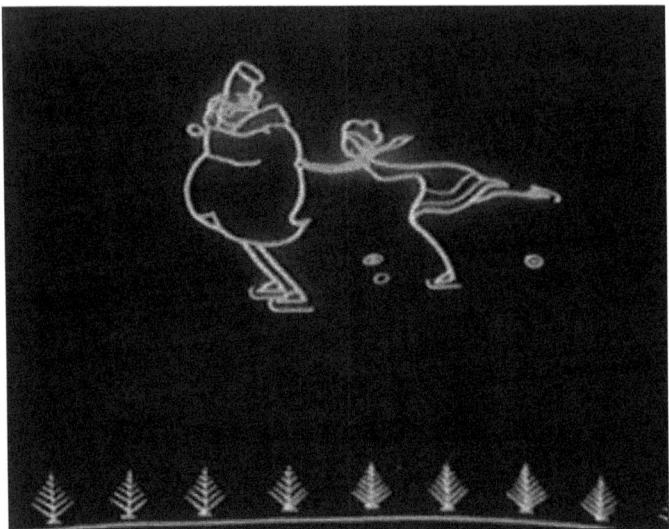

Figure 1.4. *Thin white profile on black background. Still from* The Skating Rink.

geted to an adult public, towards the end of the 1920s films for children also made their appearance. Educating the new generation was increasingly important, and animators felt the need to take advantage of the accessibility of animation to address the young public.

The first animated films for children were made in 1927, a year that saw more than one youth-oriented production. Only two of the films released in this year have been preserved:[32] *Sen'ka the African (Sen'ka Afrikanets*, Cherkes, Merkulov, Ivanov-Vano, 1927), based on the story *Krokodil* by the famous children's writer Kornei Chukovskii; and the film *The Skating Rink* (*Katok,* Ivanov-Vano, Cherkes, 1927, Fig. 1.4), whose graphic choice – a thin, white profile on a black background – is unmistakably indebted to the work of one of the world's first animators, Emile Cole. Both films used successful comic gags and a laconic but highly expressive style.

At the end of the 1920s, new artists focused on animation for children. In 1928, four talented artists, Nikolai and Ol'ga Khodataev and the sisters Valentina and Zinaida Brumberg, gathered together at the Moscow Tret'ia Fabrika Sovkino to produce one of the most successful animated films of these early years, *The Samoed Boy* (*Samoedskii mal'chik,* 1928), the story of a boy who grows up in a cold countryside, rebels

[32] Films for children were created in 1927 in more than one studio: in Ukraine, Viacheslav Levandovskii's *The Tale of the Straw Bull-Calf* (*Skazka o solomennom bychke*); in Leningrad at Sovkino, *Vintik-Shpintik* (Vladislav Tvardovskii); in Moscow at Mezhrabpomfil'm, *Moidodyr* (Maria Benderskaia, puppet film); and at Moskovskaia fabrika Sovkino, *The Huge Cockroach* (*Tarakanishche*, Aleksandr Ivanov). However, none of these films survived. For details about these films, see Macheret and Glagoleva, *Sovetskie khudozhestvennye fil'my*.

Chapter 1 From Propaganda to Children's Films

against his people's superstitions, leaves the country to study in the city, but still longs for his village and the nature that surrounds it. This film conveys an ambivalent message: the diverse features of such an immense country as the Soviet Union are glorified in the film, but at the same time "diversity" is controlled and channeled into state institutions. *The Samoed Boy* is particularly significant for its technical achievements in conveying the characters' movement; the scene of the sledge ride helped many animators in rendering the movements of animals on the run. While Nikolai Khodataev was already famous, his sister Ol'ga and Valentina and Zinaida Brumberg had started to work as directors only a year earlier and went on to become some of the most prolific animation directors of the years that followed.[33]

At the same time, at Sovkino in Leningrad, Aleksandr Presniakov and Igor' Sorokhtin, working with the artist Vladislav Tvardovskii, made a film called *The Offended Letters* (*Obizhennye bukvy*, 1928). The film's plot is simple: the letters of the alphabet revolt in protest against schoolboys' negligence; some delegates among them are sent to Narkompros (Narodnyi komissariat prosveshcheniia – The People's Commissariat of Enlightenment) with a complaint about the children. Had this film been preserved, it would constitute a historical document, since in it animation was combined with live-action sequences and the animated delegates to Narkompros were received by no less than the Commissar of Enlightenment, Anatolii Lunacharskii, in person.[34]

A particularly successful film for children was *The Adventures of Munchausen* (*Pokhozhdeniia Miunkhauzena*), an adaptation of Rudolf Erich Raspe's tales, produced in 1929 by D. Cherkes, I. Ivanov-Vano, and V. Suteev. The film's style, which recalls Gustave Doré's characters, pleased both children and adults, the latter especially impressed by R.E. Raspe's subtle irony.[35]

Towards the end of the 1920s, serial characters made their first appearance in Soviet cartoons. American cinema certainly influenced this trend, from the live-action star system with personalities such as Charlie Chaplin, Mary Pickford, and Douglas Fairbanks, to cartoon characters such as Felix the Cat, Oswald the Lucky Rabbit, and Mickey Mouse. Even earlier cartoon characters seem to have influenced

[33] Ginzburg, *Risovannyi i kukol'nyi fil'm*; Elizarov, *Sovetskaia mul'tiplikatsiia*; Macheret and Glagoleva, *Sovetskie khudozhestvennye fil'my*.

[34] Another animated film in which Lunacharskii appears in person is *Tip-Top in Moscow* (*Tip-Top v Moskve*, A. Ivanov, 1928). Macheret and Glagoleva, *Sovetskie khudozhestvennye fil'my*; also in Ivanov-Vano, *Mul'tiplikatsiia vchera i segodnia*, 19.

[35] *Animatsiia ot A do IA*, dir. Liakhovetskii and Margolina.

Soviet directors, especially Koko the Clown from Max Fleischer's series *Out of the Inkwell*, which was shown in Moscow in 1924 and which, as the director Khodataev mentions in his writings, inspired the Russian serial character Tip-Top.[36] There were two advantages to having serial characters: first, it would attract audiences willing to follow their adventures from film to film; second, it would save time and work by using some of the drawings for more than one cartoon. The drawn characters Tip-Top, Buzilka, Murzilka, and later Kliaksa appeared in some films, but the most prolific character was the puppet Bratishkin. Most of these films attempted to be entertaining while conveying a political or social message. They combined live-action footage and animation in the hope of attracting a broader audience of both adult and young spectators. However, none of these characters survived for long, mainly because animation at the end of the 1930s turned to new themes and styles.

Waiting for cel animation: drawings and flat marionettes

The type of animated films produced in the 1920s and early 1930s was strictly connected to the techniques available in Soviet Russia at that time. Soviet animators used simple outlines like those in caricatures to accelerate production, but an extraordinary amount of work was still necessary to draw frame by frame every single character's movement and the corresponding background. Russian artists waited longer than Western animators for the arrival of the advanced cel technique, that is, drawing on transparent sheets of celluloid. This delay was perhaps due to the cost of cels or to the European tradition of puppet theatre, which, as Donald Crafton ventures, strongly influenced the choice in animation of flat marionettes and cut-outs.[37] Most of the films made at the very beginning of Soviet animation were either realized through drawings on paper or through flat paper marionettes with movable joints. Cut-outs permitted animators to avoid the complete re-drawing of full figures and background and thereby accelerated the film-making process, but the movement created by adjusting, frame by frame, parts of these paper marionettes was definitely less smooth than the fluid movement achieved with the drawings. However, the brusque and jerky gestures so obtained had a mechanical character well suited to the grotesque traits

36 Khodataev, "Iskusstvo mul'tiplikatsii", 88.

37 Crafton, *Before Mickey*, 257.

of the individuals represented in the satirical and propagandistic films. Yet, flat marionettes allowed only a very limited range of movements and forced a depiction of the characters mostly in profile. In order to obtain greater flexibility, flat marionettes were replaced by paper cut-outs with autonomous body parts (such as hands, legs, head, etc.) that the animators could adjust or substitute after each take. The various phases of the characters in movement were cut out from a sheet of paper, so that the environment depicted underneath would be visible at any time around the character in motion; hence, the background did not need to be re-drawn for each frame. Still, the background was simple and characterized by a few fundamental elements in order to allow a harmonious combination of characters and surroundings.

Only with the introduction of the cel technique and the possibility of tracing the various phases of a character's movements on transparent sheets could animation develop more complicated forms with more attention to detail; but in Russia, celluloid sheets came to be available only in the mid-1930s. The new technique brought a series of consequences that influenced the entire Soviet animation system, from production to stylistic choices.

Puppet and stop-motion animation

At the same time as cut-outs and flat marionettes, puppet animation also developed in the early years of Soviet animation. Various personalities distinguished themselves in this field. Among them it is worth mentioning Iurii Zheliabuzhskii, Viacheslav Levandovskii, and especially Aleksandr Ptushko. Zheliabuzhskii was already famous for some of his agitation shorts (*agitki*) and some live-action films, such as *The Cigarette Girl from Moscow* (*Papirosnitsa ot Mossel'proma*, 1924) and *The Collegiate Registrar* (or *The Station Master*, *Kollezhskii registrator*, 1925); as well as for his camerawork for such well-known films as Protazanov's *Aelita* (1924). Zheliabuzhskii first tried animation in 1927, collaborating with Cherkes and Ivanov-Vano on *The Skating Rink*, but his major contribution to animation was *The Adventures of Bolvashka* (*Prikliucheniia Bolvashki*, 1927), in which live-action footage is combined with stop-motion animation using a wooden marionette, Bolvashka, reminiscent of

Pinocchio and his Russian version Buratino, as well as of the traditional Russian puppet Petrushka. *The Adventures of Bolvashka* was Zheliabuzhskii's second and last animated film;[38] soon thereafter he had to leave his work in cinematography, presumably for political reasons.[39]

During the mid-1930s, some puppet films were also produced in the studio Mosfil'm by the director Viacheslav Levandovskii, who had previously worked in drawn animation at the Odessa studio VUFKU, where he created *The Tale of the Straw Bull-Calf* (*Skazka o solomennom bychke*, 1927), the first Ukrainian animated film. Once Levandovskii moved to Moscow, he turned to puppet animation with the films *The Fox and the Grapes* (*Lisa i vinograd*, 1936), *Silver Rain* (*Serebrianyi dozhd'*, 1937), and later *In the Land of Puppets* (*V kukol'noi strane*, 1940).[40]

But it was at another Moscow studio, Sovkino, where puppet animation came to thrive thanks to the most famous puppet animation director of this era, Aleksandr Ptushko. Unlike his earlier colleagues who dealt with animated drawings in a sometimes crude agitational way, Ptushko was able to meet the high demand of these years for films concerning aspects of Soviet contemporary life, and in particular propaganda topics, in an original and enjoyable way. In 1928 Ptushko began to produce animated films in which he combined live-action film with stop-motion technique. His early film, *An Event at the Stadium* (*Sluchai na stadione*, Tret'ia Fabrika Sovkino, 1928), introduced Bratishkin, one of the first serial characters in the history of Soviet animation.[41] This film – the only one with Bratishkin that has been preserved – was based on a simple story that depicted Bratishkin's disappointment at having missed a Spartiakiada soccer game. The film is particularly significant in the way it engages in the broader artistic discourse on self-reflexivity and production. It exploits the characters' adventures to showcase the work of the Sovkino cameramen; thus, it artfully promotes in a self-referential way one of the major Moscow studios, much in the way Vertov used self-advertising (although less subtly) in his *Soviet Toys*. While viewing *An Event at the Stadium*, Vertov comes to mind repeatedly – the way cameramen are depicted shooting from the most original places and the words used to praise them take us back to Vertov's theories on the role of the camera as a

38 Macheret and Glagoleva, *Sovetskie khudozhestvennye fil'my*.

39 *Animatsiia ot A do IA*, dir. Liakhovetskii and Margolina.

40 Elizarov, *Sovetskaia mul'tiplikatsiia*; Macheret and Glagoleva, *Sovetskie khudozhestvennye fil'my*.

41 Bratishkin would appear in some other Ptushko films, such as *One Hundred Adventures* (*Sto prikliuchenii*, 1929) and *Let's Bring the Cinema to the Countryside!* (*Kino v derevniu!*, 1930), as well as in Merkulov's drawn films *Night Alarm – Bratishkin In The Barrack* (*Nochnaia trevoga – Bratishkin v kazarme*, 1928) and *Adventures of Bratishkin* (*Prikliucheniia Bratishkina*, 1929). The last film made with Bratishkin was Tvardovskii's *Bratishkin Competes* (*Bratishkin sorevnuetsia*, 1930). Macheret and Glagoleva, *Sovetskie khudozhestvennye fil'my*.

Chapter 1   From Propaganda to Children's Films

Figure 1.5. *Cameramen in multiple-frame imagery.
Still from* An Event at the Stadium.

privileged recording eye of reality and evoke his subsequent film *Man with a Movie Camera* (1929) (Fig. 1.5).

Another of Ptushko's puppet films, *Master of Daily Life* (*Vlastelin byta*, A. Ptushko, Moskovskaia Fabrika Soiuzkino, 1932), addresses the new Soviet life on several levels: from a spatial level (the question of living places), to promotion of hygiene, to finally an implicit political message. The story presents a family that moves to a new house in an unsuccessful attempt to get rid of the bugs that torment them. The Constructivist style of the new house is loaded with connotations of a specific moment in Soviet art and architecture, while the efficient, clear, and defined traits of this style sharply contrast with the main characters' way of living. The words that end the film: "Enough! We must be able to live in our new home!" ("Dovol'no! Nuzhno umet' zhit' v novom dome!") echo as an exhortation to Soviet citizens in general to learn the rules of the new society and banish the old "parasites" (that is, the old bourgeoisie).

Ptushko's most successful film was the feature film *The New Gulliver* (*Novyi Gulliver*, script by G. Roshal, Moskinokombinat, 1935). In a clever and careful combination of live-action sequences and stop-motion photography of conventional and grotesque puppets, Ptushko transformed Jonathan Swift's story into a contemporary tale with very strong political content: after falling asleep on the book of Gulliver's adventures, the Pioneer Petia dreams that he has become a new Gulliver and will lead the poor Lilliputians in their revolution against the rich rulers of their country.

A successful combination of puppets and live-action sequences also characterized Ptushko's last puppet animation film, *The Little Golden Key* (*Zolotoi kliuchik,* Mosfil'm, 1939), an adaptation from A. Tolstoy's story about the adventures of Buratino. After this film, Ptushko turned his efforts towards live-action films, and only sporadically collaborated as an artistic director on some other animated films.

With the introduction of the cel technique in the mid-1930s and the simultaneous tendency to abandon every reference to actuality, two factors that I shall discuss later in this chapter, experimentation with puppet films slowed down and came to an end before the beginning of World War II. Only in 1952 was a division of the studio Soiuzmul'tfil'm assigned to the production of puppet films. During its first two years, this division released only a few films, but the production of three-dimensional animated films soon increased, and greatly developed starting in the late 1960s and 1970s.

The Leningrad experience: book illustrations meet avant-garde works in Mikhail Tsekhanovskii's films

While Soviet animators were producing a variety of films in Moscow, in Leningrad, the book illustrator Mikhail Tsekhanovskii (1889–1965) was experimenting with his drawings and trying to bring animation closer to avant-garde work. Like most Soviet directors, however, Tsekhanovskii never reached the modernist extreme of complete abstraction favored by several contemporary European directors. This was not only because abstract formalism was harshly attacked by Soviet officials, but also because Soviet artists at that time were more concerned with delivering a specific message to the audience.

Tsekhanovskii came to cinema only after working in the publishing world as a book illustrator, an experience that clearly marks his distinctive style. The new and influential school of graphics for children's books founded by Vladimir Lebedev in Leningrad in the 1920s greatly influenced Tse-

Chapter 1 From Propaganda to Children's Films

khanovskii. Lebedev brought children's book illustrations to a high artistic level; the book, in fact, was conceived as a blend of literature and art and the artist's name would appear on the cover together with the author's name. Tsekhanovskii worked next to Lebedev at the children's book publisher Raduga, and at Lengiz as an illustrator of books by well-known children's writers such as Samuil Marshak and Kornei Chukovskii. His illustrations recall some peculiarities of Lebedev's drawings, such as clarity, laconism, the use of the directness of poster style, elements of journal graphics, and advertising. Among the artists coming from Lebedev's school, Tsekhanovskii was the one who first linked book illustration to animation. His films deserve some closer analysis in this study, because they not only represent the most significant works of animation of these years, but also provide a model to which some directors of the 1960s referred.

Tsekhanovskii's first film, *The Post* (*Pochta*, 1929), had its origins in his illustrations drawn for a popular text for children of the same title written by Samuil Marshak and published as an illustrated book in 1928. Marshak's verses told a story about a letter which travels around the world, passing from postman to postman following the itinerant addressee Mr. Zhutkov. While animating his book, Tsekhanovskii wished to be faithful to the original traits of his drawings and opted for the same technique as his colleagues in Moscow: cut-outs.

The following year, 1930, Tsekhanovskii added Vladimir Deshevov's music to the film, making of the sound version of *The Post* the first sound animated film in the history of Soviet animation. Unfortunately, the sound version of the film has been lost, and what has been preserved is only the original silent version. In 1964, however, Tsekhanovskii remade the film with a rearrangement of Deshevov's original musical score. For this version, Tsekhanovskii abandoned the cut-out figures of the original film and used the modern technique of drawings on cel. The result is, stylistically, a completely different film that is hardly comparable with the 1930 version. Most of the films made by Tsekhanovskii from the 1940s onward lack that special indefinable quality that characterizes works of art. The meticulous attention to characters' movements, often reproduced with the help of a rotoscope (in Russian *ekler*),

Figures 1.6. *Diagonal composition. Stairs. Still from* The Post.

deprives the film of the poetic imperfections and originality that distinguished Tsekhanovskii's first films.

In 1994, the School and Studio for Animation SHAR (director of sound Sergei Seregin) undertook to reconstruct the original score of the 1930 version of *The Post* on the basis of the 1964 film music. The project provided a version of *The Post* that is probably very similar to the original, lost sound film. Sound, however, seems to be a superfluous element in *The Post*, since the composition of the images and

Chapter 1 From Propaganda to Children's Films

Figure 1.7. *Diagonal composition. Train. Still from* The Post.

the montage produce a silent soundtrack with rich variation in rhythm. In this film, the composition inside the frame or *in-frame montage* (*vnutrikadrovyi montazh* to use Eisenstein's terminology) and the editing between the shots create a particular rhythm, a flow of images presented one after another in a sort of visual symphony (Fig. 1.6–1.7). There is a sense of uninterrupted movement, which accelerates and decelerates according to the images on the screen. Not only does movement function as a narrative element (the letter passes from hand to hand until it reaches the addressee), but movement is also used as a differentiating trait among the various postmen around the world – so we see how postmen from Brazil, England, Germany, and Russia seem to have different attitudes, expressed in distinct ways of walking. The pace of life of a given country is presented through a simple portrait of a postman; we have a Russian pace as "sostenuto" and "con forza", compared to an English "accelerato", a German "a tempo", and a Brazilian "rallentato", "semplice" and "tranquillo". Both in the book and in the film, each postman's particular walk serves to exemplify a national character and at the same time allows the reader and the spectator to experience the change of rhythm as he passes from country to country. Moreover, the specific beat in the postmen's movements is underlined by the rhythm

25

of Marshak's verses in both the printed book and the film's intertitles.

If in the book the variation of rhythm is perceptible above all through Marshak's verses, in the film the change in rhythm is conveyed through an alternation of images and intertitles. The intertitles are presented on the screen with characters of different sizes and shapes, and the diversification of the style and design of the letters together with their animation convey the declamatory tone of Marshak's verses. The letters that compose the intertitles acquire a life of their own – words appear all together in a sentence or one by one, and sometimes words emerge from the black background in discrete units, letter by letter. Letters or words appear at different speeds according to the meaning or intonation of the sentence. The graphic form of the words gains a value on its own; the words assume a plastic value that goes beyond their content. How can we not think of the Futurists' claims about the importance of the graphic effects of the written word, of a new visual language, which would maximize the iconic force of the written word? In this regard it is enough to think about the manifesto "The Letter As Such" written by Velimir Khlebnikov and Aleksei Kruchenykh in 1913. If the Futurists were mainly concerned with handwriting, later the Constructivists would develop the notion of the importance of the graphic form of words in typeface. In this vein, El Lissitzky's works on typography, such as the illustrations for a short picture book for children *About Two Squares* (*Pro dva kvadrata*, 1922), and for Mayakovsky's collection of poems *For the Voice* (*Dlia golosa*, 1923) are particularly significant.[42] In articles written in 1923 and 1925, El Lissitzky claims that the printed word should be seen, not heard, and that typographic form should express through optical means the writer's gestures and voice.[43] In Tsekhanovskii's film *The Post,* similarly, the plastic aspect of the word fills the void left by the absence of sound.

If, on the one hand, *The Post* can be placed within the heritage of Futurism and Constructivism, on the other hand, it was also influenced by modernists, especially in its use of flat objects on a white screen, geometrical shapes and essential forms with no ornaments, symmetric composition, and space cut by lines – all elements that we find for example in Kazimir Malevich's paintings. Furthermore, *The*

42 Lissitzky, *For Two Squares*; Maiakovskii and Lissitzky, *Dlia golosa*.

43 Lissitzky, "The Topography of Typography"; Lissitzky, "Typographical Facts" (1925) quoted in Mercier, "Post-Analyse du film de M. Zechanovsky 1929", 72.

Chapter 1 From Propaganda to Children's Films

Figure 1.8. *Circular Message. Still from* The Post.

Figure 1.9. *Tunnel. Still from* The Post.

Post is strictly connected to the European avant-garde cinema of the 1920s, and in particular to experimental films by directors like Viking Eggeling, Hans Richter, Walter Ruttmann, and Marcel Duchamp.[44] Even though Tsekahnovskii's films are not as abstract as Eggeling's *Diagonal Symphony*, Richter's *Rhythmus 21/23*, Ruttmann's *Opus I/II/III*, or Duchamp's *Anémic Cinéma,* they nonethe-

44 Also Mercier notes the influence of modernism and avant-garde experimental films on Tsekhanovskii.

Figure 1.10. *Train. Still from* The Post.

less share with these experimental films an interest in rotating objects, clashing lines, curves, and geometrical forms, as well as a playfulness that creates a sense of movement and rhythm. A direct similarity is found, for example, at the very beginning of *The Post*, when a boy writes a message for the postman on an envelope (Fig. 1.8); the boy's circular writing recalls the rotating spiral of Marcel Duchamp's *Anémic Cinéma*. The use of optical effects to show depth (like the tunnel in *The Post,* Fig. 1.9), the multiplication of images, blank backgrounds, quick montage, and abstract forms generated by movements and speed are all recurrent elements in the experimental films of those years; they occur frequently in Tsekhanovskii's *The Post* and subsequently in his experimental film *Pacific 231 (Pasifik 231,* 1931).

The main trait that Tsekhanovkii's films have in common with the avant-garde works is their rhythm. As Tsekhanovskii writes in his diary, the content, the essence of *The Post* is pure movement; the "pleasure in looking at this picture should arise from the sensation of an interrupted and diverse movement".[45] The rhythm that Tsekhanovskii creates in the film underlines the vitality and restlessness of modern life in general, with its dynamism, speed, energy, and the power of machines. Looking at Tsekhanovskii's drawings, we recognize the modern faith in technology, the dream of breaking down all the barriers that divide the

45 Written on 24 December 1928. Mikhail Tsekhanovskii, "Dykhanie voli", *Kinovedcheskie zapiski* 54 (2001):193. Also in Tsekhanovskii, "Dykhanie voli", in *Katalog-al'manakh. Suzdal' 2002*, 137.

Chapter 1 From Propaganda to Children's Films

Figure 1.11. *Airplane. Still from* The Post.

world. The world he depicts is the modern world always in motion, a world in which steam-engine locomotives, airplanes, and all other moving machines acquire life of their own in glorifying the new modern industrial and technological world (Figs. 1.10–1.11).

Having always been fascinated with technology, Tsekhanovskii could not witness with indifference the new technological revolution brought by the introduction of sound in cinema. He dedicated the decade before World War II to experimentation with synchronization of sound and images.

The advent of sound: Tsekhanovskii's experiments

At the beginning of the 1930s, a new technological innovation was made in cinema: the introduction of sound in film. It is well known that the main directors of the Soviet school of cinema were against this innovation when it first appeared, or at least desired to utilize this feature in non-naturalistic ways – at this propos Sergei Eisenstein, Vsevolod Pudovkin and Grigorii Aleksandrov wrote the manifesto "Statement of Sound" ("Zaiavka") published in the journal *Zhizn' iskusstva* in 1928.[46]

It is true that generally the advent of sound presented a whole series of new problems, also for animation. In fact, in

[46] Taylor and Christie, *The Film Factory*, 234–235.

animated films, sound has a complex function; image and sound have to be synchronized, so that the characters not only "talk", but also their movements produce sound and correspond to the rhythm of the music. As we know now, there are two methods for recording sound in animated films: the first is to film the images and subsequently record the sound over them (post-synchronization); the second is to work out a preliminary soundtrack and shoot the film according to the sound scheme. This latter method gives a better synchronization of image and sound, and it is in general the technique used by contemporary animators.

However, for the first Russian sound animated movie (*The Post*), sound was post-added to an already existing silent film, and in the Soviet Union of the 1930s, post-synchronization was generally used, such as in *Black and White* (*Blek end uait*, 1932), a film made by Leonid Amal'rik and Ivan Ivanov-Vano in 1932 to illustrate some of Mayakovsky's verses. Soon the animators realized that this method would not result in perfect synchronization and they started to search for new methods and techniques.

Tsekhanovskii was a pioneer in this area; he was the first in the Soviet Union to conceive of the possibility of building an animated film on an existing soundtrack.[47] For Tsekhanovskii it was not simply a question of the synchronization of image and sound; he went as far as considering sound as the organizing principle, as the dominant feature to which the entire structure of the visual images would be subordinated.

A good example of this approach to sound would be an experimental film made by Tsekhanovskii in 1931, *Pacific 231*. In this film Tsekhanovskii tried to interpret visually a famous symphonic work, Arthur Honegger's symphony *Pacific 231* (written in 1923), considered by most music critics the first example of musical inspiration derived from the modern poetry of machines, energy, and speed. The full title of the film was: *Pacific 231: a Symphonic Poem about the Steam-Engine Locomotive of Arthur Honegger, Performed by the Symphony Orchestra Conducted by A.V.Gauk* (*Pasifik 231 simfonicheskaia poema o paravoze Artura Oneggera, ispol'niaet simfonicheskii orkestr pod upravleniem dirizhera Sofila A.V. Gauk*). The finished film resulted in a live-action (thus non-animated) short, but during its creation, Tsekhanovskii

47 See his articles: Tsekhanovskii, "Spetsifika Tonfil'ma"; Tsekhanovskii, "O zvukovoi risovannoi fil'me"; RGALI, "Professional'no-tecnhnicheskii opyt: *Pasifik*", 53–54.

thought several times of introducing drawings and animated objects into the sequence of photographic images. Only gradually did he understand that animated elements would not fit harmoniously into this type of experimental film. His research and his experiments with sound for *Pacific 231*, however, were very useful for his future animated films and for Soviet animated films of that time in general.

Tsekhanovskii, in working with Honegger's symphony, sought to reach an absolute rhythmic correspondence between the music and the rhythm of the movements inside the frame, as well as between the music and the rhythm of montage. He approached Honegger's symphony in the same way as he used to approach the text of a literary work in order to create illustrations for it – this film looks like a filmic illustration of a musical work. The film follows three main visual themes: the steam-engine locomotive, the conductor directing the musicians in the orchestra, and the musicians with their instruments. An artistic unity in the work is achieved by coordinating in parallel external similarities of movements and similarities between forms of objects, and by associating precise visual elements with specific sounds. As he explained in his article about *Pacific 231*, the director meant to film synchronically the orchestra playing the symphony in several planes with different groups of instruments at the same time, in such a way that the visual frames could help the listener to perceive the rhythmic, melodic and semantic design of Honegger's work.[48]

As the spectator watches Tsekhanovskii's film, a continuous stream of images and sound captures him and brings him into a dimension where sound and visual elements from different worlds melt together. Human beings are represented in discrete units, in modernistic fragmented images (hands, lips, cheeks of the musicians and part of their instruments), and men themselves become objects, machines. As the music already intimates, the film is an apotheosis of the powerful machine, of the strength and the purposefulness of the industrial force. Images of musical instruments and musicians are superimposed over details of the steam-engine locomotive. Windows of a train wagon, telephone poles, traffic lights, and streetlamps are glimpsed fleetingly on a background representing the orchestra playing.

48 RGALI, "Professional'no-technicheskii opyt: *Pasifik*", 53–54.

Tsekhanovskii's experiments were not concerned only with formal questions; he always had in mind the revolutionary message he wanted to convey to the spectator. If *The Post* was a celebration of human work (with the aid of the most modern technological discoveries, especially in transportation), *Pacific 231* was mainly a celebration of the machine. In one of his unpublished articles, Tsekhanovskii voiced his enthusiasm for the advent of sound in Soviet film; he welcomed sound as a means of expressing completely and thoroughly the ideas that lie at the base of filmmaking, that is – he said – the ideas of the construction of socialism.

> The more paths we take over from the very outset, the more deeply we engage with the entire spectrum of sound in cinema, the more quickly we will reach our principle goal. We possess the material and the tools of this new art form in order, possibly, to fully reveal the colossal ideas of our Socialist construction.[49]

Sound was indeed strictly connected with technological evolution and technological researches in the new Socialist state, which had been seized by enthusiasm for industrialization.

Not only was Tsekhanovskii interested in sound film, but he was also fascinated with the experiments done in the Soviet Union with "drawings of sound". According to an anecdote reported by the Russian film critic and scholar Nikolai Izvolov, Tsekhanovskii was in the Leningrad studio during the sound recording of Abram Room's film *The Plan for Great Works (Plan velikikh rabot,* or *Piatiletka,* 1930), which was the first Soviet sound film. In this laboratory, three people were looking at the developed film in question: Tsekhanovskii, the composer Arsenii Avraamov, and his technical assistant, the engineer Evgenii Sholpo. They examined the soundtrack marks on the film for the first time, and noticed how they appeared in the form of a curved line; each of these three men thought that if they drew a curved line of their own instead, it should somehow generate sound.[50]

Tsekhanovskii never engaged in such a difficult enterprise. Instead, Avraamov and Sholpo began to do research in the field, producing some interesting works. At the beginning of the 1930s, after obtaining some initial successes in the creation of artificial sounds, they founded an institute in

49 RGALI, Tsekhanovskii fond 2627, op.1, d. 92, ll. 13–17 "Ne prevyshchen li protsent oshibok?" 1931.

50 Izvolov, *Fenomen kino,* 269–270.

Chapter 1   From Propaganda to Children's Films

Figure 1.12. *Priest in "Bazaar". Still from* Balda.

Figure 1.13. *Merchant in "Bazaar". Still from* Balda.

Moscow dedicated to artificial sound research – the Scientific Research Cinema and Photographic Institute. Later on, Avraamov and Sholpo were joined by Nikolai Voinov and Boris Iankovskii. While Avraamov was more interested in the sounds of the simplest, most basic geometrical forms, Voinov would look for a more practical and easily applicable system for the production of animated films, and he used paper cut-outs to reproduce specific sounds.

By 1932 Avraamov's laboratory was ready to synthesize

Figure 1.14. *Bear Show in "Bazaar". Still from* Balda.

human speech using circles, triangles, and squares, but the State blocked financial aid for the experiments and the staff could not afford to continue their research. Incidentally, it is curious to notice how at the same time that the Soviet schools of synthetic sound were exploring the possibilities of sound drawing, similar experiments were undertaken independently in Germany by Oskar Fischinger and Rudolf Pfenninger. In this regard, Ivanov-Vano recollects how he suddenly read in the German journal *Filmtechnik* (1932, N. 23) that for the first time in the world, an exhibition in Germany showed short films in which the sound was created without using a microphone. Those were works by Pfenninger.[51] The Soviet experiments on generating sound through drawings have been almost completely forgotten, even though such a famous experimental animator as Norman McLaren is believed to have been aware of this research and to have been influenced by it.[52]

Tsekhanovskii was fascinated by the theoretical possibilities of rendering sound in drawing, but he was never directly involved in the research; he would examine these experiments only in the light of his studies on the synchronization of images and sound. After *Pacific 231*, the director embarked on new experiments with sound, this time utilizing animated techniques, and created an animated opera based

51 Ivanov-Vano, *Kadr za kadrom*, 91.

52 In *Kadr za kadrom*, Ivanov-Vano mentions that Norman McLaren was well acquainted with the experiments of the Russian inventors of sound drawings because he had helped to translate into English the Russian text *Animated Film*, a book published in Moscow in 1936 in which all these experiments are systematically described (Zil'ver, ed., *Mul'tiplikatsionnyi fil'm*). Ivanov-Vano, *Kadr za kadrom*, 92.

Chapter 1   From Propaganda to Children's Films

Figure 1.15. *Woman and Cat in "Bazaar". Still from* Balda.

on Pushkin's fable *The Tale of the Pope and his Worker Balda* (*Skazka o pope i rabotnike ego Balde*, Figs. 1.12–1.15).

Dmitrii Shostakovich, who started to work with Tsekhanovskii in 1933, composed a musical score exclusively for this animated film. Ultimately, by 1936, the composer's work on this score generated fifteen pieces that became his op. 36. In his diary, Tsekhanovskii mentions that *Balda* was almost completed,[53] but the film was never released and all we have remaining from it is a few minutes of one scene entitled "Bazaar". The characters here are grotesquely depicted, and with their simplicity and the mechanical quality of their movements they look like caricatures of the merchants and priests described by Pushkin. Their mechanical movements perfectly correspond to the rhythm of the shrill and somehow mechanical (puppet-like) music of Shostakovich; they also correspond to the precise rhythm of the verses written for the film by the OBERIU poet Aleksandr Vvedenskii. It should be mentioned that there is an affinity and friendship between Tsekhanovskii and the OBERIU group on the basis of their works for children's books and of their avant-garde works. Tsekhanovskii was especially close to Aleksandr Vvedenskii, who contributed to *The Tale of the Pope and his Worker Balda*, and Daniil Kharms, who wrote the words for the *compère* of the film *The Post*.

It is unfortunate that, as happened to many experimental

---

[53] In his diary on the date 24 February 1936, Tsekhanovskii noted that he was going to finish *Balda*, a stronger and more mature film, in his opinion, than *The Post*. Tsekhanovskii, "Dykhanie voli", *Kinovedcheskie zapiski* 54, 187.

artists of the time, the increasing attacks on Tsekhanovskii's graphic style and Shostakovich's music for "formalism" prevented their completing the film. Tsekhanovskii in his diary explains how the article "Muddle Instead of Music" ("Sumbur vmesto muzyki"), which appeared in *Pravda* in 1936 attacking Shostakovich and other "formalists" (such as the theatre director Vsevolod Meyerhold) was the main cause for shutting down the work on *Balda*. Had this film been released, Soviet animated cinema might have developed differently. With the imposition of socialist realism and the subsequent creation of the centralized studio Soiuzdetmul'tfil'm in 1936, which was oriented exclusively towards animated films for children, all such experiments came to a halt.

The 1930s: the last satirical animated films

Around 1936, not only were stylistic innovations hardly accepted, but also films that aired political and social themes soon could no longer be made. In order to understand the peculiarities of the Soviet animated films made in the early 1930s and how Soviet animation could have developed if authorities did not reject in toto satire, one should think about the last satirical animated films of these years, *Black and White* (*Blek end uait*, I. Ivanov-Vano and L. Amal'rik, Mezhrabpomfil'm, 1932), *The Tale of the White Bull-Calf* (*Skazka pro belogo bychka*, V. Suteev, L. Atamanov, Mezhrabpomfil'm, 1933), *The Little Music Box* (*Organchik*, N. Khodataev, Soiuzfil'm 1933), and *The Tale of Tsar Durandai* (*Skazka o tsare Durandae*, Ivanov-Vano and B. and Z. Brumberg, Mezhrabpomfil'm, 1934). These films, based on attacks on rich, racist, and two-faced capitalists, followed the poster-style of Mayakovsky's *Okna ROSTA* (as in *Black and White*), the journal caricature style of the early 1920s (as in *The Tale of the White Bull-Calf*), or a manner closer to folk art, wood engravings, and traditional toys (as in *The Little Music Box*).

Black and White was an adaptation for the screen of Mayakovsky's homonymous poem using poster and graphic style that recalled his drawings as well as the tradition of the Revolutionary poster and agitprop films. The drawings and the words, recited in a bombastic tone following

Mayakovsky's style, matched the rhythm and structure of the poet's verses. As in the poem, inspired by Mayakovsky's visit to Cuba, the Cuban workers appear under the yoke of American domination, victims of severe racist treatment.

The Tale of the White Bull-Calf was a political satire on the theme of nuclear disarmament. In it, various animal figures representing League of Nations members – a Fox, Hyena, Snake, Lion, Tiger, Hippopotamus, and Crocodile – were depicted in ways that suggested their hypocrisy in facing the problem of nuclear disarmament, while the Soviet Union presented a contrasting positive image of a young Pioneer.

While the first two films attack capitalist countries, *The Tale of Tsar Durandai* and *The Little Music Box* deal with the touchy subject of the ineptitude of rulers. The treatment of such a topic in these two films was read by the authorities as a criticism of the contemporary system and probably helped bring about the authorities' subsequent total rejection of any type of satire in animated films.

The Little Music Box, made in 1933, was criticized by the press for its "incorrect interpretation of Shchedrin's satire",[54] and for "deviation from the social and historical concreteness of the period of reaction under Nicholas".[55] Fortunately Saltykov-Shchedrin's works were still in favor with the Soviet leaders, thus no serious consequences resulted from this criticism. In his film, Khodataev emphasized the punitive function of the rulers in Saltykov-Shchedrin's story right at a time when the country was experiencing dekulakization, forced collectivization of the peasantry, and terror unleashed because of famine. The repression of the peasants in the film could be seen as a direct allusion to the contemporary situation, while a scene where books burn in a library could be a reference to Soviet censorship. Potential allusion to contemporary society becomes even more marked towards the end of the film, when the governor arrives at a contemporary city, which has a clear Constructivist character.

The modern architectural style of the buildings in this scene sharply contrasts with the stylistic choices adopted in the rest of the film, which reflect the traits of traditional wooden toys and Vladimir Favorskii's wood engravings. In particular, the vivid character of Favorskii's engravings was faithfully reproduced by his disciple Georgii Echeistov, who

---

54 Volkov, "Mul'tiplikatsiia", 113.

55 Volkov, "Mul'tiplikatsiia", 116.

participated in the creation of this film together with Daniil Cherkes. *The Little Music Box* and *The Tale of Tsar Durandai* were the last two Soviet films that adopted this stylized manner and had satirical content. Soon animation underwent a change of direction.

A change of direction: animation for children only, the Disney influence

After the First Congress of Soviet Writers in 1934, when socialist realism became officially the mandatory canon to follow in art, most of the animators moved away from traditional Soviet animated films with ideological messages and began to create mainly films intended to entertain or educate the young audience. The decision to orient animation production towards films for children was in part a political choice, and in part due to Disney's influence on Soviet animation. In 1935 at the First International Film Festival in Moscow, some Disney animated films were screened to the general public with great success. The influence of American productions affected the choice of themes and style in Soviet films. Several Soviet animators enthusiastically embraced the American films' comic gags, slight plot development, and Disney's typical "roundness" of character outline. The adoption of Disney's style also had some political consequences, especially at a time when Stalinism insisted on cinema as an art form for the masses. Boris Shumiatskii, the head of the newly created Soiuzkino and later the deputy chairman of the GUFK (Chief Directorate of Film and Photo),[56] urged the need for "a cinema for the millions" and the necessity of following socialist realism in film, renouncing any formalism, and creating a "cheerful and joyful spectacle".[57]

Paradoxically, at a time when the import of foreign film was drastically diminishing, Shumiatskii was fascinated by American studios, and intended to build a Soviet Hollywood in the Crimea; he even traveled to the United States to study the American film industry in order to realize his project, but his dream never materialized – Shumiatskii was arrested and executed in 1938.[58] A similar visit to the United States, this time to animation studios, was made by Viktor Smirnov, who, after learning the techniques used for drawn animated films at the Disney studio[59] in 1933, came back to

56 GUKF – Glavnoe upravlenie po proizvodstvu khudozhestvennykh fil'mov, founded in 1933. In 1937 his title was simplified to GUK – Chief Directorate of the Film Industry.

57 Shumiatskii, "A Cinema for the Millions (Extracts)", 368.

58 Taylor, "Ideology as Mass Entertainment", 213–216.

59 Elizarov, *Sovetskaia mul'tiplikatsiia*, 207.

Russia bringing new technologies and a new approach towards animation in general. In 1934, a new studio, "Smirnovaia studiia", was created and linked to Mosfil'm. The eight films produced there over three years had mainly an entertainment purpose and were full of comic gags, although they were definitely of poorer quality and vividness then their American counterparts. However, not all the artists were willing to conform to the slogan "Give us a Soviet Mickey Mouse!" ("Daite nam sovetskogo Mikki Mausa!") which was announced at the 1933 All-Union Conference on Comedy (Pervoe vsesoiuznoe soveshchanie po problemam komedii), where issues concerning laughter and comedy in Soviet feature and animated films were discussed. During this meeting the supporters of Smirnov and of the Disney style he promoted clashed with some of the most talented directors (including Mikhail Tsekhanovskii, Nikolai Khodataev, and Ivanov-Vano), who tried to oppose the tendency to blindly imitate Disney-style. Some of them wrote articles in journals and publications;[60] some directly intervened with speeches at the 1933 conference, defending the singular qualities of Soviet animation and vehemently opposing American film style and themes. Nevertheless, these attempts did not succeed in arresting the shift in Soviet animation.

The quality of the films in the American style released by the Smirnovaia studiia could not compare with the American technological perfection. Smirnov introduced celluloid sheets in Russia only in 1933–1934, while in America the technique had been known for two decades, although not always used by American studios because of the high costs of royalties and of cel sheets in comparison with cheaper paper. In America, Earl Hurd, who used celluloid sheets to draw characters and then apply them over painted background sheets, patented cel technique already in 1914. Almost at the same time John Randolph Bray patented an alternative technique, which utilized cel sheets for painting scenery and then applied them over the drawings to be animated. Bray and Hurd formed together the Bray-Hurd Patent Company and earned healthy profits from royalties until 1932, when the patents expired. When the patent came into public domain, studios tended to use cel more often, since the costs diminished. Soon cel animation became the industry norm.[61] The celluloid sheets in the Soviet Union

---

[60] Especially Tsekhanovskii and Khodataev. See for example Tsekhanovskii, "Ot Murzilki k bol'shomu iskusstvu"; and Khodataev, "Iskusstvo mul'tiplikatsii", 66–69.

[61] Giannalberto Bendazzi, *Cartoons*, 2–21; Furniss, *Art in Motion*, 19–20; Crafton, *Before Mickey*, 150–155.

were of inferior quality to those available in America. The American cel sheets used at the end of the 1930s were of a good transparent quality that could allow juxtaposition of a few layers, while the Soviet cels had a slight grey or yellow tinge that would cause a considerable darkening of the drawing when more than three layers were used at the same time.[62] For a comparison of the retrograde techniques available in the Soviet Union, one can think of Walt Disney's use of the multiplane camera already in the *Silly Symphonies* film *The Old Mill* (1937) and partially in *Snow White and the Seven Dwarfs* (1937). This special device allowed the placement of cel sheets with characters and background scenery on superimposed glass planes, so that the different layers, seen from a perpendicular camera, could convey a three-dimensional composition and an enhanced quality of depth. In comparison with the results already obtained by Disney animation at the end of the 1930s, Soviet animation was developing slowly. The new system, however, enabled the Disney style to spread among Soviet animation artists and permitted the rate of production of animated films to increase drastically.

The use of drawings on cel, in fact, lent itself to a subdivision of work similar to that of an assembly line. Animated films became products of collective work, with the animators performing small and repetitive tasks. In this way production was greatly accelerated, but the end product, which had passed through several hands, tended to become standardized. Disney's style became dominant, especially the characteristically round outlines of his characters and his particular way of depicting the animals. As Crafton notes, a shift towards rounded traits had happened also in early American animation (see for example the transformation of the look of Felix the Cat). Crafton points out some aesthetic, economic, and psychological reasons for this change. Firstly, he notices how a rounded shape made Felix seem more cuddly and sympathetic; secondly, "circles were faster to draw, retrace, ink and blacken"; thirdly, animators seemed affected by what Gestalt psychologists call "shaping", a natural tendency to drift towards simple (circular) forms.[63] This approach, thus, suited animation for children and allowed increased production, but also worked against cultivating a distinctive style.

Indeed, this system made possible more centralized control over the activity of the animators, a control that followed

62 Ivanov-Vano, "Graficheskaia mul'tiplikatsiia", 172.

63 Crafton, *Before Mickey*, 313. Crafton also refers to Arnheim, *Visual Thinking*, 194–200.

Chapter 1   From Propaganda to Children's Films

the desire of the Soviet authorities to limit the artists' freedom of expression. It was not by chance that techniques such as cut-outs and puppet animation, in which the director had to follow the entire development of the film-making process, were not used again until the late 1950s.

In order to strengthen control over the activity of independent animators even further, the production of films came to be organized in a centralized location. A new studio, "Soiuzdetmul'tfil'm", was created in 1936 to centralize the animated film industry and replace production by small groups or individuals. Animators from Viktor Smirnov's studio, as well as from studios based at Mezhrabpomfil'm and Mosfil'm, began to work at Soiuzdetmul'tfil'm. The particle 'det' in the name of this studio (from detskii – for children) is symptomatic of the tendencies in animated films of these years, whose primary goal was the ideological and aesthetic education of young audiences. Later on the particle "det" was cut and the studio took its current name "Soiuzmul'tfil'm", but the tendency to produce only animated films for children lasted until the 1960s, when one began to see tentative signs of a renewal in style and theme.

With the creation of the studio Soiuzdetmul'tfil'm, the independence of several small groups came to an end; artists and directors with different artistic orientations had to work together and be subjected to direction by supporters of the Disney style. Some of the artists, realizing the impossibility of fighting against the dominance of Disney's style, left the studio. This was the case with the famous artist Nikolai Khodataev, who refused to produce frivolous and standardized films and abandoned in toto animation in order to fully dedicate himself to sculpture.[64]

Strict control over animation also broke through post-production. An increasing number of films began to be censored, including some films that did not seem to have any reference to contemporary politics. As an example it is enough to recollect how Suteev and Amal'rik's *Kolobok* (1936), a film based on the traditional Russian tale of the same name, in spite of no particular reference to actual situations, was accused of distortion of reality and caricature in its image of the kolkhoz. A year later, another film by Suteev made with the collaboration of Amal'rik, *A noisy voyage* (*Shumnoe plavanie*, 1937) was first accepted under

64 See Khodataev, "Pridia iz neizvestnosti, ia i ukhozhu v neizvestnost'", 186–190; and Khodataev, "Iskusstvo mul'tiplikatsii", 67.

41

Shumiatskii's direction, but in 1938–1939, after Shumiatskii's execution, the film was attacked on the basis of a changed attitude towards foreign music, jazz in particular, and for not representing Soviet reality.[65] Nationalist concerns began to be noticeably predominant with the approach of World War II, when Soviet animation experienced a brief revival of films for adults with political themes.

The animation of World War II and the restrained reawakening of political films

The pre-war atmosphere stirred a brief and temporary return to political films. Mythification of the past, exaltation of the present, and apotheosis of a brilliant future found expression through new patriotic films. They showed that an alternative path in the development of animation was still possible following the lesson taught by animated films of the 1920s and not limiting production to films directed at children's entertainment and education. The film *Victorious Destination* (*Pobednyi marshrut,* D. Babichenko and L. Amal'rik, 1939), after glorifying the 5-year-plans and the Stakhanovist movement, ends with a train representing the All-Union Communist Party speeding towards the direction pointed by Lenin. In other films, an accent on future successes gives way to the celebration of idealized pasts, a tendency started by live-action films of these years, such as Vladimir Petrov's *Peter I* (1937–38), Sergei Eisenstein's *Aleksandr Nevskii* (1938), and Vsevolod Pudovkin's *Minin and Pozharskii* (1939) and *Suvorov* (1941). One of the first animated films following this trend was *Militant Pages* (*Boevye Stranitsy,* D. Babichenko 1939, also translated as *War Chronicle*), a short consisting of a series of animated posters (*kinoplakaty*) that surveys the history of the Soviet Union from the Civil War to the Stalinist era.

In 1938, the idea of introducing political ideas in satirical form was actualized in the animated journal *The Political Satirical Journal No.1* (*Zhurnal politsatiry N. 1*, D. Babichenko, I. Ivanov-Vano, A. Ivanov, V. Polkovnikov, L. Amal'rik, 1938). The series released only two films in 1938 and 1941. Of these, the first issue has not been preserved; the second issue, *Political Satirical Journal No. 2* (*Zhurnal politsatiry N. 2,* I. Ivanov-Vano, A. Ivanov, O. Khodataeva, Z. and V. Brumberg, 1941) focuses on the fight against Hitler and Fascism.

65   See Borodin, "Animatsiia podnevol'naia", *Kinograf* 16, 140. See also Amal'rik's interview in the TV series *Animatsiia ot A do IA,* dir. Liakhovetskii and Margolina.

This topic reappears in other films of the same years, such as *How Vasia Terkin Went to Be Recruited* (*Kak Vasia Terkin prizyvat'sia shel*, P. Shmidt, V. Siumkin, 1941); *Cinemacircus* (*Kinotsirk*, O. Khodataeva, L. Amal'rik, 1942); and *He Surpassed* (*Prevzoshel*, V. Mudzhiri, Tbiliskaia kinostudiia, 1942). The most interesting films following these nationalistic subjects were *The Fascist Boot Won't Trample the Soil of Our Motherland* (*Ne toptat' fashistskomu sapogu nashei rodiny*, Ivanov-Vano, Ivanov, 1941), in which the popular march "The armor is strong, and our tanks are fast ..." ("Bronia krepka, i tanki nashi bystry ...") performed by the famous Aleksandrov ensemble emphasizes the patriotic spirit; and *When Goebbels Does Not Lie* (*Kogda Gebbel's ne vret*, S. Fedorchenko, Goskinprom Gruzii, 1944), which combines animation with documentary footage.

A few more films featuring patriotic themes or political caricature were produced by Dmitrii Babichenko, Ivan Ivanov-Vano, Aleksandr Ivanov, and Panteleimon Sazonov, using the style of the famous agitation posters of *Okna TASS* (*Windows TASS* – The Telegraph Agency of the Soviet Union), which were agitational political posters released during the years of World War II, continuing the tradition of the *Okna ROSTA* of the 1920s. An isolated experiment but worth mentioning, the film *Three Girlfriends* (*Tri podrugi*, P. Shmidt, Lenfil'm, 1941), about three girl-Pioneers who embark on a long flight to the Arctic, introduced in animation one of the favorite topics of the High Stalinist era: expeditions and aviators.

In general, during the war, animation production diminished considerably. In addition to the political film mentioned above, only a few films for children appeared in 1940 and 1941 at Mosfil'm, Soiuzmul'tfil'm, and Lenfil'm. In 1940 at Mosfil'm, Viacheslav Levandovskii and Georgii Elizarov, with the help of the famous puppet theater director Sergei Obraztsov as artistic consultant, produced a puppet film for children called *In the Land of the Dolls* (*V kukol'noi strane*). In the same year four animated films for children, this time drawn, were made at Soiuzmul'tfil'm, *And We, Too, to the Olympiad* (*I my na Olimpiadu*, V. Suteev), *Ivas* (*Ivas'*, Ivanov-Vano), *The Little Bear* (*Medvezhonok*, A. Evmenenko), and *Favorite Heroes* (*Liubimye geroi*, D. Babichenko), a film dedicated to the 20th anniversary of Soviet cinematography. Two other films were produced at Lenfil'm, *The*

Tale of the Stupid Little Mouse (*Skazka o glupom myshonke*, M. Tsekhanovskii) and *Circus* (*Tsirk*, A. Sinitsin). In 1941, only three films for children were made at Soiuzmul'tfil'm studio, two of them were adaptations of Kornei Chukovskii's tales, Leonid Amal'rik and Vladimir Polkovnikov put on-screen *Barmalei*, while V. Suteev adapted *The Fly-Tsokotukha* (*Mukha-tsokotukha*); P. Sazonov and Lamis Bredis, instead, referred to Krylov's fable in their *The Elephant and the Pug* (*Slon i mos'ka*).[66]

Soon the studios in Leningrad and Kiev closed, the studios in Erevan and Tbilisi released only a few films, and the Moscow studio Soiuzmul'tfil'm was evacuated to Samarkand, where, suffering from lack of means, it barely kept on functioning.

Animation after World War II: fables and folk art

When the studio Soiuzmul'tfil'm returned to Moscow, the production of animated films was slowly set in motion again. Some directors from Leningrad, such as Tsekhanovskii and Mstislav Pashchenko, and later the Armenian Lev Atamanov, joined the Moscow studio; while young artists like Lev Mil'chin, Anatolii Sazonov, and Evgenii Migunov also took part in the new collective. These new animators came from the well-known cinema institute VGIK (*Vsesoiuznyi gosudarstvennyi institut kinematografii* – All-Union State Institute of Cinematography), where in 1938 regular courses started to prepare artists for live-action and animated films. Courses came to a stop during the war, when the director Ivanov-Vano – who was one of the founders of the new department of animation inside the Faculty of Art – together with other members of the studio Soiuzmul'tfil'm evacuated to Samarkand. After the War, Ivanov-Vano continued to give courses at VGIK and at the Soiuzmul'tfil'm studio, and for the rest of his life he kept teaching as much as working in the studio.[67]

In the post-war years, animation artists working at Soiuzmul'tfil'm had to abandon once more the satirical and propagandistic films, with their poster and caricature style adopted during the war, in order to follow the studio's mandate of producing animated films for children. The animated films for children made in Soiuzmul'tfil'm had a

[66] Macheret and Glagoleva, *Sovetskie khudozhestvennye fil'my*.

[67] Ivanov-Vano, *Mul'tiplikatsiia vchera i segodnia*.

Chapter 1 From Propaganda to Children's Films

moralizing emphasis and promulgated values such as friendship, loyalty, comradeship, honesty, and the triumph of justice. Features of these animated films – a positive attitude towards the Socialist world, the victory of the good over the bad, the values of comradeship and sharing – recall themes found also in live-action films made during the Stalinist period. The language used in animation followed Lenin's dictum that cinema had to be made for the masses, even more so in the case of children's animation, in which the language is absolutely simplified in order to be comprehensible to a young audience. It seems that Soviet animation explicitly took upon itself the role of educating a particular segment of society, one that would be responsible for the future of the country. The didactic tone used in animation followed the tendency in Stalinist art to present a society that was working towards the realization of a perfect socialist world. The education of children was considered of vital importance to the creation of the new world. Youth organizations of the young Pioneers and the older Komsomol helped to spread ideological and universal humanistic values, which were promoted through children's literature and films, as well as cartoons made for children.

In terms of the aesthetics of the films, the most talented artists (such as the sisters Valentina and Zinaida Brumberg, Ivan Ivanov-Vano, Lev Atamanov, Leonid Amal'rik, Vladimir Polkovnikov, Evgenii Migunov, Panteleimon Sazonov, and Mikhail Tsekhanovskii, to mention a few), while still following the main naturalistic style brought by "Disney's revolution" and adopting Disney's style to such an extent that some of the characters and animals looked very similar, tried to infuse their work with a Russian spirit. The directors sought original aesthetic choices, looking at works by such well-known illustrators of Russian fables and fairy-tales as Ivan Bilibin, Valentin Serov, and Mikhail Nesterov. In order to do so, directors opted for adaptations of Russian classics in which elements of Russian traditions would be evident in the story; fairy-tales that would permit the introduction of elements of Russian folk-art; fables, especially animal fables, that would allow depiction of Russian nature in a realistic way; and contemporary tales that would immerse the young spectator in the specific Soviet reality.

Already during the 1930s, folk-tales and fables increasingly found their place on the screen in animated films. Fables, in particular adaptations from Krylov, fulfilled the desired didactic function for children, while folklore was seen as a re-appropriation of the past, of traditional values that started to acquire particular importance in the growing nationalistic spirit of the late 1930s. Already at the beginning of the 1930s, a general interest in folklore spread in literary circles, especially after Maxim Gorky returned from exile in 1931. After his speech in 1934 at the First Congress of Soviet Writers, in which he defined folklore as "the unwritten composition of the toiling man" and called on literature to follow folklore models,[68] a wide search for examples of oral folklore and for ways to disseminate this material was promoted. However, Clark notes that there are some contradictions in Gorky's advocating a marriage between literature and folk forms, since in his articles on literature published in the 1930s he insists on the "necessity of purifying the literary language and *expunging* all regionalism, earthiness, and *folkisms* from Soviet prose".[69]

Valentina and Zinaida Brumberg were famous for their adaptations of folk-tales – *The Tale of Tsar Durandai* (*Skazka o tsare Durandae*, 1934), *Ivashko and Baba-Iaga* (*Ivashko i baba-iaga*, 1938) – and fables such as *The Dragon-Fly and the Ant* (*Strekoza i muravei*, 1937) already in the 1930s. They also worked on adaptations of Russian literary classics with a strong folkloric content, such as *The Tale of the Tsar Saltan* (*Skazka o tsare Saltane*, 1943), based on Pushkin's story, and *The Disappeared Letter* (*Propavshaia gramota,* 1945) based on Nikolai Gogol'"s two stories "The Disappeared Letter" and "The Bewitched Place".

In adapting fables to the screen, filmmakers tried to retain some specific traits from Russian culture and especially from Russian nature. The film *The Little Grey Neck* (*Seraia sheika*, 1948), directed by L. Amal'rik and V. Polkovnikov, two of the most famous and successful directors in this genre, pioneered this new trend.[70] These films based on animal fables advocated moral lessons and inculcated such virtues as comradeship, reciprocal help, and respect for the elders and for nature. Apart from rare exceptions, the characters appearing in these fable-films often have the same characteristic traits as Disney's anthropomorphized animals, so that wolves, foxes, hedgehogs, hares, and other animals look the same in most of the films. This seems to have been one of the tendencies favored by Stalin, and one

68 Clark, *The Soviet Novel*, 147.

69 Clark, *The Soviet Novel*, 150.

70 See Pashchenko's films *Summer Travelers* (*Lesnye puteshestvenniki,* 1951) and *The Disobedient Kitten* (*Neposlushnyi kotenok,* 1953); P. Sazonov's *The Fox-Builder* (*Lisa-stroitel',* 1950), based on Krylov's fable; Aksenchuk's *On the Forest Stage* (*Na lesnoi estrade,* 1954), based on S. Mikhalkov's fables *Attention Birds* (*Ostorozhnye ptitsi*) and *The Drunk Hare* (*Zaiats vo khmeliu*). Some films made in the 1950s have a specific didactic goal, for example the film *Zai i Chik* (A. Ivanov, 1951) deals with teaching children street rules.

Chapter 1   From Propaganda to Children's Films

that several artists would oppose in the post-Stalin era. The film critic Anatolii Volkov reports that Stalin did not have a direct influence on the diffusion of the Disney style in Russian animation, but it was well known among cinema directors that the Leader liked Disney films, and in particular *Snow White and the Seven Dwarfs* (1937) and *Bambi* (1942), which had been shown in Russia in the postwar years.[71]

In the late 1940s and early 1950s, adaptations of fantastic tales became the main trend in Soviet animation and the most successful among the young audience. Examples in this genre had already begun to appear at the end of the 1930s, and later, in the Brumberg sisters' adaptation of Pushkin's *The Tale of the Tsar Saltan*.

This genre, however, was fully developed starting with Ivanov-Vano's film *The Hunchbacked Horse* (*Konek-gorbunok*, I. Ivanov-Vano, 1947, remade in 1975). With this film, Ivanov-Vano attempted to introduce a more original style, closer to Russian folklore, in particular to folk art, using achitectural styles typical of peasant villages, carved wood, embroidery, ceramics, and wooden toys. Talented directors such as Ivanov-Vano, Atamanov, and Ivan Aksenchuk produced several successful films in this genre starting from the late 1940s. Important examples include: Ivanov-Vano's *The Tale of the Dead Princess and the Seven Bogatyrs* (*Skazka o mertvoi tsarevne i semi bogatyriakh,* 1951) adapted from Pushkin's tale; *The Snow-Maiden* (*Snegurochka*, 1952), based on Aleksandr Ostrovskii's play and Nikolai Rimskii-Korsakov's music; *Twelve Months* (*Dvenadtsat mesiatsev,* 1956), an adaptation of a fairy-tale by S. Marshak; Atamanov's *The Yellow Stork* (*Zheltii aist,* 1950), based on a Chinese tale, *The Little Scarlet Flower* (*Alen'kii tsvetochek*, 1952), based on a Russian tale, *The Golden Antelope* (*Zolotaia antilopa*, 1954), based on an Indian tale, and *The Snow Queen* (*Snezhnaia koroleva*, 1957), based on a Danish tale; Aksenchuk's *A Walnut Switch* (*Orekhovyi prutik,* 1955); and Aleksandra Snezhko-Blotskaia and Polkovnikov's *The Enchanted Boy* (*Zakoldovannyi mal'chik,* 1955).

Thanks to several excellent directors, some Soviet animated films found a niche in which to blossom and several films were characterized by such an exceptional quality of graphic design and remarkable expressiveness of the animator-actor that they also appealed to adults; some of them also distin-

[71] Volkov, "Mul'tiplikatsia", 117.

47

guished themselves at festivals due to their excellent aesthetic qualities. A few of the films, though, suffer from a technique that once more was brought from the USA, rotoscoping. The method involved filming live actors, and then drawing their movements frame by frame. While this technique helped develop fluid movements in the characters, if used pedantically, providing an exact copy of each slight movement made by the actors, it would result in a slavish emulation of photography, a cold reproduction of merely external, superficial traits that lacked the imperfect and intangible, fantastic allure typical of animation. The best results with this method were obtained by choosing the most significant phases in the actors' movements; animation requires a certain degree of conventionality, and any attempt "to illustrate fantasy with realistic means"[72] gives only poor results. As mentioned earlier in the chapter, this is evident in the work of one of the most talented directors, Mikhail Tsekhanovskii, who, once he abandoned his experiments with sound and avant-garde art, dedicated himself to this naturalistic tendency. The films Tsekhanovskii made at Soiuzmul'tfilm with the rotoscope,[73] though still distinguished by the high quality of the drawings and images, lacked the spark of fantasy and originality that marked his earlier films.

A possible and brilliant alternative to this way of animating characters was shown in the film *Fedia Zaitsev* (V. and Z. Brumberg, 1948), which occupies a singular place in the history of animation of the post-war years. The stylistic choices adopted by the directors Brumberg, and in particular conceived by the artist Anatolii Sazonov, combined a naturalistic style with the convention, long avoided in Soviet animation, of using a simple animated profile of a child's drawing. The film was so successful that it was remade in 1960 with the title *I Drew the Little Man* (*Chelovechka narisoval ia*), at a time of new experiments in style, and of the Brumbergs' particular attention to children's drawings (see one of the films analyzed later in this book, *Great Troubles*, 1961). *Fedia Zaitsev* was based on an original story written by Mikhail Vol'pin and the famous satirist Nikolai Erdman. Not only was Erdman a script writer, but, until his arrest in 1933, he was also a poet and a talented dramaturge; he wrote several satirical sketches for the small-form theater (1922–1924), and he wrote two major plays, *The Warrant*

[72] Kracauer, quoted in Volkov, "Mul'tiplikatsia", 121.

[73] *The Flower with Seven Colors* (*Tsvetik-semitsvetik*, 1948), *The Tale of the Fisherman and the Fish* (*Skazka o rybake i rybke*, 1950), *Kashtanka* (1952), *The Princess-Frog* (*Tsarevna-liagushka*, 1954).

Chapter 1 From Propaganda to Children's Films

(1924) and *The Suicide* (1930), which were at first very successful, but later harshly criticized by the authorities, causing his temporary arrest and exile. Erdman and Vol'pin had started a thriving collaboration already in 1938 with the script for Grigorii Aleksandrov's hit musical *Volga-Volga*; after this success, they continued to write scripts together for live-action films[74] as well as for animated films. Their *Fedia Zaitsev* is a "contemporary tale", that is, a tale for children focused on contemporary reality. This new genre was most wanted by authorities and personalities such as Maxim Gorky who, already in 1935, during a meeting of writers and cinema workers, recommended that they pay particular attention to tales that combine magical transformations with reality: "Here there is a great space for fantasy, a great space for art, space for realism, a situation which does not preclude great flights of imagination".[75]

However, apart from *Fedia Zaitsev,* not many films focused on contemporary reality.[76] Most of the films produced in the Stalin years – adaptations of moral fables, folk-tales and fantastic tales – created an atemporal world, removed from everyday life and topical issues. One could speculate that during the difficult Stalinist years, artists considered it safer to focus on a fantastic reality and educate children through allegorical stories than to venture into actual events. It is a little simplistic to see a connection between the positive attitude of official socialist realist art and these fairy-tales, in which good always overcomes evil, but surely animated films of the Stalinist years had an additional task, to provide a diversion for adults who wanted to find refuge in a fabulous story that would take them far from the problematic and sometimes frightening life of the years following the war.

The Soviet films made after World War II had much in common with Disney's feature-length films and seem to have the same escapist role that Eisenstein noticed in Disney animation. While Disney, according to Eisenstein, served as a "consoler" to the grey reality and problems of capitalist countries, Soviet animation created a form of obliviousness that detached the spectator from any direct reference to reality. Eisenstein explains the escapism that Disney's films offered not in terms of their being a political and ideological tool used by the authorities, but as a unique form in which the "plasmaticness" of the drawings could bring the specta-

---

74 *The Actress (Aktrisa,* Leonid Trauberg, 1943), *Courageous Men (Smelye liudi,* Iudin, 1950), *The Outpost at the Mountain (Zastava v gorakh,* Iudin, 1953), *Behind the Footlights (Na podmostakh stseny,* Konstantin Iudin, 1956), *Stories About Lenin (Rasskazy o Lenine,* Iutkevich, 1957), *The Old Horseman (Staryi naezdnik,* Boris Barnet, 1959), *Father Frost (Morozko,* Aleksandr Rou, 1964, children film), *Through Fire, Water and ... Brass Pipes (Ogon', voda i ... mednye truby,* Rou, 1968, a children's film).

75 Gorkii, *Literatura i kino,* 438. Also quoted in Ginzburg, *Risovannyi i kukol'nyi fil'm,* 183.

76 Examples of successful films dealing with contemporary stories: *When the Fir-Trees Light Up (Kogda zazhigaiutsia elki,* Pashchenko, 1950), *The Magic Store (Volshebnyi magazin,* L. Amal'rik, V. Polkovnikov, 1953), *The Island of Mistakes (Ostrov oshibok,* V. and Z. Brumberg, 1955), *The Arrow Flies into the Tale (Strela uletaet v skazku,* Amal'rik, 1954).

49

tor to another dimension, "between the primal protoplasm and formed man",[77] that is, to a unique, almost atemporal dimension. One might wonder whether Russian animation of the Stalinist era, following Disney's style, would provide the spectators the same form of escapism. According to David MacFadyen, Soviet animation enacted an inclusive sense of union, providing a version of the Freudian "'oceanic feeling' of selfless union with others that has much in common with the (pre-dogmatic, romantic) goals of socialism".[78] While MacFadyen's fascinating theory and phenomenological approach link together Soviet animation between 1936 and 1999, seeing it as a fundamentally emotional, rather than a propagandistic enterprise, I will single out from this discourse the specific trend that appeared during Khrushchev's Thaw, when animation's function was not merely "emotional"; rather, it became more social and fulfilled specific needs in the cultural, social, and political Soviet world.

[77] Jay Leyda, *Eisenstein on Disney*, 69.

[78] David MacFadyen, *Yellow Crocodiles and Blue Oranges*, xvi.

Chapter 2

Russian Animation of the Thaw in its Socio-Political and Cultural Context

Khrushchev's Thaw: innovations and restrictions

The particular atmosphere that characterized the Thaw promoted the development of animation in new directions. In order to fully understand the phenomenon, it is important to look at the time in question from a broader point of view and recall the main events that determined such a distinct period of Soviet history. After the death of Stalin, radical changes occurred in the political sphere. Following 1953, the fact that Stalin was not replaced by a charismatic and strong man who would continue the tradition of the cult of personality – on the contrary, his successor attacked this same tradition – altered the Soviet people's perception of the socialist world in which they lived. Khrushchev questioned a god-like leader, revealing problems that had been hidden for a long time. The focus inevitably shifted to economic and social problems that needed to be resolved in the name of a positive future, a new path towards the "real" communism, and possible future achievements.

In promoting his vision of a better future, Khrushchev was more open to criticism of the present faults in society, and the arts experienced a moment of relative freedom. Although the Party and the official cultural institutions remained the final authority in determining what could and could not be expressed, the climate was still more open and receptive to new experiments than during Stalin's years. Changes and re-evaluations of Stalinist values for the first time appeared in an outspoken and direct way. This could be explained to some extent by the socio-economic situation of the Soviet Union after World War II, a time when the nation was recovering from the war and was more prone to paying attention to human needs, and also a time when the USSR needed more flexibility and foreign expertise in order to create a technologically advanced nation.

The entire period – named "the Thaw" after the eponymous novel written by Il'ia Ehrenburg in 1953 – was characterized by pendulum swings in the behavior of the authorities, at times granting more freedom, at other times freezing the liberal atmosphere and imposing harsher control. It was a time of contradictions as well as of instability that marked what one can define as the three waves of the thaw: the first wave started shortly after Stalin's death with the Central Committee Plenum in September 1953; the second occurred after Khrushchev's "secret speech" during the Twentieth Party Congress in February 1956; and a final thaw came in 1962, following the Twenty-Second Party Congress (October 1961).[79]

A new climate was created, and intellectuals were given more freedom already in 1954, when the Second Congress of Soviet Writers rejected the literary doctrine of "no conflict". This Soviet cultural policy, known as *Zhdanovshchina*, or *Zhdanovizm* – named after the Central Committee secretary with responsibility for ideology and culture Andrei Aleksandrovich Zhdanov, who developed it in 1946 – had forced all artists to conform to the Party line in their creative works, and had caused persecution of several writers, among them the satirist Mikhail Zoshchenko and the poet Anna Akhmatova. A more tolerant period for culture followed the Congress of Writers; yet, Party leaders maintained restrictions on artistic works and intervened in cultural affairs, often "suggesting" style and content. They understood the risk of permitting too much freedom, as Khrushchev recollects in his memoirs.

> We were scared – really scared. We were afraid that the thaw might unleash a flood, which we wouldn't be able to control and which could drown us ... . We wanted to guide the progress of the thaw so that it would stimulate only those creative forces which would contribute to the strengthening of socialism.[80]

At the beginning of the Thaw, in 1956, a series of literary rehabilitations occurred. Works by Il'f and Petrov, Isaac Babel', and Iurii Olesha became available, and in the pages

[79] See also Clark, *The Soviet Novel*, 211.

[80] Quoted in Suny, *The Soviet Experiment*, 404.

Chapter 2 From Propaganda to Children's Films

of the journal *Novyi Mir* new stories and novels were published, stretching the boundaries of what was permissible. Writers such as Viktor Nekrasov, Vladimir Dudintsev, Boris Pasternak, and Aleksandr Solzhenitsyn openly challenged the falsities of socialist realism, and younger poets like Evgenii Evtushenko and Andrei Voznesenskii appeared with verses criticizing the vestiges of Stalinism while experimenting with new forms. Poetry readings were held at the monument to Mayakovsky in Moscow's city center, and later, at stadiums. The most famous poets in these years – Evtushenko, Voznesenskii, Bella Akhmadulina and Robert Rozhdestvenskii – gathered crowds of hundreds and then thousands for their open-air poetry readings, a genre of mass entertainment that had its origins in the 1920s and was revived in 1956 with the founding of poetry days. But the authorities did not like these meetings, much less the films depicting them, such as *Il'ich's Gate* (*Zastava Il'icha*, 1961, M. Khutsiev, rel. 1965 as *I Am Twenty* [*Mne dvadtsat' let*]).

The end of 1956 marked a time of harsh and conservative moves in the political sphere. The taming of the insurrection in Poland in the summer of 1956 was followed by severe repression of the uprising in Hungary by Soviet tanks in November. The following year, 1957, Khrushchev also tried to hold back liberalization in the arts. He met with writers and artists in March and then May, reemphasizing the doctrine of mandatory artistic obedience to the Party line and the necessity to "write about what is positive in life".[81] Publishing was under strict control and reviews and articles about cinema from this time show caution, with the conservative position prevailing over the liberal.[82]

In May 1958, one major positive innovation occurred: the Central Committee revoked a decree issued by Zhdanov in 1948 that denounced "formalism" in music and signaled a campaign of persecutions against composers such as Dmitrii Shostakovich, Sergei Prokofiev, and Aram Khachaturian. At the end of the same year, however, the most striking examples of the "boundaries of the permissible" in the arts resonated both internationally with the famous "Pasternak affair", and in the sphere of cinema, with the replacement at the head of Mosfil'm of the film director Ivan Pyrev – who had fostered some innovative projects during the 1950s – by Leonid Antonov, an old Party man.[83]

81 Quoted in Suny, *The Soviet Experiment*, 406.

82 Woll, *Real Images*, 64.

83 Woll, *Real Images*, 64.

If the period 1957–1959 was characterized by a freeze in cultural policy, the subsequent period saw some relaxation, until a stronger sign of thaw came with the Twenty-Second Party Congress in October 1961, during which a new round of de-Stalinization was promised. In 1961, Evtushenko wrote his famous poem *Babi Yar*, and in October 1962 his *Heirs of Stalin* appeared in *Pravda*. New attempts to eradicate the Stalinist legacy took place. Aleksandr Solzhenitsyn's novel *One Day in the Life of Ivan Denisovich* was published in November 1962; subsequently, his novels *The First Circle* and *Cancer Ward* also found their way into the publishing world. Yet there were signs that the conservative impulse in the arts was still active, and some articles appeared attacking the innovative writers of the time, such as Ehrenburg and Voznesenskii.[84]

This third thaw began to look shaky in December 1962, when Khrushchev visited the Manezh Gallery in Moscow during an exhibition of young contemporary artists and, using foul language, attacked the abstract experimentation of the works exposed, in particular, those by Ernst Neizvestnyi. Some of the artists who took part in this modern art exhibition were also important figures in Soviet animation. The two main figures in this group, Ülo Ilmar Sooster and Iurii Nolev-Sobolev, created one of the most interesting and innovative films of the late 1960s, *The Glass Harmonica* (*Stekliannaia garmonika*, 1968).[85] The film, directed by Andrei Khrzhanovskii and written by Gennadii Shpalikov, was censored soon after its completion and not released until Gorbachev's *Perestroika*. Incidentally, the same Shpalikov was involved in another project that suffered from Khrushchev's disapproval; he was the co-author of the script for Khutsiev's film *I Am Twenty*, which was attacked by Khrushchev in March 1963 for giving a false picture of Soviet youth, and released only in 1965 after Khutsiev rewrote and re-edited it a few times.

Soon after the event at the Manezh, a campaign for "ideological purity" in art was launched, bringing with it a reshuffling in positions of prominence within the arts. However, it seems that, as Priscilla Johnson notes, maintenance of "ideological purity" in the arts was rarely at the center of Party attention, since drawn-out and contradictory decisions took place in these last two years of Khrushchev's power. For example, in December 1962, Shostakovich's

84 Johnson, *Khrushchev and the Arts*, 4.

85 See analysis in Chapter 4.

Chapter 2 From Propaganda to Children's Films

Symphony no. 13 based on Evtushenko's poems *Babi Yar* and *Fears* was cancelled after a second performance; but Bulat Okudzhava was able to perform in front of ten thousand people in January 1963. A three-month exhibition of Fernand Léger's art work was also set up in Moscow at the beginning of that year. Articles in defense of modern art appeared together with articles attacking it. At a moment in which anti-Western feeling seems to have been at its peak (especially after the Wynne-Penkovsky spy trial in May 1963), a high-level decision stopped the jamming of British and American radio broadcasts in Russia, and the jamming of Voice of America broadcasts stopped on 19 June 1963.[86]

Khrushchev rejected reactionaries' demands that the Party use force against progressive intellectuals; at the same time, he strongly asserted the control of the Party over both conservative and liberal trends. In a speech given on 24 April 1963, Khrushchev clarified his position towards the arts.

> Some creative intellectuals have drawn incorrect conclusions from the Party's work to overcome harmful consequences of the Stalin cult. They failed to grasp that struggle against the cult does not signify a weakening of leadership, a denial of authorities. Some have even begun to maintain that the time has come when everyone can determine his own line of conduct and the direction of his work, not reckoning with the interests of society and the state. This is nothing but an anarchist concept, hostile to Marxism-Leninism.[87]

It was during this particular time, characterized by inconsistent and variable cultural policy, that Soviet people saw the first innovative experiments in animation since the 1920s.

Animation shifts in new directions: from the Stalin Era to the Thaw

What did animation do to change and adapt to this particular moment in Soviet history? Animation directors reacted by giving more prominence to educational motifs in animated films for children, and also, more innovatively, by proposing new themes for the adult public. They departed from the fairy-tale worlds of Stalinist animation and attempted to bring the audience in contact with a reality that had specific referents in the Soviet Union under Khrushchev. Satire reappeared onscreen in animated films addressed to adult audiences. Khrushchev not only accepted, but also promoted satire as a "corrective tool" in the fight against social

86 Johnson, *Khrushchev and the Arts*, 52–54.

87 Quoted in Johnson, *Khrushchev and the Arts*, 48.

ills. It is not by chance that the main Soviet satirical journals enjoyed an increase in circulation in these years. However, the satire that appeared in animation did not at first constitute harsh criticism of the system, but rather tackled the same issues that concerned the establishment in these years. Production and release of films was controlled by a state department (Goskino). The presence of Party members in the artistic collective of the studio might have played an important role in pushing towards this direction, but it seems that the artists themselves felt the need to express new themes and adopt genres that reflected the general spirit of the time.

In animated films targeted to the youngsters, tales featuring children and set in a contemporary world began to appear more and more often. Educational animated films explicitly teaching principles of solidarity, friendship, duty, courage, responsibility, justice, love for nature, good behavior, and honesty now outnumbered traditional folk-tales and fantastic tales in the repertoire of Soviet animation production. Khrushchev's famous slogan "The present generation of Soviet people will live under communism!"[88] gave children hope that they would see the realization of true communism; children were charged with the great responsibility of saving the country and guiding it to the right path. The didactic stances in animated films were regarded in a new way; now children's good behavior attained the status of a heroic act performed in the name of a better future.

In general, once the past was under critical review, propaganda turned toward the present and the future, focusing on both actual everyday life and technological achievements and successes in space, thus also celebrating new kinds of hero and emblems of the future, such as the cosmonauts. This shift of attention was also reflected in the arts: a fascination with science fiction literature and cinema coexisted with stories of everyday life, presented without embellishments or the usual standardized heroes. Live-action films of the Thaw, as well as literary works, responded to Khrushchev's attack on Stalin's cult of personality, and to the desire of a population that had survived a war to see a truer representation of reality, depicting the little man rather than some bombastic "hero".

The emphasis on the future was stressed in animation on

[88] This renowned sentence was pronounced by Khrushchev at the Twenty-Second Congress of the Communist Party in 1961, and also ends the Program of the Communist Party approved on this occasion.

Chapter 2 From Propaganda to Children's Films

the one hand by the introduction of themes such as space and the development of technology, and on the other, by focusing on social criticism through satirical films for adults aimed at fostering a better society.

Space flights, sport, and the "Scientific-Technological Revolution"

The general atmosphere of these years, with new military technology, freer scientific inquiry, and space exploration, contributed to a growing interest in science and technology, the creation of a "myth" of science, and a consequent passion for the science fiction genre. In October 1957, the Soviet Union launched the first space satellite, called *Sputnik* (Fellow Traveler), and soon after, a rocket orbiting the Earth carrying the dog Laika. In April 1961, the space program's highest achievement was reached with the first human being in space, Iurii Gagarin, who became a national hero – the new Soviet hero – and a symbol of the superiority of Soviet socialism. Scientists, too, enjoyed a particular veneration in this time, symbolizing honesty and integrity in the public imagination. It was felt that their scientific truth was more objective and less questionable in comparison with all the lies that the Soviet people realized they had been living.

At this time, the genre of science fiction became widespread in cinema; live-action films based on scientific research, such as the controversial *Nine Days in One Year* (*Deviat' dnei odnogo goda*, M. Romm, 1962), appeared on screen. Themes of space and trips to the moon entered Soviet animation,[89] from Mayakovsky's utopian *The Flying Proletarian* (*Leta-iushchii proletarii,* I. Ivanov-Vano, I. Boiarskii, 1962) and the cosmonauts of *The Main Star* (*Glavnyi zvezdnyi*, R. Davydov, 1966), to the adventures of the serial animated character Murzilka, who appeared in two films dedicated to trips in space and to "contemporary miracles" presented at the VDNKh (Vystavka dostizhenii narodnogo khoziaistva, Exhibition of National Economic Achievements), namely *Murzilka and The Giant* (*Murzilka i velikan*, P. Nosov, 1960), and *Murzilka on the Sputnik* (*Murzilka na sputnike*, E. Raikovskii, B. Stepantsev, 1960), which was the first Soviet widescreen film. Moreover, in 1961, Estonian animation tackled the issue of the cosmos in the puppet film *Ott in Space* (*Ott' v kosmose*, E. Tuganov, 1961, Tallinfil'm), while in Moscow

[89] Even earlier, however, specifically in 1953, the sisters Brumberg made a film called *Flight to the Moon* (*Polet na lunu*, 1953), which presents the space adventures of the Pioneer Kolia.

in the same year, a glorious celebration of the cosmonauts Iurii Gagarin and German Titov was depicted in animated posters in a style typically used for the glorification of Soviet heroes (*Glory to You, Celestial Brothers!* [*Slava vam, nebesnye brat'ia!*], R. Davydov, I. Aksenchuk, 1961).

The significance of successes in space went beyond mere national pride. As Vail' and Genis note in their book on the Soviet people in the 1960s,[90] the Soviet achievements in the cosmos had a particular resonance in the free spirit of the Thaw. After the denunciation of Stalin, the possibility of reaching outer space seemed to be the ultimate act of liberation from a much-questioned past, and a new thrust towards the future.

If in space, Gagarin assumed the role of a new hero, on land, athletes also became the new idols, exalted as the new representatives of a better society. It is interesting to note that apart from the years 1980–1981, following the Moscow Olympics (1980), only in the years of the Thaw were numerous animated films about sports produced.[91] The reason for this is to be sought in the particular significance invested in sport in these years.

Although the importance of physical activity had always been stressed in Soviet propaganda, now more than ever excellence in sports became a matter of national pride, being another achievement of the Soviet people in an era in which space experiments put the Soviet Union on top of the world. The year of the Twentieth Congress, 1956, the Soviet Union won the most medals at the Olympics in Melbourne, for the first time surpassing the US team. In the press of the time, the new Olympic record in high jump achieved by Valerii Brumel' was compared to a further trip into space.[92] The Soviet Union had the highest medal count at the Olympics three times in a row (1956, 1960, 1964), thereby affirming its athletic superiority in the world. As Vail' and Genis note, sport was more tangible and convincing, and in this sense was actually preferable to the cosmos, which could not be seen, but only imagined.[93]

Thus the Soviet Union competed with the West on two fronts: technological achievements, and the superiority of the Soviet man in his physical strength. At international competitions, athletes played a similar role to soldiers at war, though this time in a peaceful contest. The very first

[90] In their book *60-e. Mir sovetskogo cheloveka*, Vail' and Genis perceptively discuss the peculiar state of mind of the Soviet people during the Thaw. I am indebted to their observations about the exaltation of achievements in space, sport, and science, discussed in this subchapter, as well as to their keen remarks throughout their book, which sparked my interest in the period in question.

[91] *Sportland* (*Sportlandiia*, A. Ivanov, 1958), *Samodelkin-sportsman* (*Samodelkin-sportsmen*, V. Bakhtadze, Gruziia-Fil'm, 1963), *Snow Paths* (*Snezhnye dorozhki*, B. Dezhkin, 1964), *Puck! Puck!* (*Shaibu! Shaibu!* B. Dezhkin, 1965), *Your Health* (*Vashe zdorov'e*, I. Aksenchuk, 1965).

[92] Vail' and Genis, *60-e*, 187.

[93] Vail' and Genis, *60-e*, 188.

decoration for a young athlete – that same decoration that Mitia, the main character of the cartoon *Sportland* (*Sportlandiia*, A. Ivanov, 1958) receives at the end of the film once he fights his laziness – has in its name a clear association to the soldier's task: BGTO "Bud' gotov k trudu i oborone" ("Be ready for toil and defense").[94]

Sport was a popular topic in animation because it was a good means of educating the young generation against laziness and of promoting a healthy life style, but also because it made it possible to introduce the idea of national pride to the young generation. Sport had always been publicized and considered imperative in Soviet society – it is enough to think about the sport scenes in Vertov's *The Man with A Movie Camera*, or the daily "Morning Gym Classes" on Soviet radio – but now it acquired a specific place in the ongoing comparison with the West.

Another point of confrontation between the Soviet Union and the West was in the area of achievements in science. In the Soviet Union, the importance of scientific achievements was not only a matter of national pride, but also had a specific atheistic ideological connotation. During Khrushchev's years, a propaganda campaign, the so-called "Scientific-Technnological Revolution", sought to promote science, space, and technology as substitutes for religion. The anti-religious movement was revived in 1959, first with a violent assault on the Orthodox church, and then with a calmer propaganda campaign focused more on scientific successes and a scientific credo[95] (together with a magnified cult of Lenin). As Vail' and Genis note, the measures against religious freedom were not contradictory to the liberal spirit of the time, but were actually a reflection of the time. It was not a matter of freedom of religion, but freedom from religion; religion was considered a remnant of the past, one not in harmony with science, progress, and communism: "believing in God was considered not so much harmful or dangerous as shameful".[96]

In animation the issue of science's opposition to religion, or to be more precise, how science dispels superstition, was hinted at in one of the best puppet films of this period, *The End of the Black Swamp* (*Konets chernoi topi*, V. Degtiarev, 1960), in which the famous fairy-tale characters of the wood-goblin (*Leshii*) and the water-sprite (*Vodianoi*) were

---

[94] Vail' and Genis also noticed the affinity of sport and war, see Vail' and Genis, *60-e*, 188.

[95] Stites, *Russian Popular Culture*, 145.

[96] Vail' and Genis, *60-e*, 237.

included in the category of "harmful superstition" (*vrednoe sueverie*). Symptomatic of a veneration of science is the scene in which a lecturer gives a speech on the theme "The Evil Forces in the World of Contemporary Science" ("Nechistaia sila v svete sovremennoi nauki").

> And the Russian peasant did not see a way out of the difficult reality surrounding him, and he hoped for help either from God, or from some sort of magical force, which folk imagination attributed to nature, say, the wood-goblin or the water-sprite. But at the present time, in our country, wood-goblins and water-sprites exist only in the poetic images of folk-art, as the beloved heroes of folk-tales. But if one still seriously believes in them, this is a harmful superstition, a remnant of the past.

This film does not aim to polemicize openly the question of superstition, but uses it as an element of the plot (Leshii reacts to the lecture with a sad "So I'm just a harmful superstition", and sets off back home). It is evident that such a theme and such a dogmatic speech ("It is a harmful superstition, a remnant from the past") used with a subtle satirical overtone could not have been allowed in another period of Soviet history.

In the film, life outside a big city is still presented as "active" ("We will build a Kolkhoz Vacation House on the black swamp", says the *kolkhoznik* who meets the wood-goblin in the woods) while it is counterposed to the "inactive" life of Leshii ("There's no need for you to idle around here", says the same *kolkhoznik* to Leshii). The right place for Leshii to live is pointed out by the *kolkhoznik*, the representative of the current doctrine: Leshii is supposed to live only in the world of fairy-tales, where he can finally be useful and active. These remarks hint at another topical issue in these years – the accusation of parasitism.[97]

The use of allegorical language makes this children's film also interesting for adults. In polysemantic animated films of this kind, one senses a hint of parody that takes the animation beyond blind acceptance and sharing of the authorities' points of view. Indeed, the films made in this new spirit strongly contrast with a film made in Khrushchev's early years, *The Miracle-Maker* (*Chudesnitsa*, A. Ivanov, 1957). In this film, the positive and productive activity in the countryside is promulgated in an open and direct way. There is no hidden message; it is a propaganda

[97] The most famous charge of parasitism was made against the young poet Joseph Brodsky in 1964.

film that is made appealing both to children and adults simply by using original and expressive characters and lively music, much like in live-action musicals of the Stalin era. With this musical animated film, which deals with the importance of corn to the overall Russian economy and Russian everyday life, animation took part in the promotion of Khrushchev's campaigns for the development of corn production in the Soviet Union. Films in this vein were positively received by the Soiuzmul'tfil'm studio; they represented an example to follow. Soiuzmul'tfil'm director S. Kulikov explained the themes that were favorably accepted at the studio in his reply to scriptwriters' letters.

> If you have a chance, look at our short, *The Miracle-Maker*, which outlines the advantages of corn in the national economy. The studio is interested in artistic proposals for the creation of similar films that have great political significance.[98]

The promotion of the country's achievements went parallel with criticisms of the faults of society that adopted either the tone of didactic parables, as for example when tackling the problem of alcoholism, or a satirical approach.

Propaganda and social criticism: new agitational films on the problem of alcoholism

In dealing with social ills, animation during the first years of Khrushchev's power reflected the Thaw spirit and at the same time contributed to spreading the new values of the Thaw through its power as a medium, that is, through exploiting its immediacy in conveying direct messages accessible to the masses. However, there was far from unanimous consent in the Soiuzmul'tfil'm studio. As it emerges from reports of the Artistic Council's meetings preserved in the Soiuzmul'tfil'm archive, artists within the studios had contrasting views on whether to follow new paths and address social problems, or to continue to focus on works for children. The innovators' aim was to "elevate" the perception of animated films to a mainstream art form that would reach adults as well. "Elevating" the status of animation did not mean transforming it into elite art, but insisting on its relevance in the cultural system, and bringing animation back to its origins, when it occupied an important place among artistic media.

During the mid and late 1950s, the directors' interest in early Soviet animation resulted in a return to satirical and propa-

[98] RGALI, "Stsenarnyi otdel. Perepiska s avtorami o predlogaemykh zaiavkakh i literaturnykh stsenariiakh (1958)", 21.

ganda films at least in theme, while they had to wait a few years before introducing drastic innovations in style. Animation took upon itself the role of educator not only of children, but also of an older audience; it began to confront serious and problematic social issues, with the desire of creating finer citizens, and consequently a better socialist society.

One of the issues that animation tackled in these years was the problem of alcoholism and its effect on the quality of workers' job performance. At the very beginning of Khrushchev's first thaw, in 1954, an animated film addressing this topic, *The Villain with a Label* (*Zlodeika s nakleikoi*, B. Stepantsev, V. Shcherbakov, 1954), was released. The script was written by Sergei Mikhalkov, a celebrated author of children's books and satirical fables, who wrote several animation scripts filmed in the studio Soiuzmul'tfil'm, and was also famous for composing the lyrics for the Russian national anthems. The story is quite simple: an animated bottle that personifies the evils of habitual drinking provokes a series of accidents at work with serious consequences for all the people who fall under its spell. While this film was one of the first examples of a new thematic direction chosen for animation, it also opted for a revival of old styles and material; it was, in fact, one of the first films made in the newly-founded (1953) division of Soiuzmul'tfil'm dedicated exclusively to puppet animation. Puppet animation technique was just beginning to be reconsidered after almost twenty years of absence from the studio – that is, since cel technique was introduced and the best director of puppet animation, Aleksandr Ptushko, stopped making his animated propaganda films. *The Villain with a Label* was the first tentative sign of the desire to find new stylistic choices in the studio, abandoning the dominant Disney style and cel technique specifically in order to deal with new and contemporary topics.

Using puppet animation for such topics was also indicative of the influence in Soviet animation of Czech puppet animation, which flourished during the 1950s. This connection is documented in a letter[99] that the director of Soiuzmul'tfil'm, A. Sinitsyn, sent to K. Kuzakov, the director of the Department of Cinematography (better known now as Goskino), with a request to allow the artists working on this film to view a Czech animated film against drinking

99 RGALI, "*Zlodeika s nakleikoi*: Materialy fil'ma", 26.

Chapter 2   From Propaganda to Children's Films

and driving, *A Drop Too Much* (*O skleničku víc*, 1954) – it was often necessary to have written authorization from Goskino to view foreign films. Directed by Břetislav Pojar with the collaboration of Jiří Trnka as art director, this Czech film embellishes with expressive and original visual choices some typical traits of agitational films: a plainspoken dramaturgy and the use of intertitles or, as in this case, voiceover in order to convey explicit messages to the masses.

In a similarly straightforward way, *The Villain with a Label* meant to create a propaganda film in a style typical of early Soviet animation; the film gave itself the designation of "agitational animated film" (*agit-mul'tfil'm*) in the original script,[100] while later on the screen it would appear with a designation that was still propagandistic but less agitational, "cinematic poster" (*kinoplakat*). The importance of going back to the experiments of the past in this genre was also recognized during a discussion of the film in a meeting of the Artistic Council, where it was openly stated that if the film meant to follow the genre of cinematic poster, it had to be as direct and clear as the posters in the *Okna ROSTA* and *Okna TASS*.[101]

Indeed, *The Villain with a Label* presents various situations in a simple and direct way, organizing each little story in a short independent episode, which ends with intertitles in the style of the Russian propaganda films of the 1920s. The intertitles of this film instigate the population to avoid alcohol with catchy phrases such as: "Sometimes drunkenness is just two steps away from crime" ("Inogda ot op'ianenia dva shaga do prestupleniia"); "A vodka drinker at work is a detriment to the country" ("Ushcherb strane nanosit tot, kto na rabote vodku p'et"); "After a shot of vodka, the road to the grave can be short" ("Byvaet, chto ot riumki vodki i do mogily put' korotkii"); "Remember, city and village dwellers! Fight against alcoholism. Alcoholism is evil!" ("Zapomni gorod i selo! Borites' s p'ianstvom. P'ianstvo – zlo!").

In making such a film, the artists and directors inevitably also had to consider the role of the government in the entire issue of alcoholism. During the Artistic Council meeting, discussions took place on the best way to tackle this complex and delicate question. One of the participants noted that it was necessary to change the label of the bottle from "vodka" to "drunkenness" (*p'ianstvo*), since, in his words,

[100] RGALI, "Zlodeika s nakleikoi: Materialy fil'ma", 1.

[101] See the influence that these agitational political posters had on early Soviet animation in Chapter 1.

in Mikhalkov's script vodka was shown as the enemy, as evil. This was wrong. Even politically incorrect. If vodka is to be judged, then it would be necessary to prohibit its distribution. And in the meantime, the government continues to increase vodka distribution. But from this, by no means does it follow that one should get drunk."[102]

While this film avoids blaming the authorities for not taking drastic measures against vodka distribution, it also calls attention to one of the most famous mobilization campaigns with which Khrushchev aimed to channel young people's energy into something productive and positive for the country and keep them far from the danger of alcoholism. At the end of the film, a man finally refuses the bottle and breaks it. This man is no one else but the driver of a train, a symbol of the move towards a bright future; what's more, the train has the sign "To the Virgin Lands" (*Na tselinnye zemli*) on its side. It is no coincidence that Khrushchev's Virgin Lands Campaign started in 1954, the same year that this film was released.

Trying to tackle the delicate question of alcoholism by focusing on educational – rather than aesthetic – goals produced a result that was not particularly entertaining, but rather gloomy, devoid of all hints of the humor that characterized the original script written by Sergei Mikhalkov. In 1960, Mikhalkov wrote a second script on the theme of alcoholism, *The Sober Sparrow: A Tale for Adults* (*Nep'iushchii vorobei. Skazka dlia vzroslykh*, Amal'rik, 1960), which used allegorical animal characters in the genre of animal fables. This second film was less innovative, for it was still made using a traditional genre and the dominant cel technique, which was a widely adopted style in the post-war years, especially in adaptations of Mikhalkov's fables and stories.

In the following years, the tendency to confront the problem of alcoholism using animation in different ways at different times is symptomatic of the changing attitude towards the topic on the part of authorities and the artists at Soiuzmul'tfil'm. For example, a film made in 1963 (*Check Your Watch – Prover'te vashi chasy*, Ivan Aksenchuk) focused on the question of alcoholism related to slacking and absenteeism at work. Later films, such as *Your Health* (*Vashe zdorov'e*, I. Aksenchuk, 1965) and *Heart* (*Serdtse*, B. Stepantsev, 1971), paid more consideration to the harmful consequences of alcohol for the individual's health – this was a time when

[102] RGALI, "*Zlodeika s nakleikoi*: Materialy fil'ma (1954)", 20.

Chapter 2 From Propaganda to Children's Films

animation was finally giving more attention to the individual, while authorities were giving less publicity to societal faults.

Apart from a few propaganda films of this kind, Soviet animation of these years started to focus on social ills through satirical films. The first films were realized in a traditional style, and only later, at the beginning of the 1960s, did the style of satirical animation develop in new and original ways.

Satire in Soviet animation

As mentioned earlier, the need to produce films for an adult public was highly debated inside the Soiuzmu'tfil'm studio. Some traditional artists preferred to focus on animation for children, opposing propaganda films as well as the new planned satirical cartoons for grown-ups. The first satirical films made for adults in the late 1950s constituted a compromise between more innovative and more traditional trends; they denounced some of the recognized weaknesses in Soviet society, but without introducing ground-breaking styles. The first targets of these attacks were some of the old objects of satire in Soviet satirical journals, the bureaucrats. At first, animation criticized them in allegorical form, such as in the film *The Signature Is Illegible* (*Podpis' nerazborchiva*, A. Ivanov, 1954), which deals with the ineptitude of the managers in a world populated by moles, rats, cats, and hedgehogs. Later, allegorical animals were abandoned and bureaucrats started to be berated more directly, as in the puppet film *The Ballad of the Table* (*Ballada o stole*, R. Davydov, M. Kalinin, 1956). Only in the second half of the 1960s did criticism of bureaucrats take the form of a harsh and pessimistic attack, as seen in the films *Man in the Frame* (*Chelovek v ramke*, F. Khitruk, 1966) and *There Once Lived Koziavin* (*Zhil-byl Koziavin*, A. Khrzhanovskii, 1966).[103]

It is important to notice that while satirical themes and propaganda works (such as those directed against alcoholism) appeared in the very first years of the Thaw (1954–1956), in the period of "freezing" (1957–1959), the only animated films on contemporary life that were released were two satirical films that probably began production in 1956,[104] films dealing with the Moscow World Youth Festival in 1957,[105] and cinematic posters on achievements in

103 See Chapter 4.
104 *Well-Known Pictures* (*Znakomye kartinki*, E. Migunov, 1957); *At the Dining Hall* (*V odnoi stolovoi*, G. Lomidze, 1957).
105 *Hello Friends* (*Privet druz'iam*, D. Babichenko, B. Dezhkin, M. Pashchenko, 1957), *To the Sixth Worldwide* (*Shestomu vsemirnomu*, E. Migunov, 1957), *The Song of Friendship* (*Pesnia o druzhbe*, M. Botov, I. Ivanov-Vano, 1957).

electrification and development of cotton-growing.[106] It seems that during the political reaction of the late 1950s, animators tried to avoid touching on the country's problems and waited to see the direction in which political events would turn. In the meantime, in animated films, old-style celebrations of Soviet heroes and deeds appeared on the screen: in 1957, the film *Our Sun* (*Nashe solntse*, I. Aksenchuk, 1957) commemorated the fortieth anniversary of the Revolution, and in 1958, two films celebrated the Red Army: *The Song of Chapaev* (*Skaz o Chapaeve*, M. Tsekhanovskii, 1958) and *The Tale of the Boy-Kibal'chish* (*Skazka o mal'chishe-kibal'chishe*, A. Snezhko-Blotskaia, 1958).

Already in 1959, directors expressed a desire to widen the range of themes and genres used in animation. In an article that appeared in *Iskusstvo Kino*, artists, while openly praising the first films that appeared in the mid-1950s in the satirical and propaganda genres, also ventured to suggest that they move from producing mostly fairy-tales and children's stories (which were still the main genres at Soiuzmul'tfil'm) to films dealing with topical problems.[107]

Finally, the year 1960 saw a revival in the production of films on satirical and topical themes, which also reflected the vast increase of interest in satirical journals in these years. As a matter of fact, according to Richard Stites, *Krokodil*, the most famous Soviet satirical journal, enjoyed a significant increase in circulation in the early 1960s, from 300,000 in 1953 to 1,700,000 in 1963.[108] Founded in 1922, *Krokodil* attacked imperialists, foreign spies, and enemies, and in general ridiculed domestic weaknesses such as laziness, bad work habits, parasitism, corruption, pilfering, and farm and factory mismanagement – all faults that hindered the development of Soviet society and the economy. The success of this journal during the Khrushchev era was not only due to the role and importance of satire in the Thaw, but also to the particular role performed then by laughter. As Vail' and Genis pointed out, laughter provided a relief from the "dark" times of official seriousness, and was a way to counteract Khrushchev's tragic revelations, with which 1960s Soviet society had to come to grips. Animation of these years combined in itself these two functions of laughter: it attacked negative aspects of life with withering satire, and at the same time affirmed positive principles. Once again, this new phase of Soviet animation was at the same time a

106 *An Incarnated Dream* (*Voploshchennaia mechta*, N. Fedorov, 1957); *The Children of the Sun* (*Ditia solntsa*, A. Ivanov, 1957).

107 Iskusstvo Kino [Editorial Board], "Smelee iskat' novoe v mul'tiplikatsionnom kino!" 93–100.

108 Stites, *Russian Popular Culture*, 136.

product of the Thaw, and a tool that, together with other art forms, fostered the freer atmosphere of this era and contributed to its general spirit.

Just as in the 1920s Russia started a new chapter in its history, during the Thaw, the Soviet Union seemed to take a new, although less radical, turn. As in the early post-Revolutionary years, art was invested with the role of attacking social ills mainly through satire and propaganda works in order to strengthen the new socialist world. Soviet animators, in the 1920s as well as in the late 1950s, felt the need to contribute with their work to this civic task. The experience of the early films taught animators that the most effective approach to attacking social weaknesses was through brief and witty animated films. Khrushchev himself mentioned the necessity of releasing satirical newsreels in his speeches at meetings with workers.[109] In 1960, animators decided to produce an animated journal called *Animated Crocodile (MUK – Mul'tiplikatsionnyi krokodil)*. The cinematic journal *Animated Crocodile* marked a significant step towards a return to the original civic tasks of Soviet animation. In its name, the journal referred to its forerunner, created in the early 1930s. This early satirical animated journal, *Kino-Krokodil* (1932–33), released only seven issues[110] (two of which have been preserved) before being discontinued due to changes in the political sphere – in the mid 1930s, satire against faults in Soviet society was no longer welcome, and soon all satirical animated films were banned by the authorities. Incidentally, during the war, two issues of another animated satirical cinematic journal, *The Journal of Political Satire (Zhurnal politsatiry*, 1938–1941), appeared on the screen, though this time the attacks were directed exclusively against foreign enemies.

The *Animated Crocodile* of the 1960s was what could be defined as a "cinematic journal" (*kinozhurnal*, or to be more precise, an animated journal, *mul'tzhurnal*) in which satirical subjects for adults were presented onscreen in a ten-minute issue. The original project provided for a regular series of at least three issues a month, and in order to meet this target it was proposed that a special group be created inside Soiuzmul'tfil'm to work exclusively on this journal. According to some of the artists who worked in the studio, the first issue of *Animated Crocodile* was not completely successful; it needed more biting themes and experimentation with new

109 "Govoriat mastera mul'tiplikatsii", 131.
110 Macheret and Glagoleva, *Sovetskie khudozhestvennye fil'my*.

visual forms, so that "the teeth of the crocodile would be visible and sharper".[111] The themes treated in the *Animated Crocodile* varied from poor administration, careless suppliers, lack of respect for nature, and defense of peace in the first issues to, in later issues, more concrete examples of pollution, misused energy resources, disrespect for communism, infatuation with dazzling foreign products and life styles, poor quality of consumer goods, and parents' responsibility for spoiled and "parasitical" grown-up children.

As with its 1930s forerunner, *Animated Crocodile* stopped being released after only a few issues, the sixth and last number appearing in 1961. The reasons for discontinuing the production of this new satirical newsreel were less political than in the case of its predecessor. The shutting down of *Animated Crocodile* was due to internal difficulties in organizing a constant group of animators dedicated exclusively to this project, and most of all it followed the creation of another satirical newsreel, one which was not exclusively animated. It was easier and quicker to deal with topical issues in live-action style than in animation, which requires a great number of drawings for just a few seconds. The novel newsreel, *Fitil': An All-Union Satirical Cinema Journal* (*Fitil'. Vsesoiuznyi satiricheskii kinozhurnal*), was first released in 1962 and ran for many years. *Fitil'* was a cinematic journal in which each issue comprised three or four episodes about three minutes long. Most of the episodes consisted of footage presenting real situations or staged situations, but there were consistently a few animated episodes. The editorial team for *Fitil'*, an independent group devoted exclusively to this project, was directed by the influential Sergei Mikhalkov, who always found a way to make satire acceptable to the authorities. Each issue of *Fitil'* dealt with concrete situations with wit and acuity, most of the time having to do with inefficiencies found in various areas of the Soviet Union. Particularly successful were those episodes in which the irony was derived from juxtaposing untruthful words with images showing the real facts, and those that used the most successful comedian of the time in staging a situation.

Famous actors participated not only in *Fitil'*, but were also recruited for animated satirical films. In the more liberal climate, the performing arts were given greater latitude in terms of the topics they were allowed to cover, and comic actors became bolder in their attacks on the social condi-

111 Iutkevich in "Govoriat mastera mul'tiplikatsii", 132.

tions. For example, Arkadii Raikin, one of the most famous comedians of the time, incorporated in his variety theater repertoire many topics that had become possible to air only since Stalin's death, such as the lack of day care, poor restaurant service, shoddy workmanship, careerism, dull bureaucrats, philandering, mindless pedagogy, and alcohol abuse.[112]

It was Raikin who starred as presenter in a series of drawn sequences in an animated film made in 1957, *Well-Known Pictures* (*Znakomye kartinki*, E. Migunov, 1957), which deals with a range of issues, including the influence of foreign fashion, the lack of competence and slackness of workers, dishonesty, and uncultured behavior. Raikin also contributed to another influential and satirical animated film (mixed with live-action) made in the early 1960s, *The Bath* (or *The Sauna*) (*Bania*, S. Iutkevich, A. Karanovich, 1962), based on Mayakovsky's famous play written in 1929. Another very famous comic actor, Igor' Il'inskii, appeared in *The Ballad of the Table*, one of the above-mentioned films directed against bureaucrats.

The participation of such famous actors in animated films was symptomatic of the ongoing attempt to reconceive the role of animation during the Thaw years. The presence of Il'inskii and Raikin encouraged the relations with other forms of art that animation sought in order to acquire general recognition as being on the same level as the performing arts and live-action cinema. The film *Bania* had an important role in this trend: it strengthened the relationship between animation and the performing arts not only by having theater and film actors participating in the live-action sequences, but also by the very structure of the film, which mixes theater, puppet theater, live-action film, and animation. By creating intertextual references to other artistic spheres drawn from popular culture, animation of the Thaw attempted to attract an adult public to a form of art that had been relegated to child audiences for many years.

Popular culture and western influence

During the 1960s, a light mass culture emerged with pop songs and a form of mass entertainment that borrowed from foreign shows: variety theater (*estrada*). Soviet spectators responded with enthusiasm to TV shows like "Goluboi

112 Stites, *Russian Popular Culture*, 138.

ogonek",[113] in which they could see their favorite singers and music, amuse themselves with jokes and incredible stories, and at times even enjoy the participation of cosmonauts – a Soviet touch in an entertainment form that was predominantly foreign. As far as music is concerned, clear signs of a reaction against official music appeared in the form of bard-poetry and the diffusion of Soviet pop music. Bard songs, that is, songs composed and performed on the guitar by artists who were at once singers and poets, had great popular success but were barely tolerated by the authorities. The phenomenon started in Khrushchev's era, but it developed greatly during Brezhnev's years, in which guitar poetry was – like underground poems – part of the opposition to the official culture. Most often this music was released through unofficially produced and circulated tapes, through "magnitizdat" or "tape recorder publishing", in the same way that literature circulated through "samizdat". Under the influence of these artists, Soviet youth began forming guitar groups that would get together out of doors or in people's apartments. The songs of this new genre offered a new musical mood that differed from what was heard on the radio and sold on records.

The "mass songs", with their patina of officially mandated optimism (a sign of official culture – *kazennaya kul'tura*), were still favored by the leaders, and still very popular among Soviet audiences, but in the Thaw years they were often parodied. One particular song is symptomatic of a shift in the official mood, the extensively popular song "Evenings Outside Moscow" ("Podmoskovnye Vechera", by Vasily Solovev-Sedoi, words by M.L. Matusovsky, 1956), which was so famous that in 1956 its opening bars replaced those of Isaak Dunaevskii's highly patriotic "Song of the Motherland" ("Pesnia o rodine") as the chimes that sounded the hours on Radio Moscow. This change was indicative of a shift in official and pop art, and represented the growing relevance of pop songs in Soviet culture. In Richard Stites' words, it stood for "a landmark in the depoliticization of popular song".[114]

Animation directors chose to take advantage of this shift to lighter entertainment and tried to lure a broader audience by bringing into its films elements drawn from the realm of popular culture. Not only did animators turn to well-known actors, as mentioned earlier, but they also incorporated

[113] For a brief history of the variety show "Goluboi ogonek" see Larina, "Krasno-belo-goluboi ogonek".

[114] Stites, *Russian Popular Culture*, 131.

Chapter 2 From Propaganda to Children's Films

popular songs into films that, at first sight, seemed to be addressed only to children. With such "quotations" from other spheres of Soviet culture, animation was carving out a space for adults inside animated films for children, in other words, creating something like the Bakhtinian heteroglossia, "*another's speech in another's language*, serving to express authorial intentions but in a refracted way".[115] Through this double-voiced discourse, grown-ups could interpret films for children on a different level, and perceive the messages that directors addressed to them. In doing so, animation was striving to become a unifying force that could permeate various strata of society, thus growing to be generally accepted as a cultural phenomenon.

With perhaps this purpose in mind, the director of the puppet film mentioned earlier, *The End of the Black Swamp*, used the song "Evenings Outside Moscow" in one scene. This song also expressed a shift in the official mood – from the bright urban optimism of the 1930s to a more calm and nostalgic celebration of country life and an attraction to spaces outside the city. In *The End of the Black Swamp*, even the folk character of the wood-goblin seems to envy these peaceful evenings outside Moscow ("To live in the countryside, oh that's beautiful!" – "zhit' teper' v derevne, ekh krasota!"). The idealized countryside of "Evenings Outside Moscow" sets up the context of the film and recalls Khrushchev's exaltation of rural life.

In both the literature[116] and cinema of the time, provincial life acquired an increasingly privileged place, while big cities were demystified. As Katerina Clark notes, a reversal of the Stalinist valorization of place occurs: if in the Stalinist novel Moscow signified a higher-order reality, the perfect communist society, while the provincial town, factory, or kolkhoz was a step behind on the path to perfection, now Moscow (or Leningrad) became the "false" place, where bureaucracy, careerism, and lack of sincerity reigned. Places outside the big cities, which were less urbane, were more linked with Leninist ideals and so more appealing for the new heroes.[117] Animation of the Thaw followed this tendency towards both exaltation of the countryside, as seen in *The End of the Black Swamp*, and the demystification of big cities – as shown also in an animated film analyzed in Chapter 3 of this book, *Story of a Crime* (*Istoriia odnogo prestupleniia*, Khitruk, 1962).

[115] Bakhtin, "Discourse in the Novel", 324.

[116] In particular in a new type of novel that appeared for the first time in 1956, the so-called "youth novel".

[117] Clark, *The Soviet Novel*, 227.

The song "Evenings Outside Moscow", devoid as it is of any reference to Khrushchev's predilection for the countryside, was also used in Anatolii Karanovich's film *The Song Flies Around the World* (*Pesnia letit po svetu*, 1965), in which the song is chosen simply for its extraordinary popularity, and resounds in various languages as a gesture of international solidarity.

Solidarity was certainly the prevailing spirit of an important event taking place in these years, the 1957 World Youth Festival, which signaled a great turning point in Soviet youth culture. At the festival, Soviet young people had a chance to meet youth from other countries and encounter foreign fashion, and for the first time, foreign rock and jazz were played at an official event. Jazz, in fact, was still not formally accepted, but it spread among young audiences who listened to the radio programs begun in 1955 on Voice of America, or who would gather to dance at parties or jazz clubs that started to proliferate in Soviet towns. Nevertheless, in the last year of the Khrushchev era the clubs were closed, and in a speech on March 8, 1963, Khrushchev openly attacked jazz music.[118] Rock, too, first began to be heard in the Soviet Union in the 1950s via Voice of America, and soon a large underground market developed in smuggled records and homemade recordings, often made on x-ray plates.[119] According to Kristin Joy Roth-Ey's dissertation on Soviet mass media in the 1950s and 1960s, the Festival was also the first event in Soviet history to receive extended live television coverage,[120] so while having a broad potential audience, it also assumed the status of an official event. Animators also welcomed the Youth Festival by producing some animated films dedicated to it: *Hello Friends* (*Privet druz'iam*, D. Babichenko, B. Dezhkin, M. Pashchenko, 1957), *To the Sixth Worldwide* (*Shestomu vsemirnomu*, E. Migunov, 1957), and *The Song of Friendship* (*Pesnia o druzhbe*, M. Botov, I. Ivanov-Vano, 1957). These films not only delivered a message of desirable international comradeship among youth, but also represented once again the animation directors' attempt to find a connection to the cultural events that were stirring people in these years.

Relationships with western countries have always been ambivalent in Soviet cultural history, marked by periods of slight openness toward the West, alternated with brusque closing of relations. This swing behavior particularly char-

118 See Johnson, *Khrushchev and the Arts*, 175–177.

119 See Stites, *Russian Popular Culture*, 132, and Troitsky, *Back in the USSR*, 19.

120 Roth-Ey, "Mass Media and the Remaking of Soviet Culture 1950s–1960s", 66.

acterized the Khrushchev years; a period of détente was followed by some extreme manifestations of Cold War animosity, especially with the Cuban Missile Crisis in the early 1960s and the deteriorating relationship with China – two events that had a great impact on the end of liberalization. International relations were a hot topic in satirical journals, which presented western countries and their influence on Soviet culture with specific details and nuances. In other words, they provided a specific concretization of a precise moment in Soviet history.

Animation followed the satirical journals, and in particular *Krokodil*, in attacking imperialism and foreigners' behavior, and exposing the detrimental influences of Western culture on Soviet youth and society. In such anti-imperialistic and anti-American films as *Read and Take a Drive to Paris and China* (*Prochti i katai v Parizh i Kitai*, A. Karanovich, T. Bunimovich, 1960), *Overseas Reporter* (*Zaokeanskii reporter*, G. Lomidze, 1961), *Mister Twister* (*Mister Tvister*, A. Karanovich, 1963), and *Shareholders* (*Aktsionery*, R. Davydov, 1963), animators, as in early Soviet animation, ridiculed and criticized Western people and culture. In doing so, they revived and developed some of the old techniques used in propaganda and satirical films of the 1920s, such as cut-outs and poster-like style. Other films dealt specifically with the harmful Western influence on Soviet culture: *The Puppets Have the Word* (*Slovo imeiut kukly*, A. Karanovich, 1957), *Well-Known Pictures* (*Znakomye kartinki*, E. Migunov, 1957), *Animated Crocodile* (1960–1961), *Great Troubles* (*Bol'shie nepriiatnosti*, Z. Brumberg, V. Brumberg, 1961), and a later post-Khrushchev film on similar topics, *The Passions of Spies* (*Shpionskie strasti*, E. Gamburg, 1967). A favorite subject of ridicule in all these films was the spread of foreign dance, music, and clothing style in popular culture. The type of person that most embodied these deleterious tendencies was the *stiliaga*, a term derived from the word *stil'*, style, to indicate their attitudes and their particular way of dressing and behavior. It did not seem, however, that satire and ridicule had an immediate effect in limiting the spread of these "harmful" trends. A more detailed treatment of the phenomenon of *stiliagi* will be tackled in Chapter 3 in the analysis of the film *Great Troubles*. Here I would like to point out only that the *stiliagi* were not numerous, but they were perceived as presenting a public rejection of official values.

The authorities feared that they would "contaminate" most of the youth; as a recent live-action film on *stiliagi* puts it, "Every *stiliaga* is a potential delinquent" ("Kazhdyi stiliaga – potentsial'nyi prestupnik", *Hipsters* [*Stiliagi*], Valerii Todorovskii, 2008).

In order to channel the young people's energy into something productive and positive and keep them far from the danger of alcoholism, Khrushchev initiated a series of mobilization campaigns, the most famous of which was the Virgin Lands project from 1954 onward. This scheme was devised to increase agricultural production by turning previously non-arable land in Central Asia into cultivated fields. Thousands of people took part in this enterprise, mostly youth and workers. The Komsomol was in charge of recruiting young people and did this using official pomp – such as ceremonies in the Kremlin and receptions and parades in towns – and style, namely patriotic persuasiveness, analogies with the great construction projects of the 1930s, and celebration of cult figures, such as Pavlik Morozov and Pavel Korchagin.[121] No animated films were made explicitly to promote the Virgin Lands campaign, perhaps a sign that while animation depended on the state-based Goskino, and while in these years directors often supported the authorities' views, the government itself did not commission animated films on specific projects.

Incidentally, the only animated film depicting a great state project was made later, in 1975, during the years in which the Brezhnev regime proposed the re-opening of the Baikal-Amur Mainline (BAM) project, a railroad line that would connect central Siberia with the Soviet Far East in order to increase the population in a frontier zone and augment the flow of goods through to the Pacific ports. Sections of this line were built at different times from the 1930s, but after Stalin's death in 1953, all construction work on the BAM stopped, until Brezhnev in 1974 declared that a new BAM project would become a huge Komsomol undertaking. The BAM project resembled the Virgin Lands campaign in spirit and recruitment techniques, but it enjoyed less success. In the film in question, *And My Mother Will Forgive Me* (*I mama menia prostit*, A. Petrov, 1975) the director chose to introduce this topic not by addressing adults directly as most of the animated films of the 1960s and 1970s had done, but by projecting these ideas into the

121 Stites, *Russian Popular Culture*, 144.

mind of a child who feels the need in his imagination to take part in some of the great projects of these years, performing heroic acts in order to earn his mother's forgiveness for his poor behavior.

It has been noted how, while striving for innovative choices, artists ended up, consciously or unconsciously, being subservient to the authorities' views. Only later in the 1960s would their experiments increasingly detach from the establishment's views and reflect more the individual artist's worldview. The need for innovation in animated films seems to have originated first in the search for new themes, and only subsequently in stylistic choices. The fact that the audience had to wait until the early 1960s to experience the first signs of innovations in style is symptomatic of the vicissitudes of animation in the Soviet political and economic context, as discussed in the following pages.

From thematic to stylistic changes

While in the Soviet Union the arts, including live-action cinema, had turned to a new path stylistically and thematically as early as 1956, animation took more time to develop and react to the freer atmosphere of the Thaw. Animated films slowly started to suggest new themes in the mid-1950s, but ground-breaking styles were not introduced on the screen until the beginning of the 1960s. Why this delay? Apart from the obvious reason that making an animated film takes months if not years (presenting a clear disadvantage in comparison, for example, to lyric poetry, which can be written quickly), there are several factors that one should take into consideration while analyzing this phenomenon.

These factors include the filmmaking process, with its various stages of discussion and approval, as well as the production system adopted by the studio. At Soiuzmul'tfil'm, debates between innovators and traditionalists would often take place during Artistic Council meetings.[122] These were regular meetings that would occur at different stages of filmmaking. They were usually held to discuss and approve the literary script (*literaturnyi stsenarii*) and the director's script (*rezhisserskii stsenarii*, which also included directorial choices such as movements, lighting, etc.). Furthermore, for certain films the Artistic Council had to approve also the material collected in preparation for making the film (*podgo-*

[122] See minutes of the Artistic Council (Khudsovet – khudozhestvennyi sovet) meetings at RGALI, Soiuzmul'tfil'm fond 2469, opisi 1,2,3,4, "Soiuzmul'tfil'm Archive. 1939–1974".

tovitel'nyi period), and finally had to endorse the film. After approval from the Artistic Council, the scripts (and eventually, the final film) also had to be accepted by Goskino, the central state administrative body for cinema that by the mid-1960s supervised all film studios.[123]

The studio hindered innovative steps not only with its formal approval process, but also with the techniques and the production system it embraced. In fact, since its foundation Soiuzmul'tfil'm had adopted Disney's technique of cel animation, and consequently also the Disney filmmaking process, which was similar to that of an assembly line. Even the most ingenious idea, once it passed through all of the stages in the creation of an animated film (such as the development of the various phases of movement, coloring, etc.) would become a sort of standardized creation in which the original intentions were often lost.

The Disney style of production well fitted "full animation", that is, elaborate and detailed animation characterized by constant movement, use of several drawings without recycling them, a great amount of artwork, and more detailed "phases" in order to produce smoother movement. A large number of artists and staff was necessary for producing this type of animation, and the studio Soiuzmul'tfil'm was organized to provide the necessary labor force in the various departments. The specific nature of this style permitted surveillance over the creativity of the artists and lent itself to a centralized control that suited the Soviet authorities, who had been anxious to have power over the activity of independent animators since the mid-30s. Only by creating small creative units that would take care of the entire process without delegating parts of it to other departments could artists have greater command of the filmmaking process. But small groups of artists would not be able to create full animated films, which require an enormous amount of work and can hardly be produced in a limited time. Hence, innovation in styles would be possible only after reformulating the system of production and, at the same time, adopting new methods that differed from the mainstream cel technique used in the studio.

Another factor that contributed to hampering the innovative artistic impulse was the lack of high-quality scripts that dealt with new themes while taking into account the specificities

[123] For a detailed procedure see RGALI, "Perepiska s ministerstvom o rasshirenii tematiki mul'tfil'mov".

Chapter 2   From Propaganda to Children's Films

of animation. Already in 1958, in replying to writers' inquiries about successful scripts, Soiuzmul'tfil'm director S. Kulikov stressed the significance of caricature and the grotesque in animation and explicitly stated the need for satire.

> The studio needs satirical scripts for drawn animation as well as puppet films. In these scripts merciless people, speculators on state means, bureaucrats, and so on, should be ridiculed. But it does not follow that one should get carried away in depicting only the negative and shady sides of life. While showing and revealing them, it is also necessary to juxtapose them with good and positive phenomena. This makes the work more vivid and convincing, and most of all, it rightly reflects the environment and life.[124]

In presenting a script, writers often did not take into consideration that making animation required a long process, which was usually no less than six months for a short animated film. This lengthy procedure would not allow making films quickly enough to keep pace with the most current issues facing society. Also spectators, who asked the studio to put on screen journals such as *Krokodil* or *Perets*,[125] did not understand the practical difficulties inherent in making animated films based on the caricature style of satirical journals. The long amount of time necessary to create animation explains why the first satirical animated films dealt with "long-term" problems in Soviet society, that is, themes that had been attacked in journals for many years. When the desire to tackle topics from contemporary life became pressing, animators were faced with a search for new, simplified forms that would allow them to keep pace with the quickly changing topical themes.

Animators in other countries were also looking for a more linear style, and new experiments in animation appeared abroad already during the 1950s. Unlike Soviet animation, Western animation was less politically constrained in its choice of themes but, not being state-financed, was also forced to find more convenient solutions by the demands of a free market and of the cost of producing films – as well as, sometimes, by the need to adapt animated films to other spheres, such as advertising. Thanks to several talented artists who embarked on animation in the particular postwar moment, these economic factors did not result in a deterioration of animation quality, but were instead the primary causes of the development of a simpler style that

[124] RGALI, "Stsenarnyi otdel. Perepiska s avtorami o predlogaemykh zaiavkakh i literaturnykh stsenariiakh (1958)", 16–17.

[125] RGALI, "Stsenarnyi otdel. Perepiska so zriteliami po voprosam rasshireniia tematiki mul'tfil'mov (1957)"; RGALI, Soiuzmul'tfil'm "Stsenarnyi otdel. Perepiska so zriteliami po voprosam rasshireniia tematiki mul'tfil'mov (1958)".

77

would allow animators to be more flexible without sacrificing the quality of their work.

Foreign influence on stylistic choices

One of the most influential trends that appealed to Soviet animators was a new style called "limited animation", which spread to various countries after World War II. "Limited" here is not intended as a derogatory term, but merely defines a style that is in contrast with "full animation",[126] the best example of which can be found, as already mentioned, in the classic Disney style. Limited animation is characterized by a limitation of movement (the same images are used for more than one frame), simple drawings, and a bare background delineated by only a few fundamental details. Masters of this type of animation were to be found in the East, among the Yugoslav artists of the Zagreb School of Animated Films, such as Dušan Vukotić, Vatroslav Mimica, and Vlado Kristl, who led the studio in the 1950s and early 1960s; and in the West among the American artists of the UPA (United Production of America).

The appearance of limited animation in Yugoslavia, the only socialist country with a quasi-free-market economy at the time, was due to the necessity of saving time in the production of animated films in order to meet the demands of advertising. Likewise, simplified animation helped to husband resources, since the government, unlike in the Soviet Union, did not fund animation studios extensively.

Linear backgrounds, schematic drawings, and humorous but at the same time philosophical situations characterized the early Zagreb school films. The conventionalized style used by the Yugoslav artists was well suited to the themes treated in their films, which were focused on subjects and situations drawn from contemporary life, frequently presented in a witty and parodic form.

The masters of the Zagreb school followed the worldwide tendency in animation of these years to create films without dialogue or with a restricted verbal text, a choice that accentuated the importance and expressiveness of the visual image. The different temporal value of the image and of the word has always been taken into consideration by animators in their films. While the image is instantly perceived, the word requires time to be expressed and consequently to be

126 For a detailed description of the differences between "full animation" and "limited animation" see Furniss, *Art in Motion*, 135–153.

Chapter 2   From Propaganda to Children's Films

processed. In this phase of animation, in a search for condensed time, animators tended to substitute for the word a gesture or a sound; human thoughts were represented visually rather than expressed verbally.

In searching for a new simple and effective style, the Yugoslav artists created a stylized language that recalled the one fostered by the American studio UPA[127] a few years earlier. The artists who worked at UPA were determined to create a new style in animation that would contrast with the dominant Disney style. They, too, rejected the spoken word and were interested in visual choices linked to principles of modern art, formal design, and minimalism. Their films reflected modern art practices in their attention to principles of flatness, lack of perspective or distorted perspective, use of a few primary colors, a lack of superfluous detail and of meticulously detailed backgrounds, and use of simple, conventionalized figures. The films created at UPA stood out from Disney films for the attention they paid to human characters as opposed to anthropomorphic animal characters, and they differed greatly in their production system. UPA rejected the assembly-line system of animation that was used at Disney's studio and entrusted production to small groups that formed spontaneously. While adopting "limited animation", the artists created simplified backgrounds, so that the figures, moving on a "clean" space, would underline the flatness of the screen. Flat graphics clashed with Disney's realist style and his attempt to create a verisimilar feeling of depth with the use of the multiplane camera. Stylized figures required also new types of movement – not fluid and natural movements as in Disney films, but more brusque and uneven gestures. The UPA artists' drawings introduced caricature-like, grotesque and sharp forms that greatly influenced the visual choices of the Soviet artists of the 1960s, who were already fascinated by the caricature and stylized manner of graphic masters such as the French caricaturist and illustrator Jean Effel, the Danish artist Herluf Bidstrup,[128] the Russian group Kukryniksy (Mikhail Kupriianov, Porfirii Krylov, and Nikolai Sokolov), Josef Lada in Czechoslovakia, and Saul Steinberg and James Thurber in the USA.

Thanks to the palpably more relaxed atmosphere during the Thaw, Soviet artists were exposed to pictorial art and modern designs that were unavailable in previous years. In her

---

127 For discussion of UPA history and aesthetic see Furniss, *Art in Motion*, 139–142; Barrier, *Hollywood Cartoons*, 501–568.

128 In 1967, Atamanov produced a film on the basis of Bidstrup's caricatures, *The Bench* (*Skameika*).

book on the cinema of the Thaw, Josephine Woll points out how students of the state cinema school VGIK were privileged not only to be able to view Western films, but also to hear the formerly prohibited music of Richard Wagner, Anton Webern, Arnold Shoenberg, and Alban Berg. They could also see paintings by Russian modernists whose works were still not completely officially available, like Kazimir Malevich, Vasilii Kandinsky, and Pavel Filonov, as well as read some works of still banned writers such as Nikolai Gumilev, Daniil Kharms, Evgenii Zamiatin, Boris Pil'niak, Marcel Proust, and Aldous Huxley.[129]

Besides, in this period of détente, Soviet animation directors were given a chance to participate at international festivals. The first festival dedicated exclusively to animation, the International Congress of Animation, organized by the cinema commission of the French Ministry of Education, took place in Cannes from April 25 to May 3, 1956. Ivan Ivanov-Vano and Lev Atamanov, sent to represent the studio Soiuzmul'tfil'm, met on this occasion the most influential animation directors in the world, such as the French artists Paul Grimault, Aleksandr Alekseev, Claire Parker, Henri Gruel, and Jean Image; the English filmmakers John Halas and Joy Batchelor; the Polish Włodzimierz Haupe; the Czechoslovaks Jiří Trnka and Karel Zeman; the American UPA directors Stephen Bosustow and John Hubley; the National Film Board of Canada directors Norman McLaren and Colin Low; and several other original and innovative artists.[130] This congress allowed Soviet animators to make contact with foreign artists and familiarize themselves with new, innovative techniques. Screenings, discussions, and exhibitions of works made in various countries had a great impact on the Soviet artists that participated in this event.

Ivanov-Vano in his book *Kadr za kadrom* recalls his impressions of his meetings with Stephen Bosustow of UPA, with Aleksandr Alekseev and his films made with the technique of the pin screen, and with Norman McLaren and his experiments with drawings made directly on film stock. Ivanov-Vano was also thrilled to see the Czechoslovak exhibition of puppet animation, even more so at a time when the newly founded puppet animation division in Soiuzmul'tfil'm was slowly developing. Henri Gruel's films, in particular *Gypsies and Butterflies* (*Gitanos et papillons*, 1954) and *Badabou's Journey* (*Le voyage de Badabou*, 1955), created

129 Woll, *Real Images*, 31.

130 Several countries participated at this congress: France, Soviet Union, Great Britain, USA, Holland, Switzerland, Canada, Czechoslovakia, Poland, Romania, Yugoslavia, Norway, Belgium, Hungary, Japan, and Federal Republic of Germany. Ivanov-Vano, *Kadr za kadrom*, 169–189.

Chapter 2 From Propaganda to Children's Films

by animating children's drawings with the technique of cut-outs, made an impression on Ivanov-Vano, and supposedly also influenced the Brumberg sisters' film *Great Troubles*, which I analyze in Chapter 3. In 1958, presumably due to the political freeze of these years, Soviet animators did not take part in the second congress, "International Days of the Animated Film", but in 1959, in France, Ivanov-Vano began to participate in the creation of an international union of animators. This association was soon formed with the name of ASIFA (Association International du Film d'Animation), and Ivanov-Vano, being a member of the board, became the representative there of Soviet animation for many years, thus allowing Russian directors to see works of foreign artists as well as to present their films abroad.

General characteristics of the new stylistic tendencies

The innovative style of 1960s Soviet animated films visibly endorsed limited animation. The new Soviet style tended to concentrate the content in essential visual images trying to convey something general through character types and a conventionalized depiction of the world. Essential, minimal representation of reality in a modern style conveyed concepts of rationality, functionality, and minimalism through laconic, schematic images, geometric and angled forms. The characters' movements lost the fluidity they had in Disney-style films. Now movements became basic and functional, and their mechanical quality fitted the overall tendency towards modern and rational concepts. Schematic drawings, flat marionettes, and poster-like style emphasized the predilection for marked flatness of the images, while contrasting colors also contributed to accentuating the perception of two-dimensional figures. Color was mainly used to express ideas and emotions, eschewing a mimetic representation of reality. Color set the tone of the film, but it also expressed that general feeling Eisenstein suggested that cartoons should exploit: "the key principle consists in separating color from what necessarily lies beneath it, to draw it out into a general feeling and make this general feeling become a subject again".[131]

The stylistic innovations introduced in Russian animation have been defined by some artists and film critics[132] as a

131 Eisenstein, "From Lectures on Music and Colour in *Ivan The Terrible*", 184.

132 Volkov, *Mul'tiplikatsionnyi fil'm*, 4.

"plastic revolution" ("plasticheskaia revoliutsiia"), a term that witnessed a revolution in form, but did not reflect in its name the parallel novelty in content that occurred in these years. Another definition that is probably more successful is "authorial animation" ("avtorskaia mul'tiplikatsiia"). As in the French wave of "Cinéma d'auteur" in live-action films of the 1960s, the concept of authorial animation had its core in the director as the leader of the creative process. "Authorial animation" emphasized the individual style of the artist and eluded standardized choices still adopted in the Soiuzmul'tfil'm studio. The development of the main idea of the film was now in the hands of the director, who controlled every stage of the film's creation and who would then be considered the "author" of the film. In the Soviet Union, the authors' desire to detach themselves from the collective system of film production and to express their unique style and original choices was once more a reflection of the tendency during the Thaw to attribute more importance to the personal rather than communal experience.

It is not accidental that the first film that moved away from Disney-style cel technique was made by imitating children's drawings (*Great Troubles*, V. Brumberg, Z. Brumberg, 1961). In an attempt to simplify drawn animation and introduce a conventionalized style that would free animated films from mimetic representation of reality, children's drawings seem to be the quintessence of conventionality and simplicity. Although children's drawings were not necessarily adopted for later films, this visual choice opened the path towards a stylized manner for later films. It is Fedor Khitruk's film *Story of a Crime* (*Istoriia odnogo prestupleniia*, 1962) that further developed this tendency by using a conventionalized style that had great influence on the animation of the subsequent years. The following analyses of *Great Troubles* and *Story of a Crime* are meant to clarify the role of animation during the Thaw as well as to provide examples of the new stylistic choices that began to characterize Soviet animation of the 1960s.

Chapter 3

Case Studies: The Early 1960s

Introduction

In the early 1960s, Soviet audiences finally saw innovative stylistic choices in animated films. A shift in focus from the public and collective realm to private and individual concerns was expressed through portrayals of Soviet quotidian life (Soviet *byt*) in a simplified and minimalist way. It was no longer the naturalistic style of Disney, with extensive details and a perfection of movement that resembled reality, but a laconic, conventionalized style. The first attempts to take this new approach were Valentina and Zinaida Brumberg's *Great Troubles* (*Bol'shie nepriiatnosti*, 1961) and Fedor Khitruk's *Story of a Crime* (*Istoriia odnogo prestupleniia*, 1962). These works paved the way for further experimentation in style and more films for adults.

It was because the Brumbergs and Khitruk were established masters of animation art that their vanguard films could appear on screen; indeed, their position and reputation in the studio allowed them to push for some innovations. Khitruk's influence only grew with the years. Later on, he assigned himself a similar role to the one played by famous directors in the live-action cinema world such as Mikhail Romm and Ivan Pyrev, who fostered several younger artists' careers and influenced the film industry of these years.[133] In a documentary film on Khitruk, the writer Liudmila Petrushevskaia comments on the animator's mentor-like demeanor.

> In Russia there has always been what you could call a mafia of "decent people". It is still active today. This might sound crazy, but somewhere up there were the Party, the Communists, the government, the KGB, the militia, the Druzhina.

[133] Woll, *Real Images*, 38.

And we were down here. Khitruk fought to ensure that Norshtein got a state award. If Norshtein hadn't received that award, *Tale of Tales* would probably have remained banned until 1986. Norshtein would not have had a chance if Khitruk had not been so involved. That's how the mafia of the decent people worked. And in the sphere of animation Khitruk was the ringleader.[134]

Although influential personalities in the studio, especially if they were Party members like Khitruk, could venture to create more daring films, it was under the thrust of new artists that fresh stylistic choices appeared in this new phase of animation. The art director Sergei Alimov is an exemplary case – his original style gave an innovative élan to most of Khitruk's films and greatly influenced the animation film aesthetic of subsequent years.

With *Great Troubles* and *Story of a Crime,* both the Brumberg sisters and Khitruk broke with traditional themes. Yet they moved from the tradition in a smooth way, without shifting drastically away from the ideology of the time. If on first viewing these two films, being quite original and new, seemed subversive, further analysis shows that in fact, they expressed the same concerns as those voiced by authorities in the Thaw years.

Valentina and Zinaida Brumberg directed more than forty films in their fifty years of activity at the Soiuzmul'tfil'm studio, but only in the 1960s did they create films that clearly addressed an adult public. After making *Great Troubles* (1961), the Brumbergs used mild ridicule in depicting the behavior of people in contemporary society, for example the lovers' conduct in *The Hour Before the Rendezvous* (*Za chas do svidaniia*, 1965), or the uncultured behavior of the characters in *The Little Time Machine* (*Mashinka vremeni*, 1967), as well as in the sequel *New Great Troubles* (*Novye bol'shie nepriiat-nosti*, 1973).

Khitruk, on the other hand, began his career as a director with *Story of a Crime* after working at the studio as animator, racking up a filmography of more than sixty films, one of which was Brumbergs' *Great Troubles*. After *Story of a Crime,* Khitruk followed two paths: on the one hand, he produced very successful films for children such as *Toptyzhka* (1974), *Bonifatius's Holidays* (*Kanikuly Bonifatsiia*, 1965), and the mini-series *Winnie the Pooh* (*Vinni-Pukh,* 1969–1972); on the other hand, in his films for adults, he moved to sharper

134 *The Spirit of Genius.* Dir. O. Alder. Tag/Traum, 1998. Quotation as in subtitles.

satire, directing films that harshly denounced Soviet bureaucrats (*Man in the Frame,* [*Chelovek v ramke*], 1966), or parodied the artistic world in a witty way that included subtle hints at censorship (*Film, Film, Film,* [*Fil'm, fil'm, fil'm*], 1968). Eventually he began to address more universal philosophical questions and examine the alienating effects of modern society in *The Island* (*Ostrov*, 1973).

Great Troubles (*Bol'shie nepriiatnosti*, Valentina and Zinaida Brumberg, 1961)

The sisters Valentina and Zinaida Brumberg were two of the oldest animation directors at the Soiuzmul'tfil'm studio; they had been working in the studio since the late 1930s. Their films had been original, excellent works, but it was in 1961 that the directors broke with tradition. Their film *Great Troubles* (*Bol'shie nepriiatnosti*, 1961), based on the laconic and conventionalized language of children's drawings, radically differed from the dominant Disney style; it was the first film in the new phase of Soviet animation of the 1960s that combined a fresh satirical take on contemporary life with innovative stylistic choices. The Brumberg sisters' breakthrough was significant even though they confined their ridicule to those aspects of Soviet society that were already officially under attack.

Although the style of *Great Troubles* imitated children's drawings and was accompanied by a child's narrative voice, it was not directed at an audience of children, as one might think at the very beginning of the film, but was explicitly made for an adult audience, with a clear and witty ironic undertone. It is significant that this transition from child to adult spectatorship in Soviet animation is presented in a film that brings the audience back to a child's world, and at the same time uses a language alien and incomprehensible to children.

The scriptwriter Moris Slobodskoi[135] came up with an original dramaturgic strategy: a little girl describes her family, using the same idiomatic expressions that she hears from the adults that surround her. A contrapuntal relationship between the literal meanings of the expressions as understood by the child, and the figurative meanings of the expressions as recognized by an adult spectator, has a witty and satirical effect.

---

135 Moris Slobodskoi began to write scripts for animation only a year earlier with the cinematic satirical journal *Animated Crocodile No. 2* (*Mul'tiplikatsionnyi krokodil N.2*, 1960). He subsequently worked with the Brumberg sisters on the animated films for adults *The Hour Before the Rendezvous* (*Za chas do svidaniia*, 1965), *The Little Time Machine* (*Mashinka vremeni*, 1967), and *New Great Troubles* (*Novye bol'shie nepriiatnosti*, 1973). He is also famous for his scripts for some of Leonid Gaidai's famous comedies, such as *Operation Y and other Adventures of Shurik* (*Operatsiia Y, i drugie prikliucheniia Shurika*, 1965); *Kidnapping, Caucasian Style* (*Kakazskaia plennitsa, ili novye prikliucheniia Shurika*, 1967); and *The Diamond Arm* (*Brilliantovaia ruka*, 1969).

(a) Narration and self-reflexivity

The film begins with a white screen that serves as a background for a pencil tracing a little girl. This young child is depicted holding a crayon, and indeed it is she who will hand-draw all the characters in the film and will tell us their story with her naïve voice. This reminds us of the vaudeville acts called "chalk talks", and the early years of American animation when artists would draw on white paper caricatures or portraits that would morph in accordance with their voice-over, such as in James Stuart Blackton's *Humorous Phases of Funny Faces* (1906). As mentioned in the first chapter of this book, Soviet animation used similar devices in the so-called *animated caricature* (*ozhivshaia karikatura*) in the late 1920s. This reference to the earliest animated films can be read as a desire to go back to the art form's origins in order to conceive a new way of making animated films. The white background in *Great Troubles* functions as a piece of paper on which the child protagonist will draw her family members, her house, and her brother's school. It is also symbolic of a blank page, a starting point in this new phase of Soviet animation.

The film is as self-referential as the first animated films were. But while in the earliest films the creators of the drawings would make their appearance on screen, in *Great Troubles* the authors do not become visible; instead, they introduce a mediator in the form of a drawn character. This creates once more an effect of double conventionality, in which the little girl is both a narrator and part of the story. This device underlines the layered structure of the film in which the verbal world of the adults (which is the same as the authors' world) clashes with a representation of reality as seen through the eyes of a child and her drawings. This juxtaposition of layers, typical of parody, is the key to the successful comicality of the film.

Incidentally, an interesting case of self-reflexivity appears in another animated film of this period, which was made in the traditional Disney naturalistic style, *The Huge Cockroach* (*Tarakanishche*, 1963), directed by V. Polkovnikov and written by the famous Russian writer of children's literature Kornei Chukovskii. In this film, Kornei Chukovskii – easily recognizable from his physical features – becomes a drawn character who interacts with the personages created by him.

Here again there is a double level of conventionality that serves the purpose of introducing to young spectators a well-known and beloved writer of many books and verses for children, and involving them fully in the fictional world created by him. But while *The Huge Cockroach* is set in the fantastic world created by Chukovskii, *Great Troubles* focuses on contemporary real life. The innovative aspect of this film is that reality is not relegated to the world of children or to the fantastic realm of fairy-tales, as was the case with animated films of the Stalin era, but is represented with very specific references to Soviet reality and the socio-cultural system of the Thaw years.

(b) Satire of contemporary society: stiliagi, parasitism and corruption

The device of presenting the story through the eyes of a child allowed the creators of *Great Troubles* to criticize and satirize in a new and creative way the society they were so familiar with. Other elements in the film, such as music and the organization of space, help to depict contemporary life and the characters' idiosyncrasies.

Music is used as a first clue to enter the world of the characters in *Great Troubles*. The music used at the beginning of the film is typical, old-fashioned comedic music. It anticipates the amusing tone of this film and introduces the older generation, the little girl's parents. But as soon as her elder brother and sister, Kolia and Kapa, appear on the screen, the music changes: jazz music accompanies them and underlines a clear generational gap between Kolia and Kapa, on the one hand, and their parents on the other.

At this point it is worth recalling that during the Thaw, Soviet youth were exposed to a flood of Western songs, jazz, rock, and new dance styles which were denounced by the conservatives and moralizers. Foreign music and dance were often under attack in these years. In order to supplant what was deemed "Western vulgarity" on Soviet dance floors, Igor Moiseev (the great impresario of ensemble dancing) designed popular and dynamic dances rooted in tradition. For two years, his dances were shown on TV and actively promoted by Komsomol, but people ignored them and this campaign proved a complete failure.[136] In *Great Troubles*, dancing styles and foreign influence are topics that

136 Stites, *Russian Popular Culture*, 133–134.

recur throughout the film, as in the scene when Kapa, while looking for a man who would marry and support her, a respectable man ("solidnogo muzhchina"), at the same time spends nights dancing swing with foreigners ("diadi inostrantsy").

The influence of foreign music, dance, and fashion on Soviet youth was also evident in a particular youth group called *stiliagi* (*style-hunters*), whose best representative in the film is the narrator's brother Kolia. The typical *stiliaga* disdained work, hung around foreigners, loved jazz and swing music, often visited restaurants, had a passion for stylish clothing, and dressed in a very peculiar way.[137] According to Fredrerick Starr's book *Red and Hot: The Fate of Jazz in the Soviet Union*, the *stiliaga*'s uniform was "long jackets with broad shoulders, wide-striped shirts or black shirts with white ties, narrow trousers, and thick-soled shoes (preferably foreign but also obtainable from a Soviet factory in Riga)". They also wore no beards, sideburns or mustaches, but sported long hair.[138] In the film, Kolia follows this fashion, wearing wide-striped shirts and narrow trousers, and singing and dancing to the sound of jazz. He has no job, hangs around doing nothing productive, spends all his money on drinks and cigarettes, does not apply himself in high school, and fails at university. He is accused together with his sister and parents, who are considered partially responsible for his behavior, of being a "parasite" ("darmoed"). Ridiculing Kolia, the animators associate themselves with the satirical writers in *Krokodil*, who attacked the *stiliagi* in the journal, at times even with commissioned songs, orchestrated from above.

Seeing that the *stiliagi* took foreign culture and modes as their model for living, they could not be easily accepted by the authorities. The appearance of the *stiliagi* was seen as resulting from the freer atmosphere brought about by Khrushchev after his "Secret Speech" at the Twentieth Party Congress in 1956, but in reality these young people had been around since the very beginning of the 1950s. The term *stiliaga* was coined by the journal *Krokodil* already in 1948; yet, it did not appear again during the Stalin era, and it was only in the Thaw years that the *stiliaga* started to be attacked in the press. Idleness among youth was already perceivable in Stalin's time and intensified during the Khrushchev era. The behavior of the *stiliagi* was considered offensive, since

137 Kristin Joy Roth-Ey notes that paradoxically "one of the best places to learn how to dress like a *stiliaga* was the Soviet newspaper, propaganda poster, or movie theater, which, while striving to belittle callow youth, also dispensed potentially valuable information". Roth-Ey, "Mass Media and the Remaking of Soviet Culture 1950s–1960s", 49.

138 Starr, *Red and Hot*, 237.

it was seen as a rejection of the work ethic that was supposedly always upheld by the proletariat. The Communist Youth Organization, Komsomol, berated them as spoiled children, Westernizers, and parasites. In effect, they represented a harsh critique of the Soviet mindset: while Soviet man has always been more prone to idealism, and more focused on ideas, the *stiliagi* paid attention to material and empty objects.[139] Parents, schools, and Komsomol were blamed in the press for this lost youth.

The parents in *Great Troubles* are certainly not the expected typical hard workers; instead, they are shown as partly responsible for their children's behavior. The mother overprotects and idolizes her daughter, and the father does not provide a good example for his children, either; he illicitly trades the refrigerators of his company and when he gets caught, tries to bribe the inspector in order to avoid scandal and shame. The faults of society are thus ascribed to individuals who also corrupt their own children; the children in turn will become part of harmful "subgroups" (such as the *stiliagi*), a more serious phenomenon that is tougher to eradicate. This film is innovative in its way of mounting a satire on contemporary society, yet its criticism is directed not at the system itself, but at those elements in society that are not accepted by the establishment; in other words, its condemnation of society is limited by the boundaries that the system imposed. While in this film the old generation and the new youths are under attack, the younger and naïve girl stands apart and symbolizes a light of hope for a better society founded by a new generation that, according to Khrushchev, will live under real communism.

(c) *Style and language: children's language interprets the Soviet reality*

The style of children's drawings adopted in the film introduces a level of conventionality that renders the discourse more complex. *Great Troubles* presents the viewer not with a direct image of the external world, but instead an image of this external world mediated by the conventions of an artistic language (in this case, children's drawings) that is then translated into the language of animation, creating a double mediation. In analyzing this animated film it is thus necessary to consider that we are interpreting a sign that signifies another sign, or, in Iurii Lotman's words, "an image of an

[139] Vail' and Genis, *60-e*, 55.

Figure 3.1. *"They pulled Kolya by his ears from class to class".* Still from Great Troubles.

Figure 3.2. *"He got stuck in the last class".* Still from Great Troubles.

image".[140] These two levels of conventionalized representation of reality point to the two layers of speech used in the film. All the figures of speech in this film are literally translated into images using a device often found in satirical and humorous vignettes. Two layers of meaning are juxta-

[140] Lotman, "O iazyke mul'tiplikatsionnykh fil'mov", 673.

Chapter 3 Case Studies: The Early 1960s

Figure 3.3. *"There, he sat on his father's shoulders"*.
Still from Great Troubles.

Figure 3.4. *"And now his job is shaking out his father's pocket"*.
Still from Great Troubles.

posed: the literal meanings of the idiomatic expressions pronounced by the child narrator, which take shape in the drawings as understood by her; and the figurative meaning of the same expressions, as understood by the adult audience. A parody of the world is created with this juxtaposition

Figure 3.5. *"He whips the vodka like a driver" (idiomatic for "He drinks a lot"). Still from* Great Troubles.

Figure 3.6. *"He dragged himself after her, he lost his head". Still from* Great Troubles.

and overlapping of layers, a parody perceived as amusing by an audience that can understand this play of meanings.

Sentences maintain their double meaning expressed by drawings and voice-over: "They pulled Kolya by his ears

Chapter 3 Case Studies: The Early 1960s

Figure 3.7. *"Chickens do not peck at money" (idiomatic for "There is plenty of money"). Still from* Great Troubles.

Figure 3.8. *"He let fridges pass on the left" (idiomatic for "He sold fridges under the table"). Still from* Great Troubles.

from class to class" (Fig. 3.1); "He got stuck in the last class" (Fig. 3.2); "There, he sat on his father's shoulders" (Fig. 3.3); "And now his job is shaking out his father's pocket" (Fig. 3.4); "He whips the vodka like a driver" (idiomatic for "He drinks a lot") (Fig. 3.5); "He dragged himself after her, he

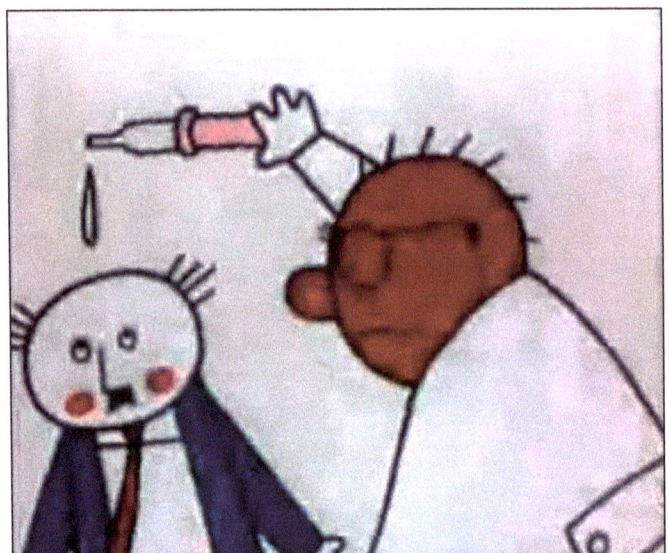

Figure 3.9. *"Now he drips on Daddy" (idiomatic for "Now he informs on Daddy"). Still from* Great Troubles.

Figure 3.10. *"Now he digs under him" (idiomatic for "Now he digs his grave"). Still from* Great Troubles.

lost his head" (Fig. 3.6); "Chickens do not peck at money" (idiomatic for: "There is plenty of money") (Fig. 3.7); "He let fridges pass on the left" (idiomatic for: "He sold fridges under the table") (Fig. 3.8); "Now he drips on Daddy" (idiomatic for "Now he informs on Daddy") (Fig. 3.9);

Chapter 3 Case Studies: The Early 1960s

Figure 3.11. *"Daddy had to oil the inspector" (idiomatic expression for "Daddy had to bribe the inspector"). Still from* Great Troubles.

Figure 3.12. *"Daddy started at once to sew himself up" (idiomatic for "Daddy was unable to cope with the situation"). Still from* Great Troubles.

"Now he digs under him" (idiomatic for "Now he digs his grave") (Fig. 3.10); "Daddy had to oil the inspector" (idiomatic expression for "Daddy had to bribe the inspector") (Fig. 3.11); "Daddy started at once to sew himself up" (idiomatic for "Daddy was unable to cope with the situ-

95

Figure 3.13. *"They have to plant him" (idiomatic for "They have to arrest him"). Still from* Great Troubles.

ation") (Fig. 3.12); "They have to plant him" (idiomatic for "They have to arrest him") (Fig. 3.13).

This laconic and simple way of representing reality without extra details reinforces the idea of the world as seen by a young child, a view that clashes with adults' perception and produces a comic outcome. The effect of Shklovskian "estrangement" (*ostranenie*), created by presenting reality from the particular view of the child, calls attention to the language itself. The colloquial language used by adults and *stiliagi* is juxtaposed with the naïve code of the child. The criticism of the family members' lifestyles and values is thus underlined by a criticism of their discourse. This brings the issue from the sphere of a single family to a more general social sphere, and thus to social criticism. Concordantly, the idiomatic expressions are organized in a sort of crescendo that starts with a depiction of personal characteristics only to move toward more serious kinds of misbehavior and eventually into crimes that have a significant negative resonance in society.

(d) Spatial choices: unstable ground

From a visual point of view, the directors made effective choices in relating the themes discussed to the formal ele-

Chapter 3 Case Studies: The Early 1960s

Figure 3.14. *"He fell through". Still from* Great Troubles.

ments in the film. Spatial relations in particular are used as symbols of a lost generation. The house does not look like a solid environment, and interiors are represented only with a line for the floor. The walls of the institute seem sturdier, but they are still not able to hold Kolia when he fails at school – the literal expression used here is "He fell through" ("On provalilsia"; Fig. 3.14). In general Kolya "cannot stay on track"; he never simply walks, but he dances, is pulled by his ears, or sits on his father's shoulders.

Kolia's sister Kapa is also depicted as not grounded. She appears hovering in the air, or in an idolized portrait hung on the wall (Fig. 3.15), or daydreaming literally "in the clouds" (Fig. 3.16).

Like parasites, both the brother and the sister "sit on the father's shoulders" (Fig. 3.17), the only place where they seem to feel comfortable. Thus, once again, the father seems to be the root of their misbehavior; on his shoulders they look like the fruits of a rotten tree.

The laconic and simple style used in this film suited the witty and contrasting juxtaposition of a verbal code with a visual one. This new, concise style conveyed the world seen in the child's mind in a straightforward way. By using the particular language of children's drawings, a device not

Figure 3.15. *An Idolized Daughter. Still from* Great Troubles.

Figure 3.16. *Kapa in the Clouds. Still from* Great Troubles.

often adopted in later films, the Brumbergs opened the door to a new stylized manner that would detach itself from the naturalistic Disney-like style that had been used by Soiuzmul'tfil'm during the previous twenty-five years. The film that followed, Fedor Khitruk's *Story of a Crime*, took advan-

Chapter 3 Case Studies: The Early 1960s

Figure 3.17. *Sitting on Their Father's Shoulders. Still from* Great Troubles.

tage of the first timid steps made by *Great Troubles* towards a more conventionalized manner in the treatment of the faults of Soviet society and developed a style that would greatly influence the films created in the 1960s.

Story of a Crime (*Istoriia odnogo prestupleniia*, Fedor Khitruk, 1962)

With *Story of a Crime,* director Fedor Khitruk and art director Sergei Alimov aimed to illustrate contemporary Soviet society through the representation of a simple man and an unembellished image of everyday life. *Story of a Crime* illustrates how the noise and behavior of 'uncultured' neighbors drives a simple accountant, Mamin, a good and meek citizen, to commit murder. At the beginning of the film, a policeman, who is about to arrest Mamin, stops the action and makes the story start anew, presenting the 24 hours prior to the murder in Mamin's life, from the moment he gets up and goes to work to a sleepless night in which he has to cope with his noisy neighbours.

(a) Violation of norms: crime and kul'turnost'

The first problem the director had to face while making the film was how to tackle such a topical theme while avoiding

99

excessive moralizing. During a discussion of *Story of a Crime* at a meeting of the Soiuzmul'tfil'm studio Artistic Council, some members expressed the desire to create a "useful" film with an edifying purpose, that is, to stress the consequences of not respecting the norms of public order.[141] Khitruk, however, aimed to shun dogmatic didacticism and opted for satire, which allowed him both to construct a deeper criticism without being either too harsh or pedantic, and to de-dramatize everyday difficulties while laughing at negative aspects of Soviet life of these years. *Story of a Crime* not only satirized contemporary society, but also offered a complex reading of Soviet reality, which included a representation of that particular moment of conjuncture of liberalization and restriction that characterized the Thaw era, when the individual strove to assert himself as an entity autonomous from society, yet still had to balance his own identity with the collective ideal of a communist world.

The film begins with the crime itself, the moment in which Mamin's private life and feelings become public – as Bakhtin notes, "the *criminal act* is a moment of private life that becomes, as it were, *involuntarily* public".[142] Mamin is stopped in his courtyard, which becomes similar to the Greek public square, the *agora*, where, in ancient times, a citizen's whole life would be laid bare and examined, and subsequently would receive its public and civic stamp of approval.[143] As Bakhtin comments: "The autobiographical and biographical self-consciousness of an individual and his life was first laid bare and shaped in the public square".[144] Here Mamin is put on trial before the public. He is completely exposed; there is nothing intimate, secret, or personal left. His private life is examined in relation to his behavior towards the collective, and everything becomes subject to public or state control and evaluation. It seems that the act of placing Mamin in the public square is the ultimate act of making him "public", a defeat of the Soviet man's efforts to obtain his own independent space in society. Indeed, in the Soviet world, in which ideological, political, social, and economic factors were explicitly part of everyday life, a person could hardly conceive of himself as functioning as an isolated and private individual. Yet, encouraged by the more relaxed atmosphere of the Thaw – although interrupted by various waves of political and cultural freeze – people were inclined to focus more on their personal needs

141 RGALI, "Delo fil'ma *Istoriia odnogo prestupleniia*", 123.

142 Bakhtin, "Forms of Time and the Chronotope in the Novel", 122; italics in the original.

143 See Bakhtin's recollection of the ancient times in Bakhtin, "Forms of Time and the Chronotope in the Novel", 131–133.

144 Bakhtin, "Forms of Time and the Chronotope in the Novel", 131.

Chapter 3 Case Studies: The Early 1960s

than, as Ronald Suny puts it, on "the demands of the officially proclaimed 'Communist morality'".[145] *Story of a Crime*, like literature and cinema of the era, reflected the tendency to reject the socialist realist canon adopted until then, which glorified a supposedly idyllic communal life, and to stress the simple individual with nothing heroic about him. The film offers an honest representation of a contemporary society that displays conflicts within itself; it is not an ideal world, but a collective composed of people violating norms of social order, people who do not fit the multifaceted criteria of *kul'turnost'* (cultured-ness).

Kul'turnost', a quite complex term, can be defined not only in terms of the degree of literary or ideological savvy an individual possesses, but also has to do with unwritten Soviet rules of etiquette which included manners and ways of behaving. The campaign for *kul'turnost'* launched in Stalin's time provided a set of norms to which the Soviet man was supposed to aspire, and these were still present in the collective mind during the Thaw years. If under Stalin the push for *kul'turnost'* was connected with an effort to ameliorate the self in order to build an ideal Soviet society, during the Thaw era it was redirected toward the true communism promulgated by Khrushchev in his "secret speech" at the Twentieth Party Congress of February 1956.[146] Catriona Kelly, in her book on Russian etiquette and culture, defines *kul'turnost'* as a "force for stability and homogeneity"[147] connected to "a dream of harmonious integration"[148] and an "Enlightenment myth of social consensus through shared behavior rules".[149] Indeed, *kul'turnost'*, while setting common norms of behavior, played a significant role in the attempt to create a homogenous communist society, and in doing so acquired a strong political value. As Svetlana Boym comments, *kul'turnost'* created a political aura around everyday life, and turned everyday misconducts into political crimes.[150]

In *Story of a Crime*, Khitruk dwells on this thin line between violation of behavioral norms and subversive behavior; he fully exploits the concept of *kul'turnost'* to represent Soviet society of the time and the complexities of relations between the individual and the system. In the film, each character represents a particular violation of the norms of *kul'turnost'* – self-centeredness or not caring for one's neighbours, breaking the rules, or idling at work – and our hero's proper

145 Suny, *The Soviet Experiment*, 406.
146 Again in 1959 at the Twenty-First Party Congress, Khrushchev defined the time as a "period of the full-scale building of Communism". Quoted Suny, *The Soviet Experiment*, 407.
147 Kelly, *Refining Russia*, 244.
148 Kelly, *Refining Russia*, 251.
149 Kelly, *Refining Russia*, 252.
150 Boym, *Common Places*, 289. See also her discussion on *kul'turnost'* in pp. 102–106.

attitude repeatedly clashes with this uncultured behavior (*nekul'turnoe povedenie*). Mamin represents an exception to the general attitude of the people around him. He is depicted as the proper Soviet man: he is nice to children and polite to his fellow man, opens doors for people, offers his seat in the subway, observes the rules, and is dedicated to his work. The paradoxical result is that *kul'turnost'* in this film is represented by a man who commits a crime.

By having the ideal character transgress, the directors undermine the boundary between right and wrong. In the film there is no distinction between a criminal deed and an uncultured behavior; both are deviations that need to be corrected. The crime Mamin commits, although blameworthy, attacks those people who threaten an ideal harmonic system with their daily uncultured behavior. The character's act, however, is not driven by any socially edifying ideals. In this, Mamin radically differs from the heroes of the socialist realist canon. He does not react with the aim of exhorting others to mend their ways, nor does he seem to be interested in socializing with others, but intervenes only when people's behavior interferes with his privacy and violates his personal space. All his activities are self-centred: he works hard, but he works by himself; he is kind and greets people but does not converse with them; he spends his free time reading or watching cultural programs on TV, but, although important for making him as a 'cultured' person, these hobbies seem oriented towards 'self-improvement', not for the benefit of society, but for his individual well being. During the Thaw, this degree of isolation was probably not regarded as suspiciously as it was in the Stalinist years, yet it was still in conflict with the collective ideal. Mamin reflects the tension between the still-required social activism and vigilantism[151] and the new tendency of the Thaw-era towards private life and polite non-interference.[152]

The behavior of the policeman who appears soon after the crime does not help to solve this tension between individual needs and the collective; on the contrary, he is a rather contradictory figure and reinforces the feeling of ambiguity permeating the film and the Thaw era itself. At first, the policeman looks threatening: the drawing simulates a low camera angle, and his figure is overbearing (Fig. 3.18); when he enters, his steps echo in the courtyard and he approaches

[151] Only a few years earlier, in 1959, *druzhiny* – voluntary bodies jointly managed by police and various Party organizations – were formally founded with the aim of helping to maintain public order.

[152] Kelly also finds this aspect reflected in behavior books. Kelly, *Refining Russia*, 326–331.

Chapter 3 Case Studies: The Early 1960s

Figure 3.18. *First appearance of the policeman. Still from* Story of a Crime.

the camera until he almost fills the entire screen – his power is presented as absolute.

But soon after, when he tries to explain the hero's behavior by presenting how his meek character is affected by the uncultured behavior of the people who surround him, the policeman introduces Mamin in a trial style but with no harshness in his voice; he sounds like a defence lawyer: "Comrades, let's investigate. Here stands before you a modest accountant, Vasilii Vasil'evich Mamin – 47 years old, never jailed, never arrested. Does he look like a criminal?" The policeman's attitude is double-edged: initially he appears menacing, but subsequently he seems kind and understanding. Nevertheless, even when the officer tries to justify Mamin, he still exerts a strict control over him; he violates the boundaries of Mamin's private life and makes it public. He also evaluates the events in terms of their ultimate repercussions for all of society and not for Mamin as a single individual, focusing in particular on that uncultured behavior that threatened Soviet society as a whole.

The original script emphasized the gravity of lack of *kul'turnost'* even more persuasively than the film. The screenwriter stood for the main character, as though the uncultured people were guiltier than Mamin himself: "The narrator says: 'Let's discuss this, comrades: Who is guilty?' And all the veritable culprits confusedly lower their gaze".[153] The

[153] RGALI, "Delo fil'ma *Istoriia odnogo prestupleniia*", 80.

103

actual film still finishes with words that stress the sharing of responsibility for the crime among the crowd, but at the same time underline the need to punish the transgression: "Who is really guilty, comrades? A crime occurred and Vasilii Vasil'evich will certainly be arrested. But we hope that the people who decide the fate of the citizen V.V. Mamin will see our film and will understand everything".

The last sentence in the film is clearly self-reflexive. The narrator draws the viewers' attention to the film itself and to the function of the film. This moment of self-reflection raises more general issues, such as the question of the role of the arts in society and the messages conveyed by the mass media. It also presents an opportunity to consider the different messages proposed to the masses during the Stalin era and in these Thaw years. The banal conclusion with an edifying speech directed to the characters in the film (but at the same time to each spectator), a speech pronounced by a figure of unimpeachable authority, is a device found in many endings of Soviet films. The edifying role of live-action films and animated films remained a paramount concern of the leaders in this period. Khitruk inserted a moral ending, yet in this last version of the film he reaches a compromise – a criminal is declared guilty, but the community shares its part of the responsibility. This is a reversal of the relationship between the individual and society as shown in a typical socialist realist canon. In the traditional Soviet novel, the hero who deviates from the norms imposed by society gradually becomes aware of his mistakes: as he develops, he achieves ideological consciousness; he eventually repents for his misconduct and in doing so, he gains acceptance by society.[154] Character development according to these rules can be found in Soviet animation only in a form lacking strict ideological content, a form suitable for children's education. The child commits a mistake, repents the bad deed, and consequently is accepted back into society, with his family and friends around him (see for example *Fedia Zaitsev*, V. and Z. Brumberg, 1948; or *The Tale of the Old Oak – Skazka starogo duba*, O. Khodataeva, 1949).

In *Story of a Crime*, a different process occurs. The character commits a crime and thereby violates the rules of society, but the spectator does not witness his repentance. It is not the hero who develops into a state of repentance and ideological consciousness; rather, a representative of authority,

[154] Clark, *The Soviet Novel*, 255–260.

Chapter 3 Case Studies: The Early 1960s

the policeman, defends him and tries to justify his acts. There is no depiction of the character after having committed the crime, and in general, no moments following the crime are shown. Instead, the film presents a reversal of time and focuses on the events that preceded the criminal act. This subtle device challenges the official canon by eliding altogether the phase of repentance, as well as by pressing a society that is far from ideal to recognize its share of the guilt.

(b) New themes bring a new graphic style

Challenges to the official canon came not only in the form of structure and themes, but also in terms of aesthetic choices. The art director Sergei Alimov was one of those young artists in Soiuzmul'tfil'm who, in the late 1950s, felt the need to keep pace with the changing times. Stimulated by the freer, although unstable, atmosphere of the Thaw, Alimov persuaded Khitruk to reject the Disney style that had been adopted by Russian animation for decades, depart from the collective system of film production, and start a new phase in animation in which only a few artists would be responsible for the creation of each film. The directors looked for aesthetic choices that would underline the specificity of animation. They aimed to avoid those perfect movements and camera-wise effects that characterized what Siegfried Krakauer defines as the "cinematic approach" of the Disney style, a method that makes the spectator forget that what we see on the screen has been devised on a drawing board, and that, according to Krakauer, "inexorably stifles the draftsman's imagination".[155] Alimov tended to elude this constriction by exploiting the conventionality of the drawings that are at the base of animation art. His drawings shun mimesis; they present characters and backgrounds in an economical way, with a few fundamental traits and no superfluous details. This particular approach resembled a new stylized manner that appeared in animation at the end of the 1950s around the world – specifically, in America at the UPA studio, and in Europe at the Czech Bratři v triku and Zagreb School.[156] In this new trend of animation, new iconic signs proposed an innovative stylistic norm that effected a conventionalized representation of reality based on modern concepts of rationality and functionality, which were perceived as congruent with contemporary life and consistent with principles of modern visual design. In *Story*

155 Krakauer, *Theory of Film*, 90.

156 However, Alimov says that he saw films from the Zagreb School only after making *Story of a Crime*, during a training session at the Yugoslavian school in 1966–1967. S. Alimov, personal interview, 31 January 2012.

105

of a Crime, modern design and minimalist features are expressed through a limited palette, schematic and clear geometric lines, flatness of figures, skewed perspective, and use of pure colors (Figs. 3.19–3.20). The geometric angularity of the images cunningly suits the satirical tone adopted in the film. This simple, direct, and concise style serves the purpose of addressing the public in a more straightforward way and recalls traits of early Soviet animation, whose simplicity and poster-like manner conveyed maximum meaningfulness in concise expression. The abrupt movements typical of animated characters in the 1920s reappear in *Story of a Crime*, and sharply contrast with the fluid gestures in Disney films. Movements here become essential and functional, and gain a mechanical quality that fits the overall tendency towards modern and rational concepts. The rhythm of the film also conveys the dynamism of modern times through a representation of what David MacFadyen – talking about this aspect of Khitruk's film in his book on Soviet animation – defines as "blocks of nervousness", that is, "flat chromatic blocks, stylized in accelerated, jerky motions to represent nervous bodies, overworked cars, and other overly mobile forms".[157] A limited palette and contrasting colors express not a mimetic representation of reality, but that particular atmosphere Eisenstein suggested a cartoon should exploit: "the key principle consists in separating colour from what necessarily lies beneath it, to draw it out into a general feeling and make this general feeling become a subject again".[158]

Patches of solid color, together with schematic drawings, skewed perspective, poster-like style, and flat marionettes deprived of shadows, all accentuate the flattening-out effect of the figures (Figs. 3.19–3.20).

This particular style brings animation closer to graphic art and caricature, and makes it take upon itself their task of criticizing and ridiculing contemporary society. By emphasizing the two-dimensionality of the sketches, the animators also underlined the very specificity of their own artistic medium, the flat surface on which a drawing is traced. The flatness of the environment highlights the differences between an animated film – in which the spectator is more interested in the reality evoked by the space on the screen than in the space itself – and live-action cinema, in which the spectator is invited to wander within the three-dimen-

[157] MacFadyen, *Yellow Crocodiles and Blue Oranges*, 144.

[158] Eisenstein, "From Lectures on Music and Colour in *Ivan The Terrible*", 184.

Chapter 3 Case Studies: The Early 1960s

Figure 3.19. *Stylized representation of space with skewed perspective. Still from* Story of a Crime.

Figure 3.20. *Flattening out effect of the figures. Still from* Story of a Crime.

sionality of the film. A parallel can be drawn with the antithesis of flatness in modern works of art and realistic illusion in earlier painting, as pointed out by Clement Greenberg: "Where the Old Masters created an illusion of space into which one could imagine oneself walking, the illusion created by a Modernist is one into which one can only look, can travel through only with the eye".[159]

[159] Greenberg, "Modernist Painting", 775.

The flat figures in *Story of a Crime* are not perceived as characters with a life of their own, but become conventional signs able to convey with a minimum of traits a general characteristic. The filmmakers play with Soviet stereotypes – the idler at work, the drunk man coming home, the noisy neighbour with an enormous stereo system, the people playing dominoes in the courtyard, the people reading on the subway, the guests singing at a party. They become "types" easily recognizable by the audience, exploiting a concept of "typage" that brings us back to Eisenstein's Soviet cinema and his practice of choosing the characters of his films on the basis of their physical characteristics, expressions, and postures. Khitruk and Alimov create similar characters, individuals who exhibit specific behavioral and external characteristics but are not psychologically fully developed.

(c) *The Soviet Union of the 1960s appears on the screen: references and concretizations*

In *Story of a Crime*, the contemporary Soviet Union of the 1960s was suggested to the audience through a representation of geographical, socio-political and economic details, which concretize the world depicted in the film. The illustration of everyday life as it was experienced in the 1960s elicited a particularly vivid reaction from the audience who experienced the time in question. The process of recognition and identification generally provoked laughter among the Soviet spectators; nonetheless, a few testimonies observe that some of the viewers perceived this film as an offence and as a sign of irreverence toward the system.[160]

In portraying the typical day of a simple citizen, Khitruk and Alimov place the character in a recognizable Moscow environment. For the first time in decades, a modern city appears in an animated film, and the spectator realizes that the story takes place in Moscow not from traditional elements of concretization[161] such as monuments or tourist attractions, but from small, specific details. Geographic concretization is achieved, for instance, through the depiction of the streets, the buildings, the courtyards, and the subway with its swinging doors, platforms with vaults, long escalators, and rows of seats packed with passengers immersed in their reading.

[160] Norshtein, "Priznanie masteru", 76.

[161] I am using the term *concretization* as delineated by Bakhtin in his essay "Forms of Time and the Chronotope", 100.

Chapter 3   Case Studies: The Early 1960s

Not only geographical, but also socio-political and economic concretizations help the viewer in this process of recognizing the fictional world. The first reference to communist economic planning occurs in a big banner pinned to the wall of Mamin's office with a slogan that exhorts the employees to fulfil the year's plan three days earlier ("Let's fulfil this year's plan by December 28!"). This incitement to complete the plan three days early sounds like a mockery of the usual larger effort to fulfil the five-year plans in fewer years. The comic effect is also emphasized by the juxtaposition of an idealistic commitment to accomplishing ambitious plans in the name of the development of the country, with the real contemporary world, in which under the above-mentioned sign people are depicted idling away their time. In more than one scene of the film the director subtly hints at this tendency toward absenteeism and apathy: people in the office are portrayed just talking and smoking instead of working, and at five when Mamin leaves the office, everyone has already left. While idleness at work was a recurrent target of satire, as for example in the pages of *Krokodil*, it began to have resonance in animated films for the first time in these years.

In another scene, the construction of a house in front of Mamin's window explicitly refers to Khrushchev's vast building projects. A visual comic gag is at the base of this scene – the house is built very quickly with all the necessary accessories (a chair, a cat, a plant, laundry hung up, curtains, etc.) and on the top of the last block is a sign that reads, "Save your money in the state bank". In the late 1950s, in order to tackle the housing problem, apartment buildings were erected all around Soviet cities in a very short time; Geoffrey Hosking notes that between 1955 and 1964, the nation's housing stock nearly doubled (from 640 to 1182 million square meters).[162] The building boom served to ease the country's serious and urgent housing problem, but the quality of these houses was quite poor. Even today, Soviet people still like to derogatively dub the standard five-storey houses built in these years *khrushchevki* (after the Soviet leader) or *khrushchoby*, by analogy with *trushchoby* (Russian for "slums").

In the film, the housing question is posed from different points of view. There is a movement from macrocosm to microcosm, from a grandiose project to its practical effects

[162] Hosking, *The First Socialist Society*, 353.

109

Figure 3.21. *Panoramic view of buildings under construction. Still from* Story of a Crime.

on daily life. A panoramic shot of a landscape full of houses and rotary cranes emphasizes the vastness of the building project (Fig. 3.21). From a narrower point of view, through Mamin's office window, the construction of the apartment building progresses block by block at the rhythm of the hero's typing and seems to suggest that it is with the honest activity of workers such as Mamin that the country is moving forward (Fig. 3.22). Finally, inside Mamin's apartment, the noise heard from the neighbours is the ultimate sign of the poor quality of the building.

The film as we know it now is a revised version of an original script[163] that had more obvious and direct allusions to the inadequate conditions of the new houses. In the protocol of the second session of the Artistic Council for the discussion of *Story of a Crime*'s literary script, an annotation reported the scriptwriter Mikhail Vol'pin's comments on the necessity of cutting the script in order to avoid clear references to the poor quality of the *khrushchevki*.[164] In the revised script, however, the reader can still perceive a subtle disapproval of the poor housing conditions, especially in the scene in which the loud noise from upstairs shakes Mamin's walls. This criticism was inevitably unwelcome at the Soiuzmul'tfil'm studio, as a member of the Artistic Council comments: "The shaking of the ceiling is annoying. It suggests that the construction is of poor quality. In general it is

163 During the various sessions of the Soiuzmul'tfil'm Artistic Council, the script of *Story of a Crime* went through numerous revisions: the first literary film script for *Story of a Crime* was approved on 19 May 1961, on the condition that some revisions would be made; the second variant was discussed and approved on June 15, 1961, and the directorial film script was discussed and approved a year later, on 15 August 1962.

164 "In the script there was a piece that we cut out in order to avoid the theme of the quality of the buildings". RGALI, "Delo fil'ma *Istoriia odnogo prestupleniia*", 122.

Chapter 3 Case Studies: The Early 1960s

Figure 3.22. *Building under construction as seen from Mamin's window. Still from* Story of a Crime.

necessary to place the main stress on the fact that norms of social order are not being observed".[165] Despite opposition, this scene was not cut out, but was maintained to achieve a comic effect.

The final version of the film lacks a direct allusion to another particularly hot issue of Khrushchev's time – the appearance of foreign products. The original script had some cues that were supposed to be pronounced by the two women struck by Mamin. These exchanges referred to the widespread passion for foreign fashion and also hinted at the fact that women greatly outnumbered men in the years following World War II:

– At the *Odezhda* they got in some Hungarian suits!
– ... Women's or men's?
– Men's!
– And what am I supposed to do with them? I'm not married.
– Give them to Fedor, maybe he will marry you![166]

Partially to avoid a controversial topic, partially to be in accordance with the general style of the film in which dialogues were reduced to a minimum, these lines had been cut in the final version of the script.

Other instances of concretization, in this case social concretization, are presented through posters and street signs. By calling on the citizens to behave properly, signs perform

---

[165] RGALI, "Delo fil'ma *Istoriia odnogo prestupleniia*", 123.

[166] RGALI, "Delo fil'ma *Istoriia odnogo prestupleniia*", 54–55. Mikhail Vol'pin, the author of the film script, is famous for witty dialogues in his scripts for animated films and for live action films (e.g., *Volga, Volga*, written with Nikolai Erdman). Both Vol'pin and Erdman were well-known cinema scriptwriters (Erdman was also a dramaturg), but they turned to animation after falling into disgrace with the authorities.

Figure 3.23. *Sign: "Drivers and pedestrians: respect each other".
Still from* Story of a Crime.

the task of civic education ("Drivers and pedestrians: respect each other", Fig. 3.23), but at times they are also obviously fictitious and constitute a self-parody, for example this all-encompassing sign: "Do not pick the flowers, do not walk, do not spit, do not litter" (Fig. 3.24). These signs once again enter the field of *kul'turnost'*.

While specific clues in the representation of space immerse the spectators in Soviet reality and activate a process of recognition, some other details provide a deeper analysis of society in this specific time of Soviet history. A semiotic reading of the film can help us to explicate how formal choices in the film are unique and original means to show the underlying ambiguities of the period in question.

(d) Lack of boundaries in the relationship between private and public: a semiotic reading

If we consider the relation of the individual with society in semiotic terms, society can be seen as a comprehensive semiotic system inside of which each individual has his own world, or in more specific semiotic language, each individual is represented by a closed system of signs; the individual, thus, is part of society and strictly connected to it. For the correct functioning of the entire community the boundaries between these two systems – that of the individual and that

Chapter 3 Case Studies: The Early 1960s

Figure 3.24. *Sign: "Do not pick the flowers, do not walk, do not spit, do not litter". Still from* Story of a Crime.

of society – should permit quite a free translation of texts from one system to the other and vice versa. In Lotman's words, the boundary is defined as

> a mechanism for translating texts of an alien semiotics into "our" language. It is the place where what is "external" is transformed into what is "internal". It is a filtering membrane which so transforms foreign texts that they become part of the semiosphere's internal semiotics while still retaining their own characteristics.[167]

In the film in question, conversely, there is no filtering of foreign texts and no translation of what comes from outside Mamin's world into his own system. The process is not one of adaptation of the external into the internal, but of violation of the boundaries and appropriation of the individual's whole by the society's order, so that the result is the presence of one comprehensive system from which the individual cannot detach himself.

On a formal level, the idea of the individual fully incorporated in an over-comprehensive society is reflected in *Story of a Crime* through the graphic representation of space. This film positions the main character, Mamin, on the border between a collective, social reality and the desire – which was tangible and strong in the Khrushchev era – to find refuge in an individual world, or at least to claim the right to do so. Every attempt made by Mamin to retreat to his own

[167] Lotman, "The Semiosphere", 136–137. In the original Russian: Lotman, "Vnutri mysliashchikh mirov", 262.

(*svoe*) space is frustrated by the invasion of its boundaries by external (or more accurately *chuzhye* – not belonging to his world) elements. The pressure on the border is powerful, because Mamin's own world is embedded in the bigger world of society. Communications and exchanges from one system to the other are generally allowed and necessary, but here it seems that, on the one hand, the characters live in a closed system with no productive interrelations; on the other hand, the characters form a society in which the very existence of the boundaries is at stake.

In order to express the idea of lack of boundaries between the individual and society, the director Khitruk and the art director Alimov opted for a stylized and symbolic representation of space. In the film no precise boundaries define the space around the individual Mamin; his space is open and visible as a public man and public life are in essence. His world is presented with no borders, as though he has no right to be detached from society, or better said, he has yet no right to be depicted in a film as a simple and independent entity.

A little coloured square on a black background defines Mamin's apartment, but those boundaries are flexible – they shrink and enlarge. Even the staircases, usually easily perceived as a liminal space between home and outside-home,[168] are practically nonexistent. The world that surrounds the character invades the scope that is supposed to be his own. Mamin's space often does not have autonomous representation; at times, it is depicted in the filmic frame together with other spaces not belonging to him. Instances of simultaneous montage are achieved with a split screen in which contemporaneous actions, taking place in different spaces, appear at the same time; two shots are spliced together in a relation of simultaneity, but at the same time they also reveal a relation of cause and effect (Fig. 3.25).

Spatial relations are not introduced in a naturalistic way, but they are suggested in a symbolic way. The space is fragmented and consists of parts put together almost like in a collage. Indeed, real collages are used in the film, made up of written-on pieces of paper, newspapers, and film advertisements. These pieces of different materials are used as synecdochic representations of newspapers read by Mamin and other characters, film advertisements posted on the

[168] "If an apartment is the focus of a 'normal' habitation, the staircases become that border space between *home* and *outside-home*". Lotman, *Universe of the Mind*, 140. In the original Russian: Lotman, "Vnutri mysliashchikh mirov", 266.

Chapter 3 Case Studies: The Early 1960s

Figure 3.25. *Example of simultaneous montage with split screen. Still from* Story of a Crime.

board, and announcements hung on the office wall. In addition, real photographs of buildings and streets are seen from the windows of Mamin's office. These pieces of material other than the drawings on cel or the cut-outs used in the films underline the sense of concretization of a specific reality and of a specific time. As in any collage, they have to be read in terms of their function with the whole, but at the same time they carry with them their own origins and specificity.

(e) Play with different artistic languages results in a comic effect

Play with different artistic languages constitutes another original feature of the film's style. The juxtaposition of animation with other art languages such as those of live-action cinema and photography has a twofold task: it emphasizes the main themes in the film – the relation between the individual and society and the opposition of cultured/uncultured (*kul'turnyi/nekul'turnyi*) – and it creates an effect of surprise that provokes the spectator's laughter.

In one scene, live-action film footage appears within the frame of Mamin's TV set (Fig. 3.26). The audience does not see a neutral, "unmarked" work, but an adaptation for the screen of Pushkin's *Evgenii Onegin*, a classic that is recog-

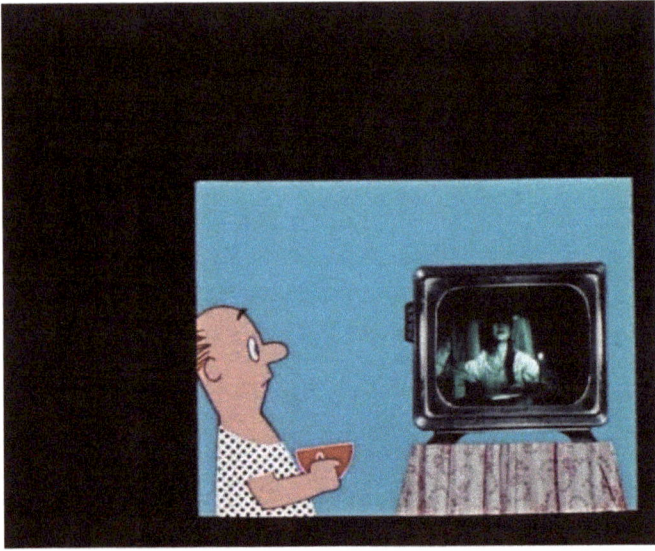

Figure 3.26. *TV scene. Still from* Story of a Crime.

nized as part of the Russian collective intellect, another element of the variegated field of *kul'turnost'*. While Mamin watches *Evgenii Onegin*, the music from his neighbor completely drowns out the sound of the film. According to Lotman, live-action film is a bilingual phenomenon – the language of the moving image, which is in film a moving photograph, is associated with the language of the spoken word. All of this is perceived, however, as a single language phenomenon (*odnoiazychnyi fenomen*).[169] In the scene in question, the two languages are separated, and the image disassociates itself from the sound: the character in the film, Tatiana, opens her mouth, and the spectator hears the neighbor's music. What happens on the screen is not perceived as a single-language phenomenon, but as two distinctive language phenomena. The language of the spoken word is substituted by music, and in this process of substitution the audience perceives a violation of norms and is forced to reconsider the relationship between form and content. Shklovskian estrangement is created, the "shape" of the work is foregrounded, and a comic effect is achieved.

A similar play with different artistic languages occurs in the scene in which the noise provoked by the neighbors' party shakes Mamin's wall to the point that a family picture hung on the wall swings sideways until it falls and breaks. The

[169] Lotman, "Fenomen kul'tury", 40.

Chapter 3 Case Studies: The Early 1960s

Figure 3.27. *Moving photograph. Still from* Story of a Crime.

photograph of Mamin's family becomes animated and moves to the rhythm of the music heard from upstairs, producing an amusing result (Fig. 3.27).

In this scene, what the viewer recognizes as a photograph hanging on the wall (even if it is not a real photograph but an animator's drawing of a photograph) enters the world of animation, becoming an image that animates itself. The animated photograph crosses the border between a static photograph and the animated world; it leaves a conventional system of signs to which the audience is accustomed, in order to enter another system, the boundaries of which are less demarcated.

The sudden and surprising passage from the language of static photography to the language of animated figures has a humorous outcome, much like the one provoked by the puppet-like movements[170] of the members of the family. In his study on laughter, Henri Bergson notes how a drawing "is generally comic in proportion to the clearness as well as the subtleness with which it enables us to see a man as a jointed puppet".[171] Bergson also observes how the human body becomes laughable when its attitudes, gestures, and movements resemble those of a machine.[172]

A comic effect is also achieved throughout the film through the substitution of music for dialogue. Whenever the characters in the film establish an act of communication where

170 The effect is created by using flat marionettes cut out from paper and putting together their joints with microscopic needles that allow them to be mobile.

171 Bergson, *Laughter*, 32.

172 Bergson, *Laughter*, 32.

dialogue would normally be used as a code for the exchange of information, the conversation is presented not through a verbal code, but through a musical code. The spectator witnesses a particularly amusing moment when a sweet clarinet sound acts as Mamin's voice, while a boastful trombone produces the rude neighbor's voice.

In the rare spoken lines in the film, verbal puns call for a humorous response. When the policeman shouts *stoite* ("stop"/"stand up"), the polysemantic value of the word materializes on screen – everyone stops and the two women (supposedly dead) stand up. A verbal pun occurs also when the guests from the neighbor's party sing a song called "Silence" (*Tishina*) out loud. Incidentally, *Tishina* was the original title of Mikhail Vol'pin's script.[173]

The film's comic tone also has the function of lightening the moralizing message. *Story of a Crime* opts for a representation of the weaknesses of society in a satirical way, rather than a moralizing manner. Satire, though, has always played a dangerous role, toeing the border of the admissible. While it is considered a good means for criticism of the weaknesses of society, it is also a mode that reveals the existence of these faults, and was generally allowed in the Soviet Union only insofar as the criticism could be manipulated by the dominant ideology. Whenever satire slips out of control, it might turn into an undesired (for the authorities) harsh criticism of the system. It seems that in the Soiuzmul'tfil'm studio, the members of the Artistic Council were aware of this danger and expressed contrasting tendencies and positions, some of them progressive, some quite conservative. Khitruk himself recalls in his memoir *Professia – animator* the opposite reactions that followed the first two screenings of his film in the Soiuzmul'tfil'm studio. Contrary to the custom of showing new films openly to the entire studio, the directors decided to limit the screening of *Story of a Crime* to a small group of people; "after all it was not a children's tale, but a satirical feuilleton. A risky and little-known genre".[174] The screening took place in complete silence and no comments followed; Khitruk's team thought their film was a complete failure. But when the film was shown to the entire studio, the audience was enthusiastic, as were the spectators and the press once the film was released. The atmosphere at the Council reflected the general climate of the Thaw, where conservative and liberal

[173] RGALI, "Delo fil'ma *Istoriia odnogo prestupleniia*", 1.

[174] Khitruk, *Professia – animator*, vol. I, 165.

positions were often in confrontation with one another. Khitruk's film cunningly played with both positions, trying to please both the audience and authorities.

In the following years, more satirical animated films appeared on the screen. Some of them, though, turned to biting satire; their harsh criticism of aspects of contemporary society was not welcomed by the new leadership, especially after 1968, when the Soviet Union fully entered the period of "stagnation" (*zastoi*).

Chapter 4

Russian Animation in the Second Half of the 1960s: Between the Khrushchev Thaw and the Brezhnev Stagnation

Context

The first years after Khrushchev's dismissal in October 1964 were still affected by the atmosphere that characterized the Thaw. Signs of relaxation were still perceivable in all spheres of the artistic world. To mention just a few examples: Viktor Nekrasov and Boris Pasternak published their works in *Novyi mir* (January 1965); in the Writer's Union some younger liberals replaced the most doctrinaire members of the secretariat; music by Rodion Shchedrin, Kara Karaev and Dmitrii Shostakovich was performed; a few controversial films were released (including Marlen Khutsiev's film *I Am Twenty*, mentioned in Chapter 2); and in late February *Pravda*'s recently-appointed editor, Aleksei Rumiantsev, ran a signed editorial in defense of artistic freedom.[175]

But by the summer of 1965 there was evidence of change. The journals *Novyi mir* and *Iunost'* were under attack for publishing "negative" work.[176] The head of the Komsomol, Sergei Pavlov, published an article in *Pravda* insisting on the role of contemporary art in supporting Party ideology, while a new article by Rumiantsev in defense of artistic freedom provoked his dismissal. Soon after, other steps towards stricter control followed. The most internationally famous event was the show trial that followed the arrest of Andrei Siniavskii and Iulii Daniel' for publishing their works in the West. With the invasion of Czechoslovakia in August 1968

[175] Woll, *Real Images*, 166.

[176] Woll, *Real Images* 166.

the new authorities sent a clear warning that they would not tolerate deviance from their rules, and would move towards more conservative positions. Stricter political, ideological, and moral criteria started to be applied in defining what was "permissible".

In the first years of Brezhnev's regime, animation still possessed the Thaw era's spirit of liberalization and innovation. Animated films for adults were still being produced alongside children's films, which constituted the majority of animation production. While some works presented humorous satire, some other films were specifically made for a grown-up public and clearly attempted to go beyond the limits of the permissible.

Films taking a polemical stance on issues concerning everyday life still appeared, but were mainly channeled into the satirical cinematic journal *Fitil'*, which continued to foreground societal problems for another two decades. Other satirical films had mainly an entertainment purpose and were accessible not only to an adult public, but also to older youth. Among the most successful and original of these were *The Bench* (*Skameika*, L. Atamanov, 1967), based on the comic drawings of the famous Danish caricaturist Herluf Bidstrup; *Othello-67* (*Otello-67*, F. Khitruk, 1967), a 30-second version of Shakespeare's play consumed as fast food for the mind at a drive-in style cinema; and *Film, Film, Film* (*Fil'm, fil'm, fil'm*, F. Khitruk, 1968), a parody of the film-making process. This satirical style is also exemplified by most of Efim Gamburg's films, from *Spies' Passions* (*Shpionskie strasti*, 1967), a parody of spy and detective films, and *Old Precepts* (*Starye Zavety*, 1968), five mini-parables on well-known sayings, to the many humorous films he made in the 1970s and 1980s.

If these films produced in the early 1960s were characterized by a caricature style, others were built on a multi-level structure that made it possible to use a naïve patina of children's language to suggest hidden messages to an adult audience. Already in Khrushchev's years one could find rare examples of films that hinted at the political situation, such as in the case of *Chipollino* (B. Dezhkin, 1961). In the film, the story is clearly addressed to a child audience, but at the same time it alludes to social and political themes familiar to the adult spectator. To choose to tell a story about the capricious whims of a despotic governor, as in this film, would have probably been too risky during the Stalin era, but it became possible and could be read as referring to the Soviet realm during Khrushchev's years, when Stalin's conduct was attacked.

In 1967, somewhat analogously, *The Mountain of Dinosaurs* (*Gora dinozavrov*, R. Strautmane, 1967), a cartoon varnished in a form typical of animated films for children, featured strong allusions to a suffocating Soviet system. This film was conceived as an educational film for children about the extinction of dinosaurs; the first script written by Arkadii Snesarev included a note that quoted as a source for the film an article published in the journal *Nauka i zhizn'* (no. 6, 1965) about theories on the extinction of dinosaurs.[177] During the discussion of the film at the Artistic Council of Soiuzmul'tfil'm, however, it was already clear that the film could be read as a political commentary on contemporary life. Nonetheless, the Artistic Council, still feeling the influence of the relaxed climate of the Thaw time and not yet experiencing the full effects of stagnation, approved the film.[178]

The film's tale of prehistoric times serves an allegorical function. The baby dinosaur's pleading to be allowed to hatch and see the light is answered with a monotone repetition of the words "I protect you, I build up a new layer, I fulfill my duty", which echo in the closed environment of the egg and are progressively accompanied by the threatening rolls of drum beating a march rhythm. A direct condemnation of the Soviet state's oppressive "care" of the individual was carefully disguised by using a simple visual form typical of educational and popular science films for children, setting the film in a prehistoric time, exploiting a subject (dinosaurs) that has always fascinated children's imaginations, and using animal characters, following an old tradition of social criticism through allegoric tales that dates back to Jean de La Fontaine, or in Russia, to Ivan Krylov.

[177] RGALI, "*Gora dinozavrov*: Literaturnyi stsenarii A.G. Snesareva", 2.

[178] RGALI, "Stenogramma zasedaniia khudozhestvennogo soveta po obsuzhdeniiu fil'ma *Gora dinozavrov*".

A more direct attempt to criticize the system was ventured by Khitruk and Andrei Khrzhanovskii in the second half of the 1960s. Khitruk's *The Man in the Frame* (*Chelovek v ramke*, 1966) and Khrzhanovskii's films *There Once Lived Koziavin* (*Zhil-byl Koziavin*, 1966) and *The Glass Harmonica* (*Stekliannaia garmonika*, 1968) marked the passage from a laconic and simple style to increasing complexity derived from the simultaneous presence of elements from different iconic systems, a convoluted symbolism, and allegoric forms. *The Man in the Frame* and *There Once Lived Koziavin* (from now on referred to as *Koziavin*) expose the same rigid and inhuman world, but bureaucratism was not the only target of the attack – on closer examination, a broader critique of the Soviet system emerges. Khitruk's *The Man in the Frame* was not censored, but its dark tone prevented it from being screened very often to the Soviet public, while Khrzhanovskii's *There Once Lived Koziavin* had a wittier overtone that allowed it to be distributed more broadly in the country. *Koziavin* was the only film made by Khrzhanovskii in the 1960s and 1970s that was released without drastic changes – though it was not submitted for screening at any international festivals.

The two films have different styles, but express a common tendency: a "situation" is more important than a series of events, and all actions are built around the character's frame of mind, which is also reflected in the organization of space – in *The Man in the Frame* the closed mind of the bureaucrat is represented by a small space delimited by a frame; while in *Koziavin,* an invisible narrow path forces Koziavin, a little cog in the bureaucratic system, to keep to one direction without going astray.

Attacks on the bureaucrat: *The Man in the Frame* (*Chelovek v ramke*, Fedor Khitruk, 1966)

Khitruk's second film directed to an adult audience (after *Story of a Crime*, 1962) deals with the story of a bureaucrat interested only in his career. The bureaucrat's narrowmindness is symbolically represented by the shape of a frame in which he forces himself to live. As he moves up towards more powerful positions, the frame becomes increasingly thicker until the character disappears in it.

In working on this film, Khitruk once again enlisted the collaboration of the artist Sergei Alimov, who tackled this topic in a stylistically original way. The visual choice adopted by Alimov and Khitruk for the representation of a bureaucrat is a flat picture of a man put in a frame. The Russian metaphor of the "paper man" (*bumazhnyi chelovek*) is literalized in a concrete form in the film with the character

Chapter 4   Russian Animation in the Second Half of the 1960s

Figure 4.1. *First emotions. Still from* The Man in the Frame.

depicted on a flat paper-like surface, which stands for his lack of spiritual depth. The frame denotes the bureaucrat's state of mind and at the same time suggests the hermetic world he builds around himself; in Khitruk's words, it is a "visual image of the man's place in society".[179] Gradually the frame becomes a character in its own right – it moves and changes shape, participates in the events depicted, gradually enslaves the bureaucrat, and ultimately swallows him. Cut-out figures and geometric forms move on screen in a deliberately mechanical way, underlining the machine-like driving force that lies behind the character and reduces him to a puppet, or rather, to an automaton, deprived of all feelings or scruples. The language spoken by the character is made up of monosyllables or mere agglomerations of letters that are voided of any meaning, as bureaucratic language often is.

Like a mechanical puppet, the character ascends in his career, ignoring all distractions. External events, temptations, and emotions do not succeed in making him capitulate, but have the opposite effect of strengthening the bureaucrat's constricting frame (Figs. 4.1–4.2).

In the first scene of the film, "Meeting with Life" (*Vstrecha s zhizn'iu*), Khitruk and Alimov juxtapose the flat drawn image of the character with series of still photographs depicting those aspects of society from which the character cuts him-

[179] Fedor Khitruk, *Professia-animator*, vol. 1, 174.

Figure 4.2. *Rejection of emotions. Still from* The Man in the Frame.

Figure 4.3. *Girl skipping rope. Still from* The Man in the Frame.

self off. A little girl appears skipping rope (Fig. 4.3); this girl will become a recurrent motif throughout the film, a sign of vitality that sharply contrasts with the main character's static and almost lifeless activity.

Festive street demonstrations, sporting activities, and smiling women and children appear on the screen. Not only does the splicing together of these photographs create a visual counterpoint similar to Eisenstein's montage, but each frame is organized according to what Eisenstein would call a "conflict inside the frame" (*vnutrikadrovyi konflikt*), that is, a conflict in the graphic direction of the lines formed by the subject in the frame, a conflict of planes, of volume and space,[180] which conveys a sense of the lively world that surrounds the inactive *apparatchik*.

Some more photographs celebrate the work force using visual choices that have their roots in the tradition of Soviet montage. The images of healthy and smiling workers are set up in opposition to Khitruk's bureaucrat, who merely sits at a desk, signing and stamping papers or simply passing files from one hand to another. The accusation of "lack of productivity" inherent in the depiction of the character resounded as a harsh criticism in a society where "parasites" were severely attacked and punished.

There is no live-action cinematic footage, but through quick editing the static images become animate, achieving an effect similar to that of Eisenstein's famous marble lion rising to its feet in *The Battleship Potemkin* (*Bronenosets "Potemkin"*, 1925). Photographs are shot frame by frame, much in the same way that in animation drawings are shot one frame at a time. The director creates a sense of movement using a series of photographs presented with slightly changed angles, different colors, or through panning camera movements, which focus on close-ups of various details, or reveal in long shots a bigger picture. The workers are depicted against several different backgrounds: an open horizon, a black background, a washed-out background, the sky, and a narrow tunnel that nonetheless has a light at its end (Figs. 4.4–4.7).

The open backgrounds emphasize the figures of the workers, making them a symbol of all the workers who contribute to the prosperity of the country. The people and their jobs are represented in a continuum, as an inseparable entity, parts of a larger vision of life. There are no delimiting frames around them; the ultimate image of the fusion of the person with the surrounding space is a picture of a doctor in his white smock and surgical mask, whose edges merge with the white background – workers and environment become one (Fig. 4.8).

The reverse situation occurs in the fictional space created in the film's animated sequences; the frame becomes increas-

[180] Eisenstein, "Za kadrom", 291.

SOVIET ANIMATION and the Thaw of the 1960s

Figure 4.4. *Workers in the sky (1). Still from* The Man in the Frame.

Figure 4.5. *Workers in the sky (2). Still from* The Man in the Frame.

ingly bigger and thicker, delimiting the character and separating him from the surrounding world. The juxtaposition of graphic images and photographs emphasizes the static quality of the bureaucrat's world and the lively and active life lying outside.

Love, friendship, human sympathy, fantasy, and freedom – all represented in the film in symbolic forms – are feelings and states that the bureaucrat lets pass him by without being

Chapter 4 Russian Animation in the Second Half of the 1960s

Figure 4.6. *Workers in the sky (3). Still from* The Man in the Frame.

Figure 4.7. *Workers in open tunnel. Still from* The Man in the Frame.

touched by them. As a symbol of love and beauty, an image from the Renaissance, Botticelli's *Venus*, appears on the screen. The Renaissance image is an iconic sign of harmony and pure beauty, of an idealized world in opposition to the down-to-earth and aseptic environment of the bureaucrat. In the collage that appears on the screen, the harmonious traits and sinuous lines that delineate the Venus contrast with the sketchy, straight, and simplified lines of the

Figure 4.8. *Doctor against white background. Still from* The Man in the Frame.

Figure 4.9. *The man and Venus. Still from* The Man in the Frame.

character in the frame. The image of Venus is cut out from the environment in which she belongs in Botticelli's painting and shares the frame with the character. No borders delimit her space, and a color that fills in the entire film frame stands for her boundless and eternal force (Fig. 4.9). To approach beauty would require the bureaucrat to step out of his enclosed space, but he refuses to venture into this world without boundaries. The moment he makes up his

Chapter 4 Russian Animation in the Second Half of the 1960s

Figure 4.10. *Breaking of the frame. Still from* The Man in the Frame.

Figure 4.11. *Renouncing emotions and restoring the frame. Still from* The Man in the Frame.

mind, the background of the film frame returns to an austere paper white and the frame is restored (Figs. 4.10–4.11).

In another scene, the outside world in the form of a kite literally breaks into the grey world of the bureaucrat, but no signs of of imagination or free-spiritedness are allowed in the character's world – he folds the kite into the shape of a letter and passes it on (Figs. 4.12–4.13). Even in this new

SOVIET ANIMATION and the Thaw of the 1960s

Figure 4.12. *The kite breaks in. Still from* The Man in the Frame.

Figure 4.13. *Reshaping the kite. Still from* The Man in the Frame.

shape the kite is dangerous and provokes the fall of another bureaucrat who holds it in his hands, while our hero, refusing to follow the same destiny, throws the kite in the garbage and rises up a notch in the hierarchy.

Attacks against the bureaucratic world are familiar topics for satire. As noted in the previous chapters, criticism of bureaucrats regularly appeared in satirical journals and was

Chapter 4 Russian Animation in the Second Half of the 1960s

Figure 4.14. *"The Cry for Help". Still from* The Man in the Frame.

Figure 4.15. *Still from* The Hand *(J. Trnka, 1965).*

often a convention of official culture. In order to strengthen the legitimate appearance of this criticism, during a discussion of *The Man in the Frame* at a Soiuzmul'tfil'm Artistic Council meeting, a suggestion was made to include a quote with Lenin's characterization of the bureaucrat.[181] This film, however, goes beyond disapproval of a single bureaucrat's behavior, and becomes a sharp but subtle critique of the Soviet system. In the scene in question, called "A Cry for Help" (*Krik o pomoshi*), a row of doors is drawn in perspec-

[181] RGALI, "Delo fil'ma *Chelovek v ramke*", 19.

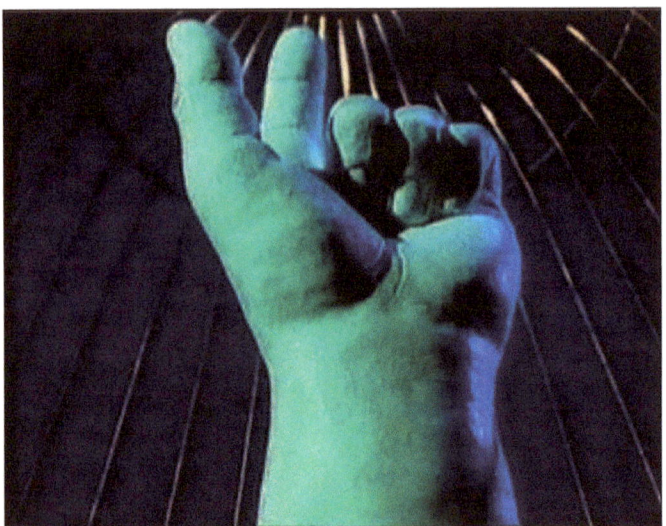

Figure 4.16. *Still (2) from* The Hand *(J. Trnka, 1965).*

tive, a rare example of three dimensional space in the film (Fig. 4.14). A man repetitively knocks at these doors and, in despair, cries for help. The bureaucrat does not answer and one last cry is heard in the distance before a deathly silence invades the entire space. On the surface, one can read this scene as another indication of the character's egoism, but on a deeper level it could be seen as referring to denunciations and arbitrary arrests. The repetition of the doors recalls the layers of the frame that surrounds the bureaucrat and emphasizes the character's willful isolation from the rest of the world. The sense of depth that the line of doors creates can also be read as a symbol of a deeper sin that lies in the conscience of the character, and at the same time can be interpreted as an issue that goes beyond a personal matter to include the system itself. Central to the interpretation of this scene is a monument that stands next to the doors: it is a pillar surmounted by a hand that seems to symbolize the way up in the character's career. The hand also stands for dictatorial power, as it recalls an identical hand that appears in a famous animated film created by the Czech director J. Trnka in 1965, *The Hand* (*Ruka*), a film that presents a sharp critique of the oppressive communist regime in Czechoslovakia (Figs. 4.15–4.16).

In this scene, gloomy music and cries resounding in empty space create a sense of anguish and oppression. The same

Figure 4.17. *Framing flowers. Still from* The Man in the Frame.

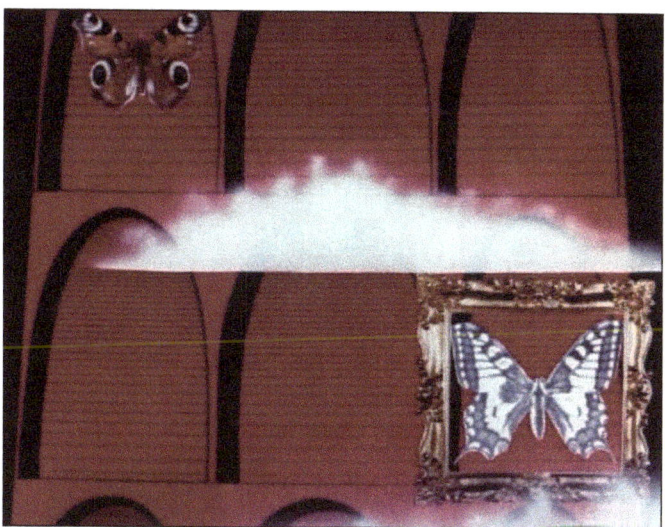

Figure 4.18. *Framing butterflies. Still from* The Man in the Frame.

oppressive feeling echoes in the last scene of the film when the bureaucrat rises to increasingly powerful positions, while his frame becomes thicker and thicker until it completely swallows him. In the background of this last scene a tower appears with various symbols of everything the character sacrificed in his life for the sake of his career. Passing by these signs of a reality that is foreign to him, not only does the bureaucrat regard them with indifference; he also appropriates them and degrades them, making them part of his world – symbolically enclosing flowers in a frame and covering butterflies with files and stamps (Figs. 4.17–4.18). The power of the bureaucrat crosses the borderline of his framed figure and impacts the outside world; with his increasing influence, he now tries to frame and seal the reality that he once consciously rejected. Once again in the film, Khitruk's criticism reaches from the small world of the character to the larger world of the entire Soviet system, and ultimately becomes a philosophical reflection on human life.

It is only the girl skipping rope that gives the film a positive ending – the bureaucrat, after all, will disappear into the world he has created, and the rhythm of the positive, naïve, and pure little girl's jumping will cause the frame that completely encloses him to fall apart (Figs. 4.19–4.20).

This positive ending was imposed on the director by some members of the Artistic Council who, appealing to remnants of the official requirements of socialist realism, were concerned to avoid gloominess in the depiction of reality. In the original conception of the film, Khitruk did not intend for things to end on such a positive note, with the destruction of the bureaucrat by the force of the little girl. "The film was conceived as a biting film; we created it with bite and we hope that it will help to fight evil. But I would not like to fall back on any epigraph. That would be an unnecessary reassurance",[182] commented Khitruk during the Artistic Council discussion of the film. Thus, the original idea was not to provide some positive image of the future, but rather to focus on the faults of certain segments of society, if not ills of the system, in order denounce and correct them.

It is worth noting that after this film, Khitruk embarked on the production of a witty and amusing film on the difficult process of filmmaking, *Film, Film, Film* (1968). While this film is mainly a parody of the cinema world, it also includes a scene in which the director and scriptwriter have to go through a long bureaucratic process and endless revisions before finally having their ideas approved (Fig. 4.21).

Khitruk in this film also pays tribute to Eisenstein, imitating scenes from *Ivan the Terrible*, offering a subtle allusion to a film that had to go through various painful revisions (Fig. 4.22).

[182] RGALI, "Delo fil'ma *Chelovek v ramke*", 20.

Chapter 4   Russian Animation in the Second Half of the 1960s

Figure 4.19. *Little girl jumping at the end of the film. Still from* The Man in the Frame.

Figure 4.20. *Frame falls apart. Still from* The Man in the Frame.

The censors surprisingly approved the scenes which had direct allusions to censorship, probably because the film was ingenious and highly entertaining, and directed its satire mainly at the artistic world. The comic quality of *Film Film Film* springs from its whimsical situations as well as an accelerated rhythm marked by music similar to that used in silent comic films, from Buster Keaton to Charlie Chaplin.

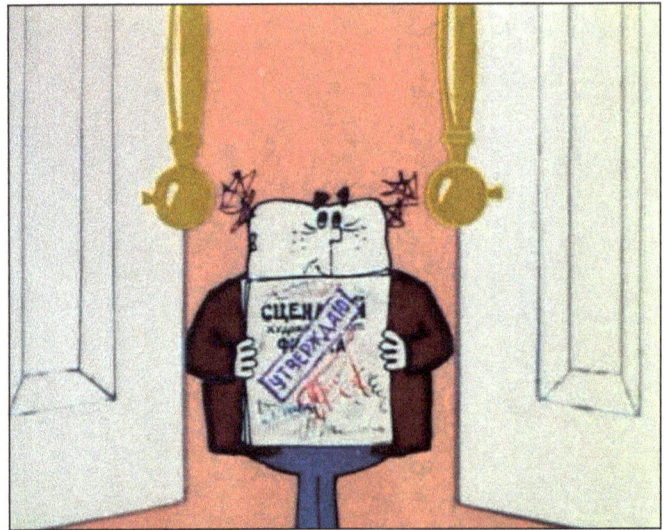

Figure 4.21. *Finally "Approved". Censorship. Still from* Film, Film, Film.

Figure 4.22. *Reference to Eisenstein's* Ivan the Terrible. *Still from* Film, Film, Film.

While the film was probably most hilarious to an audience acquainted with the cinema world, it was still accessible to a broader audience and enjoyed great success. Targeting a wide audience was probably the main strategy through which films dealing with societal problems managed to be released in the second half of the 1960s. Another humorous film that, by adopting this approach, was able to subtly touch on social issues and make its appearance on Soviet screens was Khrzhanovskii's *There Once Lived Koziavin* (1966).

Bureaucratic world once more under attack: *There Once Lived Koziavin* (*Zhil-byl Koziavin*, Andrei Khrzhanovskii, 1966)

At the same time that Khitruk was making *The Man in the Frame*, Khrzhanovskii finished the film *There Once Lived Koziavin*, the graduation piece he presented for his diploma from VGIK. As in *The Man in the Frame*, *There Once Lived Koziavin* deals with the bureaucratic world, but this time the careerist bureaucrat does not appear at the center of the action, but as one of the small cogs in the wheel. If Khitruk's film presents dark criticism of bureaucrats, *There Once Lived Koziavin*, though also a sharp satire, is presented with wit. The situations depicted in the film are absurd and paradoxical to such an extent that they provoke laughter from the audience.

The plot is simple: one day Koziavin's boss asks him to look for a colleague, Sidorov, in order to tell him that the cashier has arrived. Koziavin sets off for him and keeps on walking in the direction suggested by his boss, never going astray – he goes into drains, leaps over people, passes through buildings that are being demolished, through commission shops ignoring thieves, through construction sites, through gyms and concert theaters, through a pipe line, through a wasteland, up a mountain, through the desert on a dinosaur's skeleton, through waters, and all around the globe, to return to the office from the opposite direction from which he set out.

The comic tone of the film is created by the story, the automaton-like quality of the character, the particular use of words and music, and the choice of spaces. The laughable puppet-like behavior that Henri Bergson discusses in his book on the meaning of comedy[183] is here enhanced by the mechanical repetition of the only two lines of dialogue in the film: "Did you see Sidorov? The cashier has arrived". The repetition of the same lines, a sign of a sterile bureaucratic world, creates nonsensical situations as in the theater of the absurd. This scant and repetitive dialogue produces a comic effect, and at the same time provokes reflection on the inadequacy of language and lack of communication,

[183] Bergson, *Laughter*, 32.

which leads to a reading of the film on a broader existential level. A humorous and parodic effect also arises from the superimposition of images upon music. The film's soundtrack ranges from jazz at the beginning, to pop in the scene in which Koziavin leaves the city to the sound of an instrumental version of the famous song "Evenings outside Moscow" ("Podmoskovnye vechera"), to classical music, which accompanies an iconic image of Koziavin as the romantic Byronic hero (Fig. 4.23).

In the film, sometimes criticism adopts a darker tone, but this quickly gives way to laughable situations. When Koziavin starts his journey, he stops at an office in which legs are seen dangling from a presumably hanged body. This gloomy detail is lightened up by the body's answering Koziavin's question as it opens its legs in the same way that other people shrug their shoulders (Fig. 4.24). The lack of logic in this scene is highlighted by a chair that seems to hang from the side wall and the fact that while we see only the legs of this hanging body, we discern only the head of another bureaucrat drowned in a pile of documents, as though this senseless bureaucratic world is populated only by "half-men", or hollow bodies. While depicting an illogical world, the director insists on Koziavin's indifferent response to the "answers" given by a supposedly dead (or nearly dead) body, in this way transforming the grim scene into a witty gag.

Koziavin is a version of the "man in the frame", the man who lives in a narrow world, not able to look beyond it. All the bureaucrats depicted in the film, from those working with him – who seem to multiply in those endless and repetitive corridors – to the one he meets in the desert coming from the opposite direction, seem to have come out from the same mold as Koziavin. Both Khitruk's and Khrzhanovskii's bureaucrats are depicted going through the motions in a monotonous, nonsensical job, simply passing along pieces of paper or accumulating files in piles. The *Man in the Frame*'s actions are self-destructive, and only once he reaches the highest position does his behavior have repercussions in the world around him. Koziavin does not need power and a high position to be harmful, for he manages to damage all spheres of society by blindly performing a simple duty. Having Koziavin stop work on the production site, interrupt the sport training and the concert, or destroy the dinosaur's skeleton by walking on it demonstrates the det-

Chapter 4   Russian Animation in the Second Half of the 1960s

Figure 4.23. *Byron-like depiction of Koziavin.*
Still from There Once Lived Koziavin.

Figure 4.24. *Koziavin and half-men.*
Still from There Once Lived Koziavin.

rimental effect of bureaucracy on production, sports, art, and research. Images of workers, also found in Khitruk's film *The Man in the Frame*, create a strong contrast between the forces that are moving the country and the bureaucratic world that puts obstacles in their way and leads to stagnation (Fig. 4.25).

Figure 4.25. *Men at work in a web-like construction site. Still from* There Once Lived Koziavin.

Figure 4.26. *Intersecting lines. Still from* There Once Lived Koziavin.

Space is organized in a way that underlines the contrast between Koziavin's obtuse, regular, and constant steps straight ahead and the varied and active world that surrounds him: from lines created by a builder on the job that resemble spider webs (Fig. 4.25), to the intersecting lines of

Chapter 4   Russian Animation in the Second Half of the 1960s

Figure 4.27. *Classic works spring from the violin.*
Still from There Once Lived Koziavin.

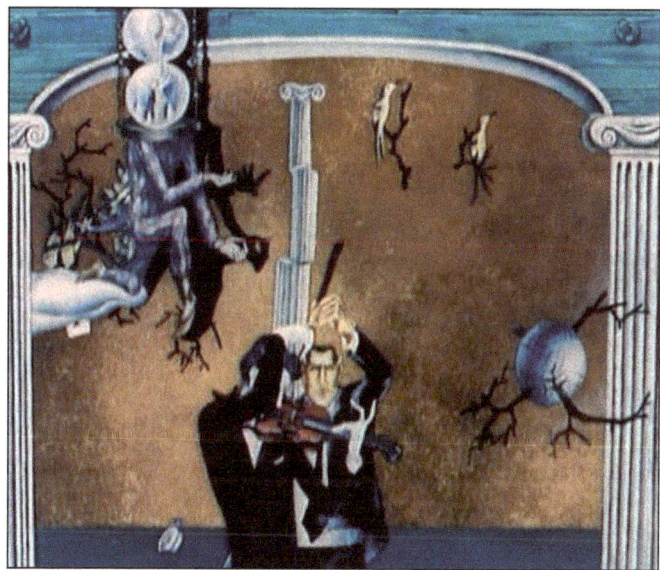

Figure 4.28. *Koziavin interrupts the violinist.*
Still from There Once Lived Koziavin.

traffic in the street, of streetcar cables, and of palaces (Fig. 4.26).

The linear path followed by Koziavin also contrasts with the multilayered artistic world that appears in a scene featuring a concert. The world of creativity is presented in the form of a collage composed of details from classic artistic works that emerge like music from a violin (Figs. 4.27–4.28).

In the same scene, timeless art concretizes into specific references to the Soviet world: famous Russian writers and directors sit among the audience (Fig. 4.29).

Personalities such as Anna Akhmatova, Aleksandr Tvardovskii with his journal *Novyi Mir* under his arm, Il'ia Ehrenburg, Marina Tsvetaeva, Boris Pasternak, Evgenii Evtushenko, Dmitrii Shostakovich, Vsevolod Meyerhold, Natan Al'tman, Nikolai Gogol', and Vasilii Kandinsky gather at this concert. What these artists have in common is that each experienced some form of repression by the system. The figure of Henri Rousseau such as in his self-portrait stands next to this special audience; in Khrzhanovskii's words, "He represents art that is alien to socialist realism".[184]

Khrzhanovskii's protest against censorship becomes even more evident with the arrival of Koziavin. The bureaucrat interrupts the violinist (Fig. 4.28), yet the violin keeps on playing, even when the background is transformed into a wooden cell (Fig. 4.30). A menace against the artist is perceived in between the visual images, but at the same time the director celebrates the power of art that would survive despite any prohibition. No matter how art is hindered, it will eternally regenerate; the images of classical art that come out of the violin turn into paper cut-outs that seem to fly in an idyllic space (Fig. 4.31), which is at the same time the park in which the concert takes place, a haven for artists, and an idealized place depicted in a painting hanging at a shop in the following scene.

The frame does not last long enough for the audience to notice, without pausing the film, that the pieces of paper are written in a foreign language, but this detail can be read as a hidden reference to the strict law governing the publication of Soviet literary works abroad, especially in light of the so-called "Pasternak affair" in 1957. Perhaps even more relevant here is an event that took place while the film was in production: the arrest and trial (1965) of Andrei Siniavskii and Iulii Daniel', the two writers and critics who were accused of anti-Soviet activity under Article 70 of the

[184] A. Khrzhanovskii, personal interview, 17 February 2012.

Chapter 4   Russian Animation in the Second Half of the 1960s

Figure 4.29. *A special audience. Still from* There Once Lived Koziavin.

Figure 4.30. *Violinist in wooden cell.*
Still from There Once Lived Koziavin.

Criminal Code for publishing their works in the West under the pseudonyms Abram Terts and Nikolai Arzhak.

The images in this scene are organized according to the principle of collage, in which images belonging to different systems are put together to convey a complex set of meanings derived from the single elements in question and from

Figure 4.31. *Paper cut-outs fly in idyllic space. Still from* There Once Lived Koziavin.

these elements in relation to the whole. This collage aims to reveal at the same time direct references to contemporary events, open denunciations of the system, and also the artist's yearning for freedom. All these issues were particularly dear to the author of the script, Gennadii Shpalikov, who was already famous for his scripts for the films *I Walk Around Moscow* (*Ia shagaiu po Moskve*, G. Daneliia, 1963) and *I Am Twenty*,[185] and for directing the film *The Long and Happy Life* (*Dol'gaia shchastlivaia zhizn'*, 1966). Shpalikov worked up the script for *Koziavin* on the basis of a tale by Lazar' Lagin entitled "The Life of Koziavin" ("Zhitie Koziavina"), which provided the original name of the film. Khrzhanovskii, however, had to omit the word *zhitie*, with its connotations of hagiography, from the title of the film to avoid any reference to the genre of church literature at a time when religion was considered "the opium of the people".[186]

After *Koziavin*, Shpalikov wrote the script for another film directed by Khrzhanovskii, *The Glass Harmonica* (*Stekliannaia garmonika*, 1968), which again was severely attacked by the censorship and shelved. Unlike *There Once Lived Koziavin*, the script of *The Glass Harmonica* offered a much gloomier and more drastic critique of the Soviet regime. This second film was a daring attempt to go beyond the limits of the permissible, and constituted a direct assault on

[185] See Chapter 2 for a brief account of the difficulties in releasing this film.

[186] Khrzhanovskii, "Drugoe kino", 116.

a system that had hindered Khrzhanovskii's free artistic expression since his early student years. In fact, in 1957, VGIK introduced disciplinary measures against students who had been too explicit in expressing their opinions.[187] Khrzhanovskii, a first year student at that time, was expelled for reading in class Gogol''s *Selected Passages from Correspondence with Friends* and was able to return as a student only with the help of the famous directors and VGIK teachers Grigorii Roshal', Mikhail Romm and Sergei Gerasimov, who undertook his defense.[188] Khrzhanovskii's on-going complex relationship with the authorities doubtless provided a reason for the recurrence of the theme of freedom of expression in his work.

Animation as a means for political criticism: *The Glass Harmonica* (*Stekliannaia garmonika*, Andrei Khrzhanovskii, 1968)

Of Khrzhanovskii's films, *The Glass Harmonica* is the one that most pointedly deals with the issue of the complex relationship between artists and the authorities. The theme would recur in later films such as a trilogy based on Pushkin's drawings: *I Fly to You in Memory* (*Ia k Vam lechu vospominan'em*, 1977), *And I am with You Again* (*I s Vami snova ia...*, 1980), and *Autumn* (*Osen'*, 1982). Khrzhanovskii's films clearly departed from the mainstream of animation for the masses and proposed a form of animation art for an intellectual audience. Pursuing directors' desire to elevate the status of animation that began in the 1960s and evolved from the wish to distinguish animation as an art form in its own right, Khrzhanovskii sought the collaboration of contemporary artists such as Ülo Ilmar Sooster and Iurii Nolev-Sobolev, who belonged to the circle of artists who took part in the famous Manezh exhibition at which Khrushchev attacked modern art. Incidentally, in 1987, in honor of Sooster, Khrzhanovskii produced a feature film, *School of Fine Arts: Landscape with Junipers* (*Shkola iziashchnykh iskusstv. Peizazh s mozhzhevel'nikom*, 1987), based on the artist's drawings and graphic works.

[187] Woll, *Real Images*, 60; and Shilova.*I moe kino*, 46.

[188] Khrzhanovskii, "Vybrannye mesta iz shkoly iziashchnykh iskusstv", 59.

The symbolism and images used by Khrzhanovskii, Sooster, and Nolev-Sobolev are more complex than those of the satirical films considered until now. By borrowing from world-renowned works of art, the director creates a common language for Western and Eastern audiences; at the same time, the increased complexity of the film calls for an elite public and contrasts sharply with the kind of superficial art that Theodor W. Adorno related to dominant ideologies. Khrzhanovskii's departure from the Disney style did not only constitute a refusal of traditional aesthetic choices, but also signified a rejection of the "official" style that Disney represented during the Stalin years. Chapter Two of this book pointed out how the adoption of the Disney aesthetic and method of production responded to the needs of official art and prevented the search for new styles. Khrzhanovskii's act of adopting a manner that contrasted with the official and approved style was in itself a protest against officialdom.

The plot of *The Glass Harmonica* revolves around the conflict between a city governor, the "Yellow Devil", personifying the evils of money, and an artist playing a glass harmonica, a rare instrument whose sound is meant "to inspire high thoughts and fine actions". The film opens with the arrival of an artist playing the glass harmonica in the Yellow Devil's grey and brutalized city. Before the sound of the harmonica reaches the population, the artist is arrested. The only sign left of the musician is a broken glass harmonica and a red carnation that has sprung from the harmonica's sound. At first, this flower seems to bring a fatal destiny – the man who picks it up is denounced and arrested – but in the hands of another young boy the flower blooms once again. The boy leaves the city and when he comes back, he awakens, with the help of the harmonica's sound, the good and beautiful side hidden in each inhabitant and finally defeats the "yellow idol".

Already in *There Once Lived Koziavin*, Khrzhanovskii briefly introduced the theme of the artist's oppression by a totalitarian system, but in *The Glass Harmonica* the director makes this issue the core of his film. Here, it is no longer the bureaucrat under attack, but a system that represses artistic freedom; thus, this film addresses an audience that is sensitive to the problems of the artistic world and understands the film's references.

In order to elude the censors, Khrzhanovskii was compelled to emphasize a plotline focused on the detrimental effect of money on society over the question of the position of the artist in an authoritarian regime. Quotations from famous

Chapter 4   Russian Animation in the Second Half of the 1960s

Figure 4.32. *The Yellow Devil. Still from* The Glass Harmonica.

etchings and paintings that depict money changers – such as Quentin Matsys's "The Money-changer and his Wife" (1514) – open the film and focus the spectator's attention on this hermeneutic key.

The "governor" of the city, the Money God or the "Yellow Devil" as he is called in the explanatory notes at the beginning of the film, is represented as a man with a bowler hat who seems to have come out of a Magritte painting. He symbolizes the bourgeois par excellence, but at the same time he represents a cold unscrupulous dictator. The aloof look in his eyes of two different colors (Fig. 4.32) suggests diabolic traits, and the mechanical way he moves and opens and shuts his mouth is not comic, but dreadful.

In the film, the director puts in relation various texts with their different codes, discourses, or voices. The *intertextuality*[189] he creates not only expresses an interplay of texts bearing specific significations, but also fulfills a dramaturgic role. The texts that interweave in the film have specific connotations that help the director to express a precise dramaturgic thought while playing with aesthetic categories. The positive heroes are represented in a mimetic form, the negative personages in a grotesque mode. In this way the film becomes structured around juxtaposed artistic categories – mimesis and the beautiful sharply contrast with the

[189] I borrow the term *intertextuality* from Julia Kristeva as in *Desire in Language: A Semiotic Approach to Literature and Art*.

Figure 4.33. *Goya-like figures. Still from* The Glass Harmonica.

Figure 4.34. *Bosch-like figures. Still from* The Glass Harmonica.

fantastic and grotesque. This complex visual code further complicates the language of the film.

Borrowed images, collages, and metamorphoses illustrate the development from a world dominated by money and a cold authoritarian regime to a harmonious world permeated

Figure 4.35. *Bruegel-like figures. Still from* The Glass Harmonica.

Figure 4.36. *Arcimboldo-like figures. Still from* The Glass Harmonica.

by art and beauty. A grey atmosphere typical of Goya's paintings (Fig. 4.33) and grotesque figures – inspired by paintings by Bosch, Bruegel, and Arcimboldo as well as original works by the art director Sooster and Nolev-Sobolev – introduce the theme of the brutalization of the people in this city (Figs. 4.34–4.36). Conversely, images

SOVIET ANIMATION and the Thaw of the 1960s

Figure 4.37. *Egg-face breaking once touched by the harmonica sound. Still from* The Glass Harmonica.

Figure 4.38. *Beautiful Renaissance face is revealed. Still from* The Glass Harmonica.

drawn from the Italian Renaissance paintings of Raffaello, Botticelli, and Perugino, as well as from 16th century Flemish painters, represent the population as touched by the sound of the Glass Harmonica (Figs. 4.37–4.38).

The lively spirit of a joyful, carnivalesque world that usually

Chapter 4 Russian Animation in the Second Half of the 1960s

Figure 4.39. *Grotesque figures. Still from* The Glass Harmonica.

Figure 4.40. *Grotesque figures (2). Still from* The Glass Harmonica.

accompanies grotesque figures, as for example in François Rabelais's work as seen by Mikhail Bakhtin, is toned down in this film in order to create a darker effect typical of surrealist painting (Figs. 4.39–4.44). The kind of grotesque achieved in this film is what Wolfgang Kayser describes in his *The Grotesque in Art and Literature* as an expression of the absurd and the uncanny, of a demonic rather than joyful laughter. The atmosphere in some scenes seems to come out

Figure 4.41. *Grotesque figures (3). Still from* The Glass Harmonica.

Figure 4.42. *Grotesque figures (4). Still from* The Glass Harmonica.

of a E.T.A. Hoffmann or Franz Kafka story; people at times resemble insects, and at other times are depicted as fantastic figures. As is typical in the grotesque, most of the characters have a mixture of human and animal qualities.

The grotesque body is subjected to repeated transformations, which are not the fruit of a carnivalesque regenerative force, but instead of a destructive power that turns people into animals – as happens, for example, in a scene in which

Chapter 4   Russian Animation in the Second Half of the 1960s

Figure 4.43. *Grotesque figures (5). Still from* The Glass Harmonica.

Figure 4.44. *The couple's fight. Still from* The Glass Harmonica.

a couple fight until annihilation to get possession of a gold coin (Fig. 4.44).

The unresolved nature of the inhabitants' bodies is more dreadful than humorous. The comic quality of the grotesque is lost and an atmosphere of doom, as in Bosch's paintings, prevails instead.

The use of the grotesque has been historically perceived as a stance in opposition to rules and authorities, even more so

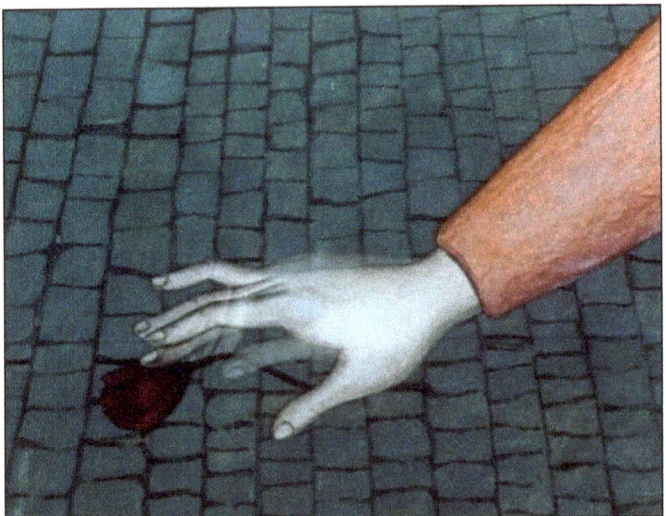

Figure 4.45. *Solemn gestures and juxtaposed images. Still from* The Glass Harmonica.

in the Soviet realm, in which grotesque stands in contraposition with the mandated optimism of Soviet socialist realism. Not only do texts with this specific connotation turn the film's intertextuality into a political act, but by depicting the authorities' supporters in a form officially rejected by the system, Khrzhanovskii attacks the Soviet establishment on multiple levels.

The dualism of the world depicted is stressed further by associating various pictorial styles with different animation techniques. Most of the characters are realized in the form of flat marionettes, but while mechanical movements suit the grotesque imagery, the positive characters' body language is expressed in solemn gestures that preserve the gravity these figures are meant to carry. In order to convey a more harmonious movement of their limbs, sometimes the director juxtaposes images in a way that reveals the flow of a gesture (Fig. 4.45).

The close relationship between the story and the visual images is intensified in that not only do the characters change as a consequence of the governor's influence or of the artist's music, but the surrounding space and inanimate objects modify their symbolic meanings accordingly. On the screen, space is represented with an intricate play of

Chapter 4 Russian Animation in the Second Half of the 1960s

Figure 4.46. *Complex perspective. Still from* The Glass Harmonica.

perspective points that generates an optical illusion (Fig. 4.46).

The city ruled by the Yellow Devil is organized on different levels, with repetitions of the same patterns and streets opening up to an invisible horizon. The complex perspective designs a fantastic and unusual space, which is illusory but at the same time concrete; it creates a sense of confusion and instability that contrasts with the harmonious, symmetrical order of the world conquered by the harmonica sound. The effect of this space is dreadful, for it seems to reflect the immensurable power of the governor of the city. The succession of these streets provokes an uncanny feeling in the spectator, as if they were led to some hellish place on the border of reality. There is only one road that leads to a brighter place on the horizon – the road walked by the harmonica player (Fig. 4.47).

The interior spaces are no less dreadful than the exterior. Piled up objects, remnants of a harmonious world, lose in the inhabitants' hands any aesthetic quality, becoming pure kitsch (Fig. 4.48). In a scene in which a house interior is shown, a row of doors creates a "conventionalized perspective" (*uslovnaia perspektiva*, in the art-director Nolev-Sobolev's words) by means of an optical illusion often used in folk-art.[190] This repetition of doors emphasizes the vastness of the space, producing an exaggerated effect that com-

[190] RGALI, "Delo fil'ma *Stekliannaia garmonika*", 92.

Figure 4.47. *The artists' road. Still from* The Glass Harmonica.

Figure 4.48. *Couple's kitsch. Still from* The Glass Harmonica.

plements the hyperbolic situation and the metamorphoses of the characters into an increasingly bestial state. These doors also build a functional space through which the neighbors can spy on each other, and so they underline the frightful theme of denunciation that recurs in the film.

The interiors of the houses – built with rooms without walls, absent ceilings, and endlessly repeating doors – echo the structure of the town. Houses follow a similar linear pattern, as if to signify that no scope for original creation is

Chapter 4 Russian Animation in the Second Half of the 1960s

Figure 4.49. *Row of doors and neighbor peeping through the keyhole. Still from* The Glass Harmonica.

Figure 4.50. *Linear pattern of the houses. Still from* The Glass Harmonica.

given in this city (Fig. 4.50). The entire city is under the gaze of the Big Brother/Money Idol, and every activity is under his control.

Play of light and shade seems to indicate how the artist can be confined, but his art will never die. The Yellow Devil comes from a road that loses its end in a dark horizon, and he will leave the city through the same path. Only the

Figure 4.51. *The road lights up. Still from* The Glass Harmonica.

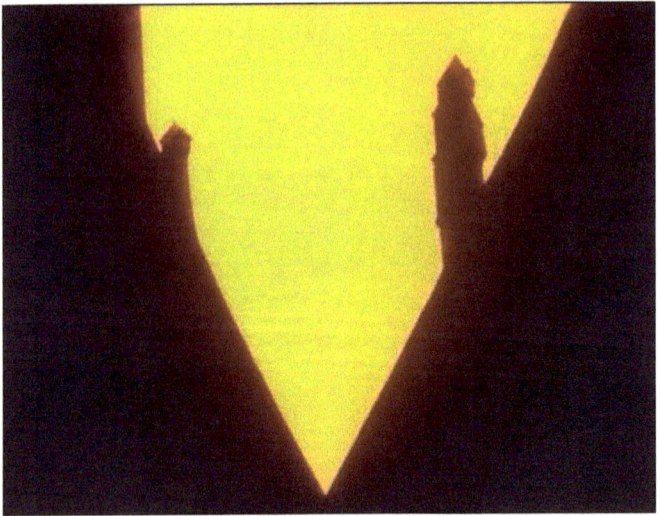

Figure 4.52. *Flash of light on the road at the end.
Still from* The Glass Harmonica.

passage of the artist lights up this road (Figs 4.51–4.52), and at the end of the film, when the devil retreats, for a fraction of a second the space gets brighter as if to emphasize the enlightenment of art that overcomes darkness.

The sound of the harmonica has an effect on the overall space that surrounds the characters. Once it becomes stronger, the cityscape itself transforms into places that, with

Figure 4.53. *Idyllic space after harmonica effect. Still from* The Glass Harmonica.

Figure 4.54. *Restored perspective. Still from* The Glass Harmonica.

their idyllic atmosphere, harmonious symmetry, and restored perspective radically differ from the confusing and frightening grey city (Figs. 4.53–4.54).

The transformation and openness of the space reaches its ultimate manifestation when all the people rise up from the ground and fly into the sky. Chagall-like figures, they are

Figure 4.55. *People rise up. Still from* The Glass Harmonica.

Figure 4.56. *Chagall-like people in the sky. Still from* The Glass Harmonica.

free to wander in the open space, to release their imagination, and to try to reach a spiritually higher order (Figs. 4.55–4.56). The oppressive governor's hand reappears and pulls them down to earth. But this time his power does not last for long; too many people have experienced freedom, and their united force is stronger than the power of the devil, who, finally defeated, leaves the town.

When the governor leaves, the town seems to return to a normal life and pace. A clock signifying the passage from progress to stagnation is repaired. The stagnant atmosphere established by the Yellow Devil's power and manifested symbolically in the demolition of the clock is now reversed. Only by giving themselves over to art and beauty and refusing any form of oppression, of money and dictator alike, is stagnation overcome and progress restored. The choice of shades of color used in depicting the broken clock (grey tones) versus the representation of the same clock at work at the end of the film (this time in pink and orange tones) is significant. The color tones play a particular role in the film – they underline the dichotomy within the world depicted. As the art director Nolev-Sobolev pointed out during a discussion of the film, the shades of the colors are organized with consecutive transitions, as in musical compositions,[191] and in fact they harmoniously and expressively follow the original musical score, written by the nonconformist composer Alfred Schnittke.

It might be useful to recall some more observations made during the discussion of the film at Soiuzmul'tfil'm and consider the genesis of the film in order to understand its evolution as well as the director's and art directors' intentions. The history of this film exemplifies the shift towards stricter official controls that artists experienced during the early Brezhnev era.

It was within the Artistic Council of Soiuzmul'tfil'm that Khrzhanovskii encountered his first obstacles. Clashing opinions among artists in the studio delayed the making of the film by two years. Khrzhanovskii and scriptwriter Shpalikov had to re-write both the literary and the director's script multiple times in order to make the film acceptable to the studio. The first version of the script was written as early as 1966 but it was not discussed for the first time until the Artistic Council meeting on 7 February 1967. The approval of the film was processing very slowly, and Khrzhanovskii asked for the support of the famous director Sergei Gerasimov to clear it for production.[192] The script had to be presented in three variants before being endorsed. In the last version of the script the negative atmosphere of the city was softened, the ending was changed to provide a more positive conclusion, and all elements that could refer to a specific Russian context (such as an inhabitant who nibbles sun-

[191] RGALI, "Delo fil'ma *Stekliannaia garmonika*", 93.

[192] A. Khrzhanovskii, personal interview, 12 april 2003.

flower seeds or scenes from Russian folklore and *lubok*) were deleted.[193]

During the Artistic Council meetings, discussions revolved around issues concerning the theme of the film, the complexity of the script, and the need for such intricate films. The members of the Artistic Council realized the risk of "political tactlessness" within such a script, and the director of the studio, Mikhail Val'kov, was not keen on proceeding with a project that showed clear references to the difficult position of the artist in the Soviet Union (a point of view that he seemed not to share).

> In its current form, the danger of political tactlessness is hidden in the script ... Let's talk openly – the script deals with the relations of the artist towards society and of society towards the artist. If the author of the script intends to talk about the Soviet artist in these terms, (I am laying it out here, because no one talks about it, while everyone thinks about it, so I am consciously revealing this), then I would not like to do this film, because it would not correspond to the reality.[194]

In addition to attacking the film for its content, some criticism was reserved for its complex style. By using citations that bring with them specific connotations, Khrzhanovskii had turned the language of the film into a code that would not be accessible to the masses, but recognizable and appreciated by an elite audience. Besides, the drawings were deprecated for their "pathology" (*patologiia*) and "morbidity" (*boleznennost'*). The surreal and anguished settings of some scenes recalled a kind of animation widespread in Europe, especially among artists like the Polish émigré director Jan Lenica (Fig. 4.57). The gloomy and disturbing atmospheres and grotesque characters of the films discussed in this chapter clashed sharply with the generally positive character of Russian animation, and could hardly be accepted by the members of the Artistic Council.

During the Artistic Council discussion of *The Glass Harmonica*, the composer Nikita Bogoslovskii raised a general question about the reception of films in the Soviet Union. He pointed out how in the Soviet Union, this new complex language of animation had appeared too suddenly. This abrupt shift created problems with distribution, provoked the unreceptive response of a biased press, and clashed with the audience's lack of readiness and preparation.[195] Thus, not only were the members of the Council not eager to

[193] N.I. Radionov: "... The second variant is more interesting and rich... the instrument – the glass harmonica – and the same *syuzhet*, which migrates widely across the folklore of several peoples of the world, allow [the filmmakers] to avoid making this film on Russian material, so as to avoid direct political analogy and facilitate the destiny of the script and of the film". RGALI, "Delo fil'ma *Stekliannaia garmonika*" 27.

[194] RGALI, "Delo fil'ma *Stekliannaia garmonika*", 30.

[195] RGALI, "Delo fil'ma *Stekliannaia garmonika*", 5.

Chapter 4   Russian Animation in the Second Half of the 1960s

Figure 4.57. *Lenica-style figure. Still from* The Glass Harmonica.

accept these films, but the audience might not have been ready to receive them favorably. Nonetheless, not all the artists in the studio opposed these new tendencies; some of them, including the same Bogoslovskii, welcomed new artistic pursuits in original forms, despite the fact that these experiments would not be accessible to the masses.[196] Some other artists, however, and especially the director of the studio, were not willing to allow a new kind of animation for an intellectual public – an attitude that came from political and ideological motivations, as well as from a concern for practical problems in the production system.

The methods of production used in the studio, based on a strict division of labors, did not allow for easy reproduction of complex images. In M. Val'kov's words:

> Still we have a factory, and we have to take this into consideration, and the artistic process has to reckon with this situation. Since we also have to deal with such difficult ideas, the requirements for the script rise immeasurably. ... Andrei Iur'evich [Khrzhanovskii], you work with a collective, and it is necessary to take this into consideration; one cannot detach oneself from the collective of the studio.[197]

The conveyer system adopted by the studio once again seems to have been an obstacle in the search for new artistic forms. After a long process of re-writing, the authors obtained permission from the Artistic Council to start produc-

[196] RGALI, "Delo fil'ma *Stekliannaia garmonika*", 5a.

[197] RGALI, "Delo fil'ma *Stekliannaia garmonika*", 74–75.

tion. On August 8, 1968, a section of the Artistic Council met to discuss the film, but only a few days later, Soviet troops crossed the border into Czechoslovakia, bringing the "Prague Spring" to an end. In this delicate moment, Goskino could not accept for distribution such a subversive film, and returned it for amendments. The only existing copy of the first version of the film, which had been seen and kept only in the Soiuzmul'tfil'm studio, was ordered destroyed.[198]

In order to have their film accepted, the artists decided to try again and conceal what they believed to be the real oppressor with the image of a capitalist ruler, the Money Devil. The beginning of the film, thus, started with some explanatory titles: "Although the events of this film are of a fantastic character, its authors would like to remind you of boundless greed, police terror, isolation, and brutalization of humans in modern bourgeois society".

This addition, however, was perceived as false not only by the authors, but also by the small privileged circle of viewers who understood the real message the director meant to convey.[199] The new titles, some changes in the representation of the governor, the appearance of the yellow coins and other minor changes were enough to avoid censorship and start production, but not to enable a release. At first Goskino granted authorization for a new version of the film. The next day, Khrzhanovskii, already in his 30s, received a letter from the enlistment office and had to serve in the navy for two years. When Khrzhanovskii came back from the navy, Val'kov showed him the document with which Goskino had reversed permission to release the film on the absurd grounds that there were no copies of the film; the order stated: "Revoke the authorization on the grounds of absence of circulation".[200] Khrzhanovskii still suspects that the rejection of the film was pushed by the leadership after they viewed it privately. It was customary to send new films from the studio to what were called "government dachas" (*pravitel'stvennye dachi*), that is, summer houses that belonged primarily to members of the Politburo. Some of the influential people who saw the film on this occasion might have complained about its release and urged against its distribution. The director considered it an "exemplary action, like the demonstrative exiling of Joseph Brodsky, in order to discourage others to do the same".[201]

[198] A. Khrzhanovskii, personal interview, 12 april 2003.

[199] A. Khrzhanovskii, personal interview, 12 april 2003.

[200] A. Khrzhanovskii, personal interview, 12 april 2003.

[201] A. Khrzhanovskii, personal interview, 12 April 2003.

Chapter 4 Russian Animation in the Second Half of the 1960s

In Moscow, the film was shown on the big screen only a few days after its completion. This was possible only because the Rossiia Theater on Pushkin Square, as per an agreement with Soiuzmul'tfil'm, automatically presented, in a small screening room dedicated to animated films, all the films that were released by the studio. In addition to the spectators and artists at Soiuzmul'tfil'm, a small group of intellectuals from outside the studio saw the film at that time, among whom were Nikolai Erdman, Mikhail Vol'pin, Erast Garin, Khesia Lokshina, Vera Trauberg, Valentin Khodasevich, Andrei Tarkovskii, Innokentii Smoktunovskii, and Iurii Lotman.[202] Subsequently the film was shelved for many years. The prohibition on releasing *The Glass Harmonica* was in force until the Fifth Congress of the Union of Cinematographers in 1986, when the film was rehabilitated. At that time, there was still no money to spend on distribution, and since then, the film has only rarely been shown at the Muzei Kino in Moscow.[203]

In a system where cinema and animation had primarily been considered mass art, films that addressed only an elite audience were obviously not received with favor. Some of the artists in the studio who considered animation primarily a form of art for children – among them the talented children's film directors Degtiarev and Suteev – defended the idea that the films made in Soiuzmul'tfil'm should address a wider public and not only an intellectual audience.[204] Also the structure of the studio Soiuzmul'tfil'm, which required a rigid subdivision of the production into specialized departments, surely did not lend itself to authorial cinema. Not only did Khrzhanovskii's film introduce innovative style and complex visual choices, but it also tackled a daring issue: the question of the artist in an authoritarian system. That this film was accepted for production (although with enormous difficulties) is an indubitable sign that at the beginning of the Brezhnev years the atmosphere was still relatively liberal, though slowly changing. However, the final destiny of the film clearly indicates a change in attitude. After this film was censored, no more films overtly critical of the system were produced for several years.

[202] Khrzhanovskii, "Vybrannye mesta iz shkoly iziashchnykh iskusstv", 61.

[203] According to Khrzhanovskii, copies of the film exist only at the VGIK, at the Muzei Kino, at the Gosfil'mofond and at the studio Soiuzmul'tfil'm. In 1992, the American company Jove Films, Inc. bought temporary distribution rights to an entire collection of Russian films, including this film, and *The Glass Harmonica* was released on VHS and DVD as part of a collection called "Masters of Russian Animation".

[204] RGALI, "Delo fil'ma *Stekliannaia garmonika*", 18.

Chapter 5

Conclusion: The Beginning of New Tendencies

Starting from the last years of the 1960s, and especially during the 1970s, Soiuzmul'tfil'm took a new path that attempted to reconcile different trends inside the studio: it began to produce films with no definite target audience, inasmuch as they addressed both children and adults. Some of these films were entertaining and captivated the adult public with "real", recognizable situations rather than fantastic worlds or typically childish settings; still others turned towards a poetic vein that focused on the author's personal artistic expression. The latter approach went along with a lyric trend in live-action films that began in the 1960s and was further developed in the 1970s, particularly, but not exclusively, in the work of Andrei Tarkovskii.

With regard to the first group of films based on contemporary settings, it is worth mentioning the appearance in 1969 of the most famous long series of Russian animated films, *Just You Wait!* (*Nu, pogodi!*, 1969–1993). Similar in structure to the American series *Tom and Jerry*, the episodes revolve around the rivalry of two anthropomorphized animals, a wolf and a hare; the first is a blatant hooligan, while the second is an astute traditional folk character. *Just You Wait!* repeated itself in each episode, but still proved appealing to the large TV public because of its comic gags, and its references to popular music and familiar images and settings.[205] The first episode of *Just You Wait!* (Viacheslav Kotenochkin, 1969) draws its characters from a brief film with the same name made by Gennadii Sokol'skii in 1969[206] as one of the three-minute-long shorts of the "animation anthology" *The Merry Go Round* (*Veselaia karusel'*, 1969–2002).

Both releases of the *Just You Wait!* series and the "almanac"

[205] For a good review of the series, see Vartanov, "Sekret uspekha".

[206] The first film and the series were made by different directors and followed distinctive styles, but the episodes were still written by the same Aleksandr Kurliandskii, Arkadii Khait, and Feliks Kamov (the latter until 1973).

The Merry Go Round show the effects of the increasing diffusion of TV. *Just You Wait!* was made for the big screen, but since it was presented on TV soon after its release, it gained immense popularity. The series kept producing episodes, with some interruptions, until 1993. *The Merry Go Round* was also very successful, and gave some young artists the chance to prove their talent and their original style in short films (only three minutes long), which were made, although irregularly, until the early 2000s. Some other "anthologies" of films such as *Kaleidoskop* (1968–1971) saw only a few releases.

Mini-series also appeared in these years. The famous characters of Cheburashka, Gena the Crocodile, Winnie the Pooh, and Karlson[207] emerged for the first time on screen at the end of the 1960s. While still oriented mainly to children, these films fascinated adults, too; their characters became so popular that Cheburashka came to be the logo for the Soiuzmul'tfil'm studio. Their stories are set in a contemporary world, in which values such as comradeship and loyalty are unshakable, yet they distinguished themselves by a lyrical atmosphere that still makes them appealing to a broad audience.

It is this tendency towards the poetic that characterizes a new kind of animation, which engages lyrically with some philosophical concepts and simple worlds rather than presenting political messages or providing pure entertainment. The movement of animation from social criticism to a purely poetic function reflected the particular moment of transition from the ideals of the first years of the Thaw to the realization at the end of the 1960s that a "bright future" (*svetloe budushchee*) was not on the horizon. The attention paid to man vis-à-vis society gave way to a desire to focus on man's subjective world; as Vail' and Genis note, idealism was replaced by cynicism and a tendency to take refuge in oneself.[208]

Films in this lyrical genre took the form of simple stories that served the task of conveying poetic situations or atmospheres, often using original stylistic choices. In particular, puppet animation films mastered this genre, from the series of *Cheburashka* and *Gena the Crocodile* to other films by Roman Kachanov and the artistic director Leonid Shvartsman, such as *The Mitten* (*Varezhka*, 1967), and films

207 *Gena the Crocodile* (*Krokodil Gena*, R. Kachanov, 1969); *Cheburashka* (R. Kachanov, 1971); *Shapokliak* (R. Kachanov, 1974); *Cheburashka Goes to School* (*Cheburashka idet v shkolu*, R. Kachanov, 1983); *Winnie the Pooh* (*Vinni Pukh*, F. Khitruk, 1969); *Winnie the Pooh Goes on a Visit* (*Vinni Pukh idet v gosti*, F. Khitruk, 1971); *Winnie the Pooh and the Day of Worries* (*Vinni Pukh i den' zabot*, F. Khitruk, 1972); *The Little Boy and Karlson, who Lives on the Roof* (*Malysh i Karlson, kotoryi zhivet na kryshe*, B. Stepantsev,1968); *Karlson Returned* (*Karlson vernulsia*, B. Stepantsev, 1970).

208 Vail' and Genis, *60-e*, 134.

by two exceptionally original masters: Nikolai Serebriakov and Vadim Kurchevskii. Their works are characterized by essential elements in the background, often made with various unconventional materials, and simple – but very expressive in their scant gestures – puppets, which often are mingled with drawings and cut-out figures, as for example in the film *The Life and Suffering of Ivan Semenov* (*Zhizn' i stradaniia Ivana Semenova*, N. Serebriakov, V. Kurchevskii, 1964) and Serebriakov's *I'm Waiting for the Bird* (*Ia zhdu ptentsa*, N. Serebriakov, 1966).

A poetic language built from associations, repetitions, allegories, metaphors, and symbols dominates all their works. Their films focus on the poetry inherent in children's fantastic worlds, as in *Frantishek* (V. Kurchevskii, 1967); in the complex world of feeling of *My Green Crocodile* (*Moi zelenyi krokodil*, V. Kurchevskii, 1966); in an ethereal space, a special dimension between dream and reality, such as in *The Great Cold* (*Velikie kholoda*, N. Serebriakov, 1969) and *Happiness is Not in the Hat* (*Ne v shliape schast'e*, N. Serebriakov, 1968); and in imaginary settings such as in the moral tale against greed *The Ball of Wool* (*Klubok*, Nikolai Serebriakov, 1968). While *The Ball of Wool* employs traditional knitting patterns and embroidery, another film, *The Seasons* (*Vremena goda*, Ivan Ivanov-Vano, with the collaboration of Iurii Norshtein, 1969), made the following year, uses lace and traditional toys. Both these films exemplify a new tendency to boldly experiment with the texture of material previously never adopted in Russian animation. In *The Seasons*, the particular material used, together with wise selections of color tone, serve to visualize Pyotr Tchaikovsky's music. By setting the life-long journey of its characters in the symbolic world of the four seasons, the film seeks to convey less a precise message than a poetic atmosphere.

Music plays a distinctive role in several films of these years, especially in works by Boris Stepantsev, in which classical music melds with a painterly style to create a particular lyrical ambience. Examples are his *The Window* (*Okno*, 1966), a poetic sentimental and philosophical film of idealized love, with music by Sergei Prokofiev; *The Song of the Falcon* (*Pesnia o sokole*, 1967), a film made by painting on glass, an adaptation of Maxim Gorky's homonymous poem, with music by Aleksandr Skriabin; and later his *Nutcracker* (*Shchelkunchik*, 1973), a successful adaptation for animation of Hoffmann's tale and Tchaikovsky's music. While on the subject, it is worth pointing out that in the 1970s a new trend of musical films developed in animation. Music in these films often constituted the dramaturgy of the movie, from the 1969 *The Bremen Musicians* (*Bremenskie muzykanty*, I. Kovalevskaia, 1969), to other films by Inessa Kovalevskaia, such as *Songs of the Inflamed Years* (*Pesni ognennykh let*, 1971), *How the Little Lion and the Turtle Sang a Song* (*Kak l'venok i cherepakha peli pesniu*, 1974), *Children's Album* (*Detskii al'bom*, 1976), *The Mountain Master* (*Gornyi master*, 1978), and many more in the 1980s.

The painterly style that characterizes Stepantsev's films constituted a peculiar way to soften up the typically well-defined drawings used in Disney cartoons. Fedor Khitruk and Sergei Alimov, too, ventured towards a style that would achieve the same effect while using different techniques. In their film *Toptyzhka* (1964), cut-out movements convey the goofy stride of the main characters, a bear and a hare, while the elimination of precise contours in the drawings suggests a change in texture, making the animals' furry coats more perceivable.

In his drawings for the film, Alimov strove to reappropriate the style and spirit of the famous artist and author of children's stories Evgenii Charushin. Alimov's style links the film to the tradition of children's illustrated books of the 1920s, as well as to graphic works from children's journals of those years, CHIZH *(Chrezvychaino interesnyi zhurnal – Extremely interesting journal)* and EZH *(Ezhemesiachnyi zhurnal – Monthly journal)*. Charushin shared with the artists at the Leningrad children's department of the publisher Gosizdat the desire to depict his characters in a laconic but expressive way with a few strokes and blots of color, but he distinguished himself by the pictorial way in which he drew the animals in his stories, avoiding his colleagues' use of sharp contours and poster-like visual choices. His particular technique allowed him to convey the texture of his animal characters, which appeared so furry, soft, and fluffy. Following Charushin's style, Alimov and Khitruk achieved in *Toptyzhka* a lyric harmony between the background and the characters. They finally avoided what, according to Sergei Eisenstein, was "incorrect" in Disney's lyric films, that is, "a tightly closed contour line, and a continuous bordering of colors", that provokes a lack of "stylistic unity of surround-

Chapter 5   Conclusion: The Beginning of New Tendencies

ings and figures".²⁰⁹ Despite his admiration for Disney, Eisenstein expressed his disappointment about this fault in the Disney style (especially in the film *Bambi*).

> In a correctly drawn landscape, the figures would genuinely blend together, drawn with *an unclosed stroke* – such as we know again in Chinese *drawing* – and with soft dabs of colour with eroded edges. ... The totally drawn film which is incapable of finding a *graphic and pictorial manner* for a full expression of its aspirations, the totally drawn film, which is incapable of finding *a stylistic unity of surroundings and figures*, is, of course, a very sad spectacle.²¹⁰

Eisenstein's suggestion about how to avoid some of Disney's mistakes is of particular significance in the years of the Thaw, given the overall context of rejection of Disney's graphics and the desire to search for new solutions.

In the 1960s, original styles appeared in the form of new drawing traits, as well as in a re-discovery of traditional Russian style.²¹¹ Although during the Stalin years, Soviet animation had already presented typical elements of traditional Russia in the depiction of costumes, houses, villages, and landscape, Russian folk art was re-appropriated during the Thaw in more direct and expressive forms. Perhaps in response to the shattered illusions of a better and ideal world, and maybe also as a rejection of the early Thaw era's infatuation with foreign products and art, starting from the mid-1960s, a general tendency to turn to the past and to folk art and national traditions began to develop.

Already in *Toptyzhka*, the influence of folk art could be seen in the depiction of the environment and in the use of a narrative voice in the old oral storytelling tradition. Other animators of the mid-1960s, seeking a way to give a "national" character to Russian animation, turned to the popular narrative art form of the *lubok*. The first film which tried to imitate the *lubok* style, *The Lefthander* (*Levsha*, I. Ivanov-Vano, 1964), was an adaptation from Nikolai Leskov's story about the ability of a talented craftsman to put a shoe on an English flea. In *The Lefthander*, the style of old Russian engravings and *lubok* harmoniously suited Leskov's *skaz* narration, typical of oral folklore. The chosen technique of cut-outs and flat marionettes with mobile joints allowed the artists to keep the style of the *lubok* intact while adapting it for the screen. The art directors in this film – Arkadii Tiurin, Marina Sokolova, and Anatolii Kuritsyn – together with

---

209 Eisenstein, *Izbrannye proizvedeniia*, vol. 3, 426–427. Quoted and translated in Leyda, *Eisenstein on Disney*, 99–100.

210 Leyda, *Eisenstein on Disney*, 99–100.

211 Eisenstein had repeatedly raised the question of whether filmmakers should use folk-art motifs (especially the traditional toys from Viatska) in their work instead of blindly following Disney. Eisenstein, "Viatskaia loshadka", vol. 3, 500–501.

director Ivan Ivanov-Vano researched and studied old carvings on wood, traditional painted boxes, folk embroidery, and ornaments.[212] Three main styles are used in this film to depict three different environments. The first style, employed to illustrate life in Tula and the Russian countryside, is based on traditional folk art, mainly *lubok* and traditional toys and ornaments (one example of which materializes in vivid and colorful images in the representation of a carnival at the beginning of the film). Conversely, the theme of the aristocratic world in Petersburg was represented with the austere style of the old prints of the nineteenth century to convey the coldness and emptiness of the court. A third style, similar to old English engravings, rendered a cold, cheerless, and foggy London.[213] *The Lefthander* laid the foundation for subsequent films made in folk-art style, the most successful being: *How One Man Fed Two Generals* (*Kak odin muzhik dvukh generalov prokormil*, V. Danilevich, I. Ivanov-Vano, 1965), based on Mikhail Saltykov-Shchedrin's story about two Russian generals on a desert island; *Go There – I Don't Know Where* (*Podi tuda – ne znaiu kuda*, I. Ivanov-Vano, 1966), based on a Russian folk-tale; and Serebriakov's *Golden Foreheads* (*Zolochennye lby*, 1971). In more recent days, this traditional style is still reproduced through cut-outs, but with the help of computer animation. A successful example of this artful combination of old and new techniques can be seen in *About Ivan the Fool* (*Pro Ivana Duraka*, M. Aldashin, O. Uzhinov, 2004).

Among the innovative films of the 1960s, cut-outs played a fundamental role in various styles and forms, from the above-mentioned examples of *lubok* images and contourless figures, to flat marionettes colored with bright and eye-catching hues that bring to life the playful world of children, as in *Bonifatius's Holidays* (*Kanikuly Bonifatsiia*, F. Khitruk, 1965), or *I'm Waiting for the Bird*. Other experiments with style did not always result in successful films. Sometimes, stylized backgrounds were ineffectively combined with figures drawn in the traditional Disney style. This fault is evident in Tsekhanovskii's film *Wild Swans* (*Dikie lebedi*, 1962), in which the director mixed a conventional background that recalls the organization of space of his early book illustrations with the naturalistic characters typical of animation of the Stalin years (Figs. 5.1–5.2).

In other films of the decade, the 1920s graphic style was fully

212 Volkov, *Mul'tiplikatsionnyi fil'm*, 33.

213 The authors' style was influenced by the works of Boris Kustodeev, Ivan Bilibin, and Nikolai Kuz'min (especially his remarkable illustrations to Leskov's story). See Efimov's review of the film, "Ozhivshie graviury".

Chapter 5   Conclusion: The Beginning of New Tendencies

Figure 5.1. *Conventional background and naturalistic characters (1). Still from* Wild Swans.

Figure 5.2. *Conventional background and naturalistic characters (2). Still from* Wild Swans.

embodied, this time attaining a successful, harmonious combination of figures and background, but still often producing inexpressive characters and arid works. Examples would include the film *The Flying Proletarian* (*Letaiushchii proletarii*, I. Boiarskii, I. Ivanov-Vano, 1962) with its flat paper marionettes set in a stylized futurist world, or the adaptation of Iurii Olesha's story *The Three Fat Men* (*Tri Tolstiaka*, V. and Z. Brumberg, 1963), which employed visual choices similar to those of innovative pre- and post-Revolutionary works. The characters in *The Three Fat Men* were depicted in geometrical forms that evoked the dresses made by Kazimir Malevich for the 1913 production of the trans-sense opera *Victory Over the Sun* (*Pobeda nad solntsem*);

Figure 5.3. *Stylized characters (1). Still from* The Three Fat Men.

the background echoed Constructivist sets, and the scenes of the Revolution, as well as most of the rest of the film, were depicted in a manner typical of graphic design of the 1920s (Figs. 5.3–5.5). The style aimed to convey the radical spirit of the time in which Olesha's story was written, but the characters seem to lack the liveliness and Revolutionary enthusiasm proper of the original works of the 1920s.

A more successful attempt to appropriate post-Revolution Soviet avant-garde style is visible in Iurii Norshtein and Arkadii Tiurin's *25th – The First Day* (*Dvadtsat' piatoe – pervyi den'*, 1968). This film conveys the spirit of the first day of the October Revolution by coordinating the interweaving images that appear on screen with a musical score by Dmitrii Shostakovich. Russian and European avant-garde paintings of the 1910s–1920s, as well as Revolutionary posters and caricatures, find a place in the film. "Paintings of this era", comments Norshtein, "are incredibly cinematographic; in them is hidden a succinct metaphysics of the time […] Art of this time … is permeated by kinetics. It embodies the time in static forms".[214] Specific works are superimposed in double exposure on Norshtein and Tiurin's drawings, namely Kuz'ma Petrov-Vodkin's Madonna from his painting *1918 in Petrograd* (*1918 god v Petrograde*, 1920), Aleksandr Deineka's *The Defense of Petrograd* (*Oborona Petrograda*, 1928),

[214] Norshtein, *Sneg na trave*, vol.1, 58, 76.

Chapter 5 Conclusion: The Beginning of New Tendencies

Figure 5.4. *Stylized characters (2). Still from* The Three Fat Men.

Figure 5.5. *Stylized characters (3). Still from* The Three Fat Men.

and Sergei Chekhonin's red figures for the cover of John Reed's book *Ten Days that Shook the World* (Fig. 5.6).

Vladimir Mayakovsky's caricatures are also clearly identifiable in the film, which owes its title to a line (quoted at the beginning of the movie) from his poem "Vladimir Il'ich

Lenin".[215] Some other paintings provided the inspiration for visual choices adopted in the film, such as works by the Soviet artists Aleksandr Deineka, Kazimir Malevich, Vladimir Pimenov, Vladimir Lebedev, Iurii Annenkov, Marc Chagall, Vladimir Tatlin, Natan Al'tman, and El Lissitzky, and by the foreign cubist painters Georges Braque and Pablo Picasso. On the screen, images clash and intersect, accompanied by the *sostenuto* rhythm of Shostakovich's music, which effectively provides the compositional structure of the film, and constitutes a *dominant* around which the entire film is organized. The short animated film does not have a precise plot, but, in Tiurin's words, tries to convey the pathos of the Revolution through music and works by famous masters of the 1920s.[216] Norshtein called it an "etude on the Revolution" ("revoliutsionnyi etiud").[217]

The original version of *25th – The First Day* was subjected to numerous attacks and requests from the authorities for revisions; indeed, such a non-narrative and visually complex film could not easily be accepted. A film like *The Eaglet* (*Orlenok*, V. Bordzilovskii, 1968), made in the same year, telling the story of a young hero of the civil war, was probably more responsive to the establishment's requests for celebration of the Revolutionary years. Some avant-garde works originally included in Norshtein's film were forcibly cut. For example, at the end of the film, the directors intended to reproduce the compositional principle of *The Formula for Revolution* by Pavel Filonov (*Formula Revoliutsii*, 1920) and an animated figure of Lenin cut out from a small engraving by Vladimir Favorskii (*Lenin and the Revolution*, 1928), but the idea was vetoed.[218] The engraving had to be replaced with an image of Lenin drawn from a Revolutionary poster that Norshtein considered "monstrous".[219] Instead of culminating the film with the original finale – Filonov's paintings, Paul Éluard's verses on fraternity among people, and Chagall's angel flying over a festive street demonstration[220] – the film trivially ends with Lenin's voice accompanied by his image intercut with some footage of a crowd at Red Square. Norshtein still regrets introducing these changes, for "an artist should not compromise, but always try to be faithful to his own creative idea".[221] This, however, was not the last time Norshtein would have to make concessions.

Already in his next film, *The Battle of Kerzhenets* (*Secha pri*

215 "Kogda ia/itozhu/to, chto prozhil,/I roius' v dniakh -/iarchaishii gde/ia vspominaiu/odno i to zhe -/dvadtsat' piatoe,/pervyi den'". 'When I/will sum up/what I lived through/ and rummage in the days - / the brightest is where/ I remember/ one and the same – 25th – the first day". From *Vladimir Il'ich Lenin* (Maiakovskii, 1924). Maiakovskii, *Izbrannye sochineniia*, 241.

216 RGALI, "Stenogramma zasedaniia khudozhestvennogo soveta po obsuzhdeniiu fil'ma *25-oe – pervyi den'*", 24.

217 Norshtein, "Sneg na trave", *Iskusstvo kino* 11 (2001): 116. For an account of this film see also Norshtein, *Sneg na trave*, vol. 1, 58–86; and Borodin, "Animatsiia podnevol'naia", Unpublished book, 9–14 (Chapter 6). In English: Kitson, *Yuri Norstein and Tale of Tales*, 38.

218 Norshtein, Iu. Personal interview. 25 September 2005.

219 Kitson, *Yuri Norstein and Tale of Tales*, 38.

220 Norshtein, *Sneg na trave*, vol. 1, 73.

221 Norshtein, Iu.

Chapter 5 Conclusion: The Beginning of New Tendencies

Figure 5.6. *Reference to Deineka's "The Defense of Petrograd" and Chekhonin's illustrations. Still from* 25th – The First Day.

Kerzhentse, I. Ivanov-Vano, Iu. Norshtein, 1971), Norshtein had to find a middle ground with his co-director Ivan Ivanov-Vano. This film was based on the juxtaposition of art reproduction from medieval times with Nikolai Rimsky-Korsakov's music from the opera *The Legend of the Invisible City of Kitezh and the Maiden Fevroniia* (*Skazanie o nevidimom grade Kitezhe i deve Fevronii*).²²² As the Russian music historian Iurii Keldysh notes, already in the opera one could sense a correspondence of the music to particular visual choices. In particular, he maintains, "The description of the characters of the opera recalls the strong and stark faces of the ancient religious paintings".²²³ In order to keep intact the images from the traditional frescoes, icons, and miniatures of the XIV-XVI centuries, the directors opted for the technique of flat marionettes. Surprisingly, in addition to the evident use of ancient icons, Norshtein also borrows discreetly from Malevich's *Red Cavalry* (circa 1932) in the scene in which the Tatars storm across the steppes to attack the Russians.²²⁴ No individual heroes are depicted but the Russian people as a whole, thus enhancing the patriotic character of this film and the heroic pathos that accompanies its lyric tone. Though it depicts war, in reality this film, made during the years in which the war in Vietnam was taking place, supports peace. Incidentally, another film, *Ave Maria* (I. Ivanov-Vano, 1972), addressed the issue of the Vietnam

---

Personal interview. 25 September 2005.

222 *The Battle of Kerzhenets* constitutes a symphonic interlude between two scenes of the third act of *The Legend of the Invisible City of Kitezh and the Maiden Fevroniia.*

223 Quoted in Lagina, "Mul'tiplikatsiia: lirika i epos", 84.

224 Norshtein, Iu. Personal interview. 25 September 2005, and in Kitson, *Yuri Norstein and Tale of Tales*, 40.

179

War, but this time in a more direct way, providing references to the war in question by illustrating characters with particular Oriental traits and using real footage of the war.

In making *The Battle of Kerzhenets*, two strong personalities came into conflict: the older established director Ivan Ivanov-Vano, and the younger, unconventional Iurii Norshtein. The disagreement between these two artists about the film ending is emblematic of an evolution in animation between the 1960s and the 1970s, from a narrative approach to a poetic, less tangible mode, made of atmospheres. The ending of the film we see today represents the position of Ivanov-Vano: the audience gets a glimpse into a bright, new life through a panorama of the construction of a white and gold city. By depicting the reconstruction of the city, Ivanov-Vano met the traditional socialist realist demand for positive endings and glorification of the workers; still, these choices had to do with his artistic point of view and his desire to convey explicit messages through his films. Norshtein, however, had proposed a different ending, one more in tune with the poetic atmosphere of the entire film. As Norshtein puts it: "He [Ivanov-Vano] did not understand what I was talking about, because I wanted the ending to be devoid of mandatory optimism. It was abominable. I wanted it to be reflected as a glitter of water, when it stops being matter. I wanted it to be immaterial, only as supposition, not as material fact".[225]

The *Battle of Kerzhenets* was a disappointment for Norshtein, but it spurred him on his search for an original approach to animation. It gave him "a sense of the resonance, the musicality of forms, the musicality of action. This has nothing to do with superficial musical rhythm, but a feeling for internal structure".[226] Norshtein gradually developed his own artistic views in films such as *The Fox and the Hare* (*Lisa i zaiats*, 1973), *The Heron and the Crane* (*Tsaplia i zhuravl'*, 1974), and *Hedgehog in the Fog*(*Ezhik v tumane*, 1975). But it was with his unique *The Tale of Tales* (*Skazka skazok*, 1979) that he ultimately expressed his philosophy of animation, a visual art form that reflects the mind of an author who is both an artist and a poet.

Soviet animation's shift from a means to critique contemporary society to a vehicle for personal artistic expression, adopting musical structures and poetic devices, further de-

[225] Norshtein, Iu. Personal interview. 25 September 2005.

[226] Quoted in Kitson, *Yuri Norstein and Tale of Tales*, 40.

Chapter 5 Conclusion: The Beginning of New Tendencies

veloped in the 1970s. By choosing a lyrical approach, directors set their characters in a poetic, atemporal world that answered only the demands of the artist's subjective *Weltanschauung*. A new chapter of Soviet animation had begun.

Bibliography

Archival material
All archival sources are drawn from the archive RGALI (*Rossiiskii gosudarstvennyi arkhiv literatury i iskusstva* – State Russian Archive of Literature and Art).

In particular I consulted:
RGALI, Fond Soiuzmul'tfil'm 2469, opis' 1, 2, 3, 4 "Soiuzmul'tfil'm Archive. 1939–1974"
RGALI, Fond Tsekhanovskii 2627, opis' 1 and 2
RGALI, Fond Kuleshov 2679, op.1

Files cited:
RGALI, Soiuzmul'tfil'm fond 2469, op.1, d. 41, ll. 1–85 "Perepiska s ministerstvom o rasshirenii tematiki mul'tfil'mov, o kul'turnoi sviazi s inostrannymi firmami, ob uluchshenii uslovi truda (1956)".

RGALI, Soiuzmul'tfil'm fond 2469, op.1, d. 67, ll. 1–45 "Stenogramma zasedaniia khudozhestvennogo soveta po obsuzhdeniiu literaturnogo scenariia fil'ma *25-oe – pervyi den'* (1967)".

RGALI, Soiuzmul'tfil'm fond 2469, op.1, d.149, ll. 1–17 "Stsenarnyi otdel. Perepiska so zriteliami po voprosam rasshireniia tematiki mul'tfil'mov (1957)"

RGALI, Soiuzmul'tfil'm fond 2469, op.1, d. 151, ll. 1–89 "Stsenarnyi otdel. Perepiska s avtorami o predlogaemykh zaiavkakh i literaturnykh stsenariiakh (1958)".

RGALI, Soiuzmul'tfil'm fond 2469, op. 1, d. 152, ll. 1–12 "Stsenarnyi otdel. Perepiska so zriteliami po voprosam rasshireniia tematiki mul'tfil'mov (1958)".

RGALI, Soiuzmul'tfil'm fond 2469, op.1, d. 259, ll. 1–26 "Zlodeika s nakleikoi: Materialy fil'ma (1954)".

RGALI, Soiuzmul'tfil'm fond 2469, opis' 1, d. 272, ll. 1–131 "Delo fil'ma *Istoriia odnogo prestupleniia* (1960–1962)".

RGALI, Soiuzmul'tfil'm fond 2469, op.4, d. 39, ll. 1–24 "Stenogramma zasedaniia khudozhestvennogo soveta po obsuzhdeniiu fil'ma *Gora dinozavrov* (1967)".

RGALI, Soiuzmul'tfil'm fond 2469, op.4, d. 225, ll. 1–12 "*Gora dinozavrov*: Literaturnyi stsenarii A.G. Snesareva (1966)".

RGALI, Soiuzmul'tfil'm fond 2469, op. 4, d. 607, ll. 1–129 "Delo fil'ma *Stekliannaia garmonika* (1967)".

RGALI, Soiuzmul'tfil'm fond 2469, op.4, d. 659, ll. 1–21 "Delo fil'ma *Chelovek v ramke* (1965)".

RGALI, Tsekhanovskii fond 2627, op.1, d. 92, ll. 53–54 "Professional'no-tekhnicheskii opyt: *Pasifik*".

RGALI, Tsekhanovskii fond 2627, op.1, d. 92, ll. 13–17 "Ne prevyshchen li protsent oshibok? (1931)".

Soviet animation bibliography and works cited

Abramov, Nikolai. "Just You Wait". *Soviet Film* 3 (1973): 31.

—-. "Mul'tfil'm: politika, filosofiia, poeziia". In *Mify i real'nost' zarubezhnogo kino segodnia. Sbornik statei, shestoi vypusk.* Ed. M. Shaternikova. Moscow: Iskusstvo, 1978. 192–211.

Adorno, Theodor W. *Aesthetic Theory*. London: Routledge & K. Paul, 1984.

Agranovskaya, Ella. "Puppets Know A Lot About Us People". *Soviet Film* 4 (1981): 34–35.

Akarzh, Lana. "Fragment iz vospominanii 'Kaliaevskaia, 23a'". In *Otkrytyi rossiiskii festival' animatsionnogo kino*. Suzdal': Izdanie Otkrytyi rossiiskii festival' animatsionnogo kino, 1999. 103–110.

Akopov, Kh. "Svoboda prostranstva". *Iskusstvo kino* 8 (1965): 79–81.

Aldashin, Mikhail. "Zhivaia i nezhivaia mul'tiplikatsiia (beseda so studentami Moskovskoi Mezhdunarodnoi Kinoshkoly, fevral' 2004)". *Kinovedcheskie zapiski* 73 (2005): 257–260.

Aldoshina, O. "U beregov slova". *Iskusstvo kino* 7 (1997): 72–75.

Aleksandra, Vasil'kova. "Pochemu medved'". In *Katalog-al'manakh Suzdal' 2002*. Suzdal': Izdanie otkrytogo rossiiskogo festivalia animatsionnogo kino, 2002. 111–113.

Alekseev, Aleksandr. "Zabveniie, ili Sozhalenie: Vospominaniia peterburgskogo kadeta. (Publikatsiia V.G. Nepevnogo)". *Kinovedcheskie zapiski* 52 (2001): 271–294.

—-. "Zabvenie, ili Sozhalenie: Vospominaniia peterburskogo kadeta (Okonchanie)". *Kinovedcheskie zapiski* 60 (2002): 345–371.

Alimov, Sergei. "Rezervy mul'tiplikatsii". *Tvorchestvo* 9 (1967): 18.

Annotirovannyi katalog mul'tiplikatsionnykh i kukol'nykh fil'mov. Moscow: Mosgorkinoprokat, 1982.

Anoshchenko, N. "Za sovetskuiu tonfil'mu". *Kino i zhizn'* 14 (1930): 3–5.

Antronov, V., and E. Dobnia. "Andrei Khrzhanovskii". *Kinograf* 8 (2000): 51–76.

Antropov, Vladimir. "Wladyslaw Aleksandrowicz Starewicz". In *Testimoni silenziosi. Film russi 1908–1919*. Biblioteca dell'immagine, 1989.

Arnheim, Rudolf. *Visual Thinking*. Berkeley: University of California Press, 1969.

Aronov, Aleksandr. "Nemudrenaia programma". *Iskusstvo kino* 1 (1996): 46–50.

Asenin, Sergei. "Andrei Khrjanovski: animation navigates between literature and painting". *AnimaFilm* 2 (1985): 21–23.

—-. "Cheburashka". *Soviet Film* 1 (1973): 22.

---. "Dobraia ulybka 'kukol'nika'". *Iskusstvo kino* 10 (1967): 56–58.

---. *Mir Mul'tfil'ma*. Moscow: Iskusstvo, 1986.

---. "Mudrost' vymysla". *Iskusstvo kino* 6 (1968): 44–57.

---, ed. *Mudrost' vymysla. Mastera mul'tiplikatsii o sebe i svoem iskusstve*. Moscow: Iskusstvo, 1983.

---. "Mul'tiplikatsiia sotsialisticheskikh stran kak sotsial'no-esteticheskii fenomen (khudozhestvennye printsipy, napravleniia razvitiia, natsional'nye shkoly, mastera). Avtoreferat". Abstract. VGIK, 1989.

---. "Smeshnoe i vysokoe". In *Ekran 79/80*. Eds. Iu. Tiurin and G. Dolmatovskaia. Moscow: Iskusstvo, 1982. 78–81.

---. "Sovremennye volshebniki ekrana". *Iskusstvo kino* 10 (1962): 62–68.

---. "Tallinskie chudodei". *Iskusstvo kino* 6 (1976): 44–55.

---. "Tendentsiia poiska". *Iskusstvo kino* 9 (1978): 123–129.

---. "Vernost' izbrannomu puti". In *Kino Panorama. Sovetskoe kino segodnia*. Vol. 3. Moscow: Iskusstvo, 1981. 180–193.

---. *Volshebniki ekrana. Esteticheskie problemy sovremennoi mul'tiplikatsii*. Moscow: Iskusstvo, 1974.

---. "Vozmozhnosti mul'tiplikatsii". *Iskusstvo kino* 8 (1964): 56–63.

---. "Vozmozhnosti mul'tiplikatsii". *Iskusstvo kino* 7 (1966): 40–43.

Asenin, Sergei, ed. "Nakazanie smekhom". *Iskusstvo kino* 4 (1963): 100–104.

Atamanov, Lev. "... A perestraivat'sia nado bylo ... (Publikatsiia G. Borodina)", *Kinovedcheskie zapiski* 80 (2006): 201–209.

---. "Avtobiograficheskie nabroski". *Kinovedcheskie zapiski* 92/93 (2009): 84–92.

---. "Mul'tiplikatsiia - eto vse chto ugodno plius eshche koe-chto". *Kinovedcheskie zapiski* 92/93 (2009): 61–84.

---. "Protiv naturalizma". *Iskusstvo kino* 5 (1959): 123–124.

---. "Puteshestvie L'va Atamanova v Kitai. Iz istorii nesostoiavshegosia fil'ma 'Nachzha vozmushaet spokoistvie moria', 1958". *Kinovedcheskie zapiski* 92/93 (2009): 92–110.

---. "'Risuiut bi ef ef', 'Petrushka' i nerealizovannye zamysly. (Publikatsiia i predisloviia Georgiia Borodina)". *Kinovedcheskie zapiski* 92/93 (2009): 110-117.

Babakhina, Elizaveta. "'Ponachalu bylo strashno'". *Iskusstvo kino* 4 (1995): 65–67.

Babichenko, Dmitrii. "Dovol'no mul'tshtampov". *Iskusstvo kino* 10 (1961): 32–43.

---. *Iskusstvo mul'tiplikatsii*. Moscow: Iskusstvo, 1964.

---. "Talantlivo, ostroumno!" *Iskusstvo kino* 12 (1961): 62–65.

---. "Tridtsat' minut". *Iskusstvo kino* 9 (1958): 71–74.

Bakhtin, Mikhail M. "Discourse in the Novel". In *The Dialogic Imagination: Four Essays*. Ed. Michael Holquist. Austin: University of Texas Press, 1981. 259–422

---. "Forms of Time and the Chronotope in the Novel". Trans. Caryl Emerson. In *The Dialogic Imagination: Four Essays*. Ed. Michael Holquist. Austin: University of Texas Press, 1981. 84–258.

---. *Rabelais and His World*. Bloomington: Indiana University Press, 1984.

Baklin, Nikolai. "Vospominaniia o dorevoliutsionnom periode v kinematografii", *Kinovedcheskie zapiski* 64 (2003): 171–174, http://www.kinozapiski.ru/ru/article/sendvalues/132/

Baklin, Nikolai, and A. G. Kalashnikov "Pervye shagi nauchnogo kino v Rossii. (Publikatsiia A.S. Deriabina, kommentarii S.V. Skovorodnikovoi pri uchastii A.S. Deriabina)". *Kinovedcheskie zapiski* 64 (2003): 184–189, http://www.kinozapiski.ru/ru/article/sendvalues/133/

Ban'kovskii, Georgii, and Eduard Ioganson. "*Simfoniia mira*: Zvukovoi tsvetnoi mul'tiplikatsionnyi stsenarii (1932) (Publikatsiia P. A. Bagrova)". *Kinovedcheskie zapiski* 65 (2003): 77–86.

Barabanov, Boris. "Reanimatsiia animatsii". *Kommersant den'gi* 37 (442) (2003): 98–100.

Bardin, Garri. "Prekrasnaia neznakomka". *Sem'ia i shkola* 8 (1987): 54–56.

—. "Zhivem kak v skazke". *Iskusstvo kino* 3 (1997): 71–72.

—. "Professionalism and something else". *Soviet Film* 1 (1988): 29.

Barrier, Michael. *Hollywood Cartoons: American Animation in Its Golden Age.* Oxford: Oxford University Press, 1999.

Bazin, André. "The Ontology of the Photographic Image". In *What is Cinema?* Ed. Hugh Gray, vol. 1. Berkeley and Los Angeles: University of California Press, 1967. 9–16.

Begizova, Irina Sergeevna. "Vzaimodeistvie muzyki i izobrazheniia v obraznoi strukture mul'tiplikatsionnogo fil'ma. Avtoreferat." Abstract. Leningradskii gosudarstvennyi institut teatra, muzyki i kinematografii im. N.K. Cherkasova, 1985.

Belaev, Ia. *Spetsial'nye vidy mul'tiplikatsionnykh s"emok.* Moscow: Izdatel'stvo Iskusstvo, 1967.

Beliakov, V. "Elektronnaia proba pera". *Iskusstvo kino* 2 (1973): 126–130.

Bendazzi, Giannalberto. *Alexeieff: Itinerary of a Master.* Paris: Dreamland, 2001.

—. *Cartoons: One Hundred Years of Cinema Animation.* London: John Libbey, 1994.

Bergson, Henri. *Laughter: An Essay on the Meaning of the Comic.* Trans. Cloudesley Brereton and Fred Rothwell. Copenhagen: Green Integer, 1999.

Bezvestnyi russkii – znamenityi frantsuz. Biblioteka Vsemirnogo kluba peterburzhtsev. St. Petersburg: Izdatel'stvo Bukovskogo, 1999.

Beumers, Birgit, Victor Bocharov, and David Robinson, eds. *Alexander Shiryaev, Master of Movement.* Le Giornate del Cinema Muto, 2009.

Bocharov, Eduard. "Problemy est', trebuiutsia resheniia". *Iskusstvo kino* 2 (1984): 23–29.

Bodiul, Natal'ia. "Mnogoe ishchesh' zanovo". *Iskusstvo kino* 7 (1980): 72–74.

Bogdanov, M.A. *O tvorchestve khudozhnika v kinematografe.* Moscow: VGIK, 1976.

Bogdanova, S. "O zhizni i tvorchestve A. G. Snezhko-Blotskoi". *Kinograf* 19 (2008): 207-240.

Boiarskii, Iosif. *Literaturnye kollazhi.* Tsentr psikhologii i psikhoterapii, 1996.

Borodin, Georgii. "Animatory: kratkaia istoriia obucheniia professii". In *Katalog-al'manakh. Suzdal' 2002.* Suzdal': Otkrytyi rossiiskii festival' animatsionnogo kino, 2002. 121–127.

—. "Animatsiia podnevol'naia". Unpublished manuscript, MS Word file.

—. "Animatsiia podnevol'naia (1 glava)". *Kinograf* 16 (2005): 54–153.

"Kastratsiia begemota (glava iz knigi 'Animatsiia podnevol'naia')". *Kinovedcheskie zapiski* 80 (2006): 210–236.

"Kastratsiia begemota (glava iz knigi 'Animatsiia podnevol'naia')". *Kinovedcheskie zapiski* 81 (2007): 140–167.

—. "Nikolai Erdman i animatsiia". *Kinovedcheskie zapiski* 61 (2002): 175–191.

—. "'Skazka o glupom myshonke': Istoriia 'nekhrestomatiinoi' kartiny (Publikatsiia i predislovie G. Borodina)". *Kinovedcheskie zapiski* 73 (2005): 216–234.

—. "*Skoraia pomoshch*: Sud'ba mul'fil'ma Medvedkina (Publikatsiia i predislovie G. N. Borodina)". *Kinovedcheskie zapiski* 49 (2000): 83–85.

—. "Slovarvarstvo". In *Katalog-al'manakh. Suzdal' 2003*. Suzdal': VIII otkrytyi rossiiskii festival' animatsionnogo kino, 2003. 136–145.

—. "Soiuzmul'tfil'm. Nenapisannaia istoriia". *Kinovedcheskie zapiski* 80 (2006): 149–152.

—. "Unesennye vetrom. Katalog redkikh i nesokhranivshikhsia mul'tiplikationnykh fil'mov". *Kinovedcheskie zapiski* 52 (2001): 295–312.

—. "V bor'be za malen'kie mysli: Neadekvatnost' tsenzury (glava iz knigi 'Animatsiia podnevol'naia')". *Kinovedcheskie zapiski* 73 (2005): 261–309.

Bortnikov, I. "The best tale". *Soviet Film* 4 (1985): 22.

Bossart, Alla. "Vertepnyi mir". In *Katalog-al'manakh. Otkrytii Rossiskii Festival' animatsionnogo kino*. Berezovaia Roshcha: Tretii otkrytii festival' animatsionnogo kino, 1998.

Boym, Svetlana. *Common Places: Mythologies of Everyday Life in Russia*. Cambridge, Mass.: Harvard University Press, 1994.

Brumberg, V. "Zvukovaia mul'tiplikatsiia". *Proletarskoe Kino* 2–3 (1931): 63.

Bugoslavskii, S. "Muzyka i zvuk v mul'tiplikatsionnom fil'me". In *Mul'tiplikatsionnyi fil'm*. Moscow: Kinofotoizdat, 1936. 258–286.

Burmistrova, Alla. "Krok à la Kiev". *Soviet Film* 4 (1990): 38–39.

Bushkin, A. "Mul'tiplikatsiia: Kadro-s"emka". *Kino-zhurnal ARK* 2 (1926): 20–21.

—. *Triuki i mul'tiplikatsiia*. Moscow: Kinopechat', 1926.

"Bytie na svalke kul'tury. Razroznennye zametki k teme 'Mul'tiplikatsiia i intelligentsiia'". In *Kino detiam. Kino-molodezhi*. Vol. 3. Moscow: Soiuzinformkino, 1989. 15–18.

Chegodaev, Andrei. *Stranitsy istorii sovetskoi zhivopisi i sovetskoi grafiki*. Moscow: Izdatel'stvo sovetskii khudozhnik, 1984.

Cherednichenko, Tat'iana. "Podobno zhivomu shutu". *Iskusstvo kino* 1 (1996): 42–44.

Cherkasova, Oksana. "'V fol'klore byta net'". *Iskusstvo kino* 3 (1997): 82–83.

Cherkes. "Dve minuty". *Sovetskii ekran* 41 (1928): 9.

Cherniaev, Petr. "Posadil ded repku". *Sovetskii ekran* 10 (1989): 2.

Cholodenko, Alan. "The Illusion of the Beginning: A Theory of Drawing and Animation". *Afterimage* 28.1 (2000): 9–12.

"Chto nam pokazhut v 1927 g". *Sovetskoe kino* 8 (1926): 5–11.

Ciment, Michel. "'Le cinéma, c'est une somme de choses inachevées'. Entretien avec Youri Norstein". *Positif* 346 (1989): 58–64.

Clark, Katerina. *The Soviet Novel: History as Ritual*. 3rd ed. Bloomington: Indiana University Press, 2000.

Crafton, Donald. *Before Mickey: the Animated Film, 1898–1928*. Cambridge, Mass.: MIT Press, 1982.

—. *Emile Cohl, Caricature, and Film*. Princeton: Princeton University Press, 1990.

"Mul'tiplikatornaia fil'ma". *Ekran kino-gazety* 7 (1925): 2.

Dabizha, Nataliia. "Rezhisser". *Iskusstvo kino* 9 (1985): 55–57.

Danin, D. "Oslik, kotoromu dvazhdy povezlo". *Iskusstvo kino* 12 (1973): 93–96.

—. "Polemichnost' nauki i nadezhdy kino". *Iskusstvo kino* 2 (1973): 122–126.

De Blois, Marco. "Youri Norstein - chercheur d'âme". *24 Images* 43 (1989): 36–37.

De Zharvil', Rober. "Zametki o kino". *Sovetskii ekran* 52 (1927): 10.

Deriabin, Aleksandr. "Vertov i animatsiia: roman, kotorogo ne bylo". *Kinovedcheskie zapiski* 52 (2001): 132–144.

Derobert, Eric. "Le conte des contes: de la Révolution à l'enfance". *Positif* 288 (1985): 61–62.

Dinov, Todor. "Gorizonty mul'tiplikatsii". *Iskusstvo kino* 7 (1970): 157–163.

Dmitrieva, M. "Na ekrane - mul'tiplikatsiia". In *Informatsiia o vedushchikh fil'makh 1985–1986 g*. Ed. N.G. Amashukeli. Vol. 6. Moscow: Soiuzinformkino, 1985. 44–48.

"Dossier animation". *Positif* 297 (1985): 31–62.

Duganov, R. "Maiakovskii v 'Kine-zhurnale'". *Iskusstvo kino* 7 (1983): 119–125.

Efimov, Boris. "Maiakovskii-khudozhnik". *Tvorchestvo* 7 (1963): 17–19.

—. "Ozhivshie graviury". *Iskusstvo kino* 12 (1964): 18–19.

Eisenstein, Sergei. *Film Form: Essays in Film Theory*. Ed. Jay Leyda. New York: Harcourt Brace Jovanovich, 1949.

—. "From Lectures on Music and Colour in *Ivan the Terrible* (1947)". *The Eisenstein Reader*. Ed. Richard Taylor. London: BFI Publishing, 1998.

—. *See also* Eizenshtein, Sergei.

Eisenstein, Sergei, V. Pudovkin, and G. Aleksandrov. "Statement of Sound". In *The Film Factory: Russian and Soviet Cinema in Documents 1896–1939*. Eds. Richard Taylor and Ian Christie. London: Routledge, 1988. 234–235.

Eizenshtein, Sergei. "Disnei". In *Metod. Tom vtoroi. Tainy Masterov: Stat'i i etiudi*. Ed. N. I. Kleiman. Vol. 2. Moscow: Muzei Kino, Eizenshtein-tsentr, 2002. 255–295.

—. "Disnei (publikatsiia i kommentarii N. I. Kleimana)". In *Problemy sinteza v khudozhestvennoi kul'ture*. Eds. Anatoly Prokhorov, B. Raushenbakh and Fedor Khitruk. Moscow: Nauka, 1985. 209–284.

—. *Izbrannye proizvedeniia v shesti tomakh*. 6 vols. Moscow: Iskusstvo, 1964.

—. "K issledovaniiu 'Disnei'". In *Metod. Tom vtoroi. Tainy Masterov: Stat'i i etiudi*. Ed. N.I. Kleiman. Vol. 2. Moscow: Muzei Kino. Eizenshtein-tsentr, 2002. 494–529.

—. "Viatskaia loshadka". In *Izbrannye proizvedeniia v shesti tomakh*. Vol. 3. Moscow: Iskusstvo, 1964. 500–512.

—. "Za kadrom". In *Izbrannye proizvedeniia v shesti tomakh*. Vol. 2. Moscow: Iskusstvo, 1964. 283–296.

—. "Zametki ob iskusstve Uolta Disneia. (Publikatsiia, predislovie i kommentarii N.I. Kleimana)". *Kinovedcheskie zapiski* 52 (2001): 98–114.

Eizenshtein, Sergei, V. Pudovkin, and G. Aleksandrov. "Zaiavka". *Zhizn' iskusstva* (1928): 4–5.

Eliseev, G. "Bez shineli". *Iskusstvo kino* 4 (1995): 160–161.

—. "Igra - raskrytaia sut' veshchei". *Iskusstvo kino* 2 (1995): 169.

Elizarov, Georgii. *Sovetskaia mul'tiplikatsiia: Spravochnik*. Moscow: Komitet po kinematografii pri sovete ministrov SSSR Gosfil'mofond, 1966.

Erofeev, Vl. "Zabytaia oblast' kino". *Sovetskii ekran* 34 (1926): 4.

Evteeva, Irina Vsevolodovna. "Protsess zhanroobrazovaniia v sovetskoi mul'tiplikatsii 60–80x godov. Avtoreferat." Abstract. Leningradskii gosudarstvennyi institut teatra, muzyki i kinematografii imena N. K. Cherkasova (NIO), 1990.

Fedorova, Elena. "Khudozhnik-postanovshchik". *Iskusstvo kino* 9 (1985): 57–59.

Fedulov, Aleksandr. "Mul'tiplikatsiia i zritel'. Tochki zreniia rezhissera". In *Kino detiam. Kino-molodezhi*. Vol. 3. Moscow: Soiuzinformkino, 1989. 25–28.

Fefer, V. "Kino-polit-sharzh – ostreishee orudie propagandy". *Sovetskoe kino* 5–6 (1927): 4–6.

Filmy-skazki. Stsenarii risovannykh fil'mov. Vol. 1–8. Moscow: Iskusstvo, 1950–1964.

Filmy-skazki. Stsenarii risovannykh fil'mov. Vol. 9. Moscow: Iskusstvo, 1970.

Filmy-skazki. Stsenarii risovannykh fil'mov. Vol. 10. Moscow: Iskusstvo, 1972.

Fomina, R. "Yuri Norshtein: first winner of the Andrey Tarkovsky prize". *Soviet Film* 8 (1989): 2.

Furniss, Maureen. *Art in Motion: Animation Aesthetics*. London: John Libbey, 1998.

Gailan, Eleonora. "Kogda-to. Vospominaniia o leningradskoi predvoennoi mul'tiplikatsii". *Kinovedcheskie zapiski* 73 (2005): 238–254.

Gal'perin, A. "Novaia model' professional'nogo kino-s"emochnogo apparata 'Ekler'". *Kino i kul'tura* 4 (1929): 58–60.

Gamburg, Efim. *Tainy risovannogo mira*. Moscow: Sovetskii khudozhnik, 1966.

—. "Trizhdy risovannyi mir". *Khimia i zhizn'* 5 (1986): 46–51.

Gapanovich, M. "Dlia mass ili dlia elity?" *Sovetskaia kul'tura* 110 (1986): 7.

Garin, V. *O trekh russkikh skazkok: Ivashko, Pro Emeliu, Kolobok*. Moskva: Goskinoizdat, 1939.

—. *Okhotnik Fedor*. Moskva: Goskinoizdat, 1939.

Gel'gar, A. "V pomoshch' mul'tiplikatoram". *Kino i kul'tura* 9–10 (1929): 57–58.

Gessen, Daniil. "Sovetskii sharzh". *Kino-nedelia* 12 (1924): 3.

Ginzburg, Sergei. "Iskusstvo mul'tiplikatsii vchera, segodnia i zavtra".

Voprosy kino-iskusstva. Ezhegodnyi istoriko-teoreticheskii sbornik 13 (1971): 142–192.

———. "Kogda khudozhnik ishchet". *Iskusstvo kino* 11 (1957): 110–113.

———. "Mastera risovannogo fil'ma". *Tvorchestvo* 2 (1959): 23–25.

———. *Risovannyi i kukol'nyi fil'm: Ocherki razvitiia sovetskoi mul'tiplikatsionnoi kinematografii*. Moscow: Iskusstvo, 1957.

———. "Skazka o schast'e". *Iskusstvo kino* 1 (1962): 83–84.

———. "Sovetskaia mul'tiplikatsiia v borbe za realizm". In *Voprosy kinoiskusstva. Sbornik statei*. Ed. Iu. S. Kalashnikov. Moscow: Gosudarstvennoe izdatel'stvo Iskusstvo, 1955. 381–411.

———. "*Toptyzhka*, ili vozvrashchennye emotsii detstva". *Iskusstvo kino* 4 (1965): 25–26.

———. "Znak i obraz". *Iskusstvo kino* 12 (1970): 69–70.

Glazova, V.N., ed. *Rezhissery sovetskogo mul'tiplikatsionnogo kino*. Moscow: Soiuzinformkino, Goskino SSSR, 1983.

———, ed. *Soiuzmul'tfil'm*. Moscow: Soiuzinformkino, Goskino SSSR, 1981.

Goodwin, James. *Eisenstein, Cinema, and History*. Urbana: University of Illinois Press, 1993.

Gor'kii, Maksim. *Literatura i kino. Sobranie sochinenii v tridtsati tomakh*. Vol. 27. 30 vols. Moscow, 1953.

Gorlenko, Aleksandr. "Professiia: khudozhnik-mul'tiplikator". In *Kino detiam. Kino-molodezhi*. Vol. 3. Moscow: Soiuzinformkino, 1989. 21–25.

Goryachev, Oleg. "Animated Cartoons Off the Screen". *Soviet Film* 12 (1989): 38–39.

Gosudarstvennoe izdatelstvo. *Kinematograf: Sbornik statei*. Moscow: Gosudarstvennoe izdatelstvo, 1919.

"Govoriat mastera mul'tiplikatsii". *Iskusstvo kino* 3 (1962): 130–142.

Greenberg, Clement, "Modernist Painting". In *Art in Theory, 1900–2000: An Anthology of Changing Ideas*, 2nd ed. Oxford, UK; Cambridge, Mass., USA: Blackwell, 2003. 773–779.

Grigor'ev, V. "Pionery leningradskoi mul'tiplikatsii". In *Iz istorii Lenfil'ma. Stat'i, vospominaniia, dokumenty 1920-e gody. Vypusk 2*. Ed. N.S. Gornitskaia. Leningrad: Izdatel'stvo "Iskusstvo" Leningradskoe otdelenie, 1970. 202–210.

Gromov, Evgenii S. *Alimov: mul'tiplikatsiia, knizhnaia i stankovaia grafika*. Mastera sovetskogo iskusstva. Moscow: Sov. Khudozhnik, 1990.

Guliev, A. "Napriamik". *Iskusstvo kino* 8 (1962): 96–98.

Gurevich, Mikhail. "Animatsiia po Kovalevu". In *Katalog-al'manakh. Otkrytyi Rossiiskii festival' anim. kino Tarusa 2001*. Berezovaia Roshcha: Izdanie otkrytogo rossiiskogo festivalia animatsionnogo kino, 2001. 123–124.

———. "Animatsiia veshchi i oveshchestvlenie maski. O nekotorykh chertakh kinopoetiki Maiakovskogo". *Kinovedcheskie zapiski* 33 (1997): 172.

———. "Ne ob etom fil'm". In *Mul'tiplikatsiia, animatograf, fantomatika*. Kiev: Izdanie Pervogo Vsesoiuznogo Festivalia mul'tiplikatsionnykh fil'mov "Krok-89", 1989. 122–147.

———. "Otkryvaem rubriku". *Mul'tpanorama* 8 (1988): 18.

Hosking, Geoffrey. *The First Socialist Society: a History of the Soviet Union from Within*. 2nd ed. Cambridge, Mass.: Harvard University Press, 1992.

Iampol'skii, Mikhail. "'Organicheskaia mashina' u Eizenshteina i Disneia". *Kinovedcheskie zapiski* 34 (1997): 52–61.

—. "Ot eposa k grotesku". *Iskusstvo kino* 9 (1984): 42–48.

—. "Palitra i ob'ektiv". *Iskusstvo kino* 2 (1980): 94–104.

—. "Problema vzaimodeistviia iskusstv i neosushchestvlennyi mul'tfil'm Fernanda Lezhe 'Charli-kubist'". In *Problemy sinteza v khudozhestvennoi kul'ture*. Eds. Anatoly Prokhorov, B. Raushenbakh, and Fedor Khitruk. Moscow: Nauka, 1985. 76–99.

—. "Prostranstvo mul'tiplikatsii". *Iskusstvo kino* 3 (1982): 84–99.

—. "Starevich: Mimika nasekomykh i kul'turnaia traditsiia". *Kinovedcheskie zapiski* 1 (1988): 84–90.

Iampolski, Michel. "Derrière l'image visible sur l'écran: entretien avec Youri Norstein". *Positif* 297 (1985): 48–50.

Iarbusova, Francheska. "Detskie chasy". *Iskusstvo kino* 3 (1977): 66–69.

Iarbusova, Francheska, and Iurii Norshtein. "Razgovor, kotorogo ne bylo". *Iskusstvo kino* 3 (1997): 52–69.

Iensen, T. "Beseda Iuriia Norshteina s Tatianoi Iensen". *Iskusstvo kino* 2 (1985): 88–98.

—. "'Zhertvoprinosenie'. Final". *Iskusstvo kino* 6 (1990): 99–107.

Iskusstvo. *Istoriia sovetskogo kino*. 4 vols. Moscow: Iskusstvo, 1973–1978.

Iskusstvo Kino [Editorial Board]. "Smelee iskat' novoe v mul'tiplikatsionnom kino!" *Iskusstvo kino* 2 (1959): 93–100.

Iutkevich, Sergei. "Maiakovskii na ekrane. (Opyt' mul'tiplikatsionnoi ekranizatsii p'esy 'Bania')". *Voprosy kino-iskusstva. Ezhegodnyi istoriko-teoreticheskii sbornik* 8 (1964): 86–114.

—. "Maiakovskii vykhodit na ekran. Bania". *Iskusstvo kino* 9 (1960): 37–64.

—. "Maiakovskoe kino". *Iskusstvo kino* 6 (1976): 58–82.

—. "Tret'e reshenie. Iz tvorcheskogo opyta raboty nad mul'tfil'mami po stsenariiam i p'esam V. Maiakovskogo". In *Problemy sinteza v khudozhestvennoi kul'ture*. Eds. Anatoly Prokhorov, B. Raushenbakh, and Fedor Khitruk. Moscow: Nauka, 1985. 114–148.

Ivanov-Vano, Ivan. "'Ekler' - za i protiv. Stenogramma doklada 'Primenenie eklernogo metoda v proizvodstve risovannykh fil'mov, 1951". *Kinovedcheskie zapiski* 80 (2006): 174–187.

—. "Graficheskaia mul'tiplikatsiia". In *Mul'tiplikatsionnyi fil'm*. Moscow: Kinofotoizdat, 1936. 101–196.

—. "Izobrazitel'noe reshenie mul'tiplikatsionnogo fil'ma". In *O khudozhnikakh teatra, kino i TV*. Ed. V.V. Vanslov. Leningrad: Khudozhnik RSFSR, 1984. 136–146.

—. *Kadr za kadrom*. Moscow: Iskusstvo, 1980.

—. *Mul'tiplikatsiia vchera i segodnia (iz lektsii, prochitannykh na khudozhestvennom fakul'tete VGIK)*. Moscow: VGIK, 1974.

—. *Mul'tiplikatsiia vchera i segodnia (chast' 2)*. Moscow: VGIK, 1975.

—. *Mul'tiplikatsiia vchera i segodnia (chast' 3)*. Mul'tiplikatsiia vchera i segodnia.

—. *Mul'tiplikatsiia vchera i segodnia (chast' 4)*. Moscow: VGIK, 1977.

—. *Ocherk istorii razvitiia mul'tiplikatsii (do vtoroi mirovoi voiny)*. Moscow: VGIK, 1967.

—. *Risovannyi fil'm*. Moscow: Goskinoizdat, 1950.

—. "'S chem my prokhodim k etomu postanovleniiu'. Sovetskaia mul'tiplikatsiia, 1960-62 gg." *Kinovedcheskie zapiski* 80 (2006): 192–200.

—. *Sovetskoe mul'tiplikatsionnoe kino*. Moscow: Izdatel'stvo Znanie, 1962.

—. "Vechno iunoe iskusstvo". *Iskusstvo kino* 11 (1977): 62–63.

—. "Vstrecha s Pushkinym". *Iskusstvo kino* 11 (1982): 86–87.

"Iz dnevnikov M. Tsekhanovskogo". In *Iz istorii Lenfil'ma. Stat'i, vospominaniia, dokumenty 1920-e gody. Vypusk 2*. Ed. N.S. Gornitskaia. Leningrad: Izdatel'stvo "Iskusstvo" Leningradskoe otdelenie, 1970. 216–221.

Izvolov, Nikolai. "Aleksandr Alekseev, nevol'nik chetvertogo izmereniia (zametki ob ideologii 'igol'chatogo ekrana')". In *Katalog-al'manakh. Otkrityi Rossiiskii festival' anim. kino Tarusa 1999*. Berezovaia Roshcha: Izdanie otkrytogo rossiiskogo festivalia animatsionnogo kino, 1999. 103–108.

—. *Fenomen kino: Istoriia i teoriia*. Moscow: Izdatelstvo Egsi, 2001.

—. "The History of Drawn Sound in Soviet Russia". *Animation Journal* 6.2 (1998): 54–59.

—. "Otpravlenie i pribytie parovoza *Pasifik 231*". In *Fenomen kino. Istoriia i teoriia*. Moscow: Izdatel'stvo EGSI, 2001. 250–262.

—. "Plennik chetvertogo izmereniia". *Iskusstvo kino* 6 (1999): 80–85.

—. "Velemir Khlebnikov i Arsenii Avraamov: Ideia futurizma i risovannyi zvuk v kino". *Katalog-al'manakh. Otkrytie Rossiiskogo festivalia animatsionnogo kino 1998* (1998): 100–104.

Johnson, Priscilla. *Khrushchev and the Arts: The Politics of Soviet Culture 1962–1964*. Cambridge, Mass.: The M.I.T. Press, 1965.

Joris, Luc. "Konstantin Bronzit. Just Making People Laugh". *Plateau* 20 (1999).

Joubert-Laurencinm, Hervé. "Entretien avec Youri Norstein". *Vertigo* 6–7 (1991): 204–210.

—. *La lettre volante. Quatre essais sur le cinéma d'animation*. Paris: Presses de la Sorbonne Nouvelle, 1997.

—. "*Le conte des contes*. Un palimpseste russe". In *La lettre volante. Quatre essais sur le cinéma d'animation*. Paris: Presses de la Sorbonne Nouvelle, 1997. 177–240.

Kabalkina, E. "Chto mozhet mul'tiplikatsiia". *Sovetskii Ekran* 2 (1980): 21–22.

Kachanov, Roman. "Napravlenie poiskov". *Iskusstvo kino* 2 (1984): 45–54.

Kapkov, Sergei. "Golosa animatsii". In *Katalog-al'manakh. Otkrytii Rossiskii Festival' animatsionnogo kino*. Berezovaia Roshcha: Otkrytii festival' animatsionnogo kino, 1998. 106–111.

—. "Komu eto nuzhno?" In *Katalog-al'manakh. Otkrityi Rossiiskii festival' animatsionnogo kino Tarusa 1999*. Berezovaia Roshcha: Izdanie otkrytogo rossiiskogo festivalia animatsionnogo kino, 1999. 118–120.

—. "Mastera durakavalianiia. Fragmenty nenapisannoi knigi." *Kinovedcheskie zapiski* 80 (2006): 237–251.

Kapkov, Sergei, ed. *Entsiklopediia otechestvennoi mul'tiplikatsii*. Moscow: Algoritm, 2006.

Karanovich, Anatolii. *Moi druz'ia kukly*. Moscow: Iskusstvo, 1971.

Katalog-al'manakh. Otkrytyi Rossiiskii festival' animatsionnogo kino Tarusa 1998–2001. Berezovaia Roshcha: Izdanie otkrytogo rossiiskogo festivalia animatsionnogo kino, 1998-2001.

Katalog-al'manakh. Otkrytyi Rossiiskii festival' animatsionnogo kino Suzdal' 2002–2011. Berezovaia Roshcha: Izdanie otkrytogo rossiiskogo festivalia animatsionnogo kino, 2002-2011.

Kayser, Wolfgang Johannes. *The Grotesque in Art and Literature*. Bloomington: Indiana University Press, 1963.

Kelly, Catriona, *Refining Russia: Advice Literature, Polite Culture, and Gender from Catherine to Yeltsin*. Oxford: Oxford University Press, 2001.

Kenez, Peter. *Cinema and Soviet Society: From the Revolution to the Death of Stalin*. London: I.B. Tauris, 2001.

Kh., N. "God raboty v oblasti mul'tiplikatsii". *Kino-zhurnal ARK* 4 (1925): 40.

Khafiz, Ikhlas Abdel'. "Obraznye vozmozhnosti ploskoi marionetki v mul'tiplikatsionnom fil'me. Avtoreferat". Abstract. VGIK, 1976.

Khaidar, Iazdzhi. "Dvizhenie v risovannom fil'me. Avtoreferat". Abstract. VGIK, 1981.

Khalatov, N. "Kogda otkazyvaiutsia ot zhanra". *Iskusstvo kino* 3 (1957): 114–116.

—. "Rasti, Murzilka!" *Iskusstvo kino* 4 (1957): 106–107.

—. "Vozrozhdenie vazhnogo zhanra". *Iskusstvo kino* 2 (1958): 97–98.

Khaniutin, A. "Samoe 'detskoe' iskusstvo". *Iskusstvo kino* 7 (1982): 39–52.

Khanzhonkov, A. "Rasskazy o proshlom". In *Iz istorii kino*. Ed. Tsentral'nyi gosudarstvennyi arkhiv literatury i iskusstva SSSR Institut Istorii iskusstv. 7 ed. Moskva: Iskusstvo, 1968. 197–205.

Khersonskii, Khrisanf. "Lektsiia o mul'tiplikatsii. (Publikatsiia, predislovie i kommentarii A.S. Deriabina pri uchastii A.S. Troshina i G.N. Borodina)". *Kinovedcheskie zapiski* 52 (2001): 145–170.

Khitruk, Fedor. "From Thought to Image". *Soviet Film* 8 (1981): 27–28.

—. "The Future is our Responsibility". *Soviet Film* 10 (1973): 30–32.

—. "Iskatel'". *Iskusstvo kino* 4 (1980): 128–129.

—. "Kuda idet mul'tiplikatsiia". *Iskusstvo kino* 9 (1977): 59–69.

—. "Moi 'Soiuzmul'tfil'm'". *Iskusstvo kino* 6 (1996): 36–39.

—. "Mul'tiplikatsiia v kontekste khudozhestvennoi kul'tury". In *Problemy sinteza v khudozhestvennoi kul'ture*. Eds. Anatoly Prokhorov, B. Raushenbakh and Fedor Khitruk. Moscow: Nauka, 1985. 7–24.

—. "Poniat' dazhe to, chto trudno voobrazit'". *Iskusstvo kino* 6 (1986): 18–26.

—. "Pridumav mir, v nego poverit'". *Iskusstvo kino* 9 (1985): 51–61.

—. *Professia – animator*. 2 vols. Moscow: Live Book, 2008.

—. "Proverit' praktikoi!" *Iskusstvo kino* 7 (1968): 55–56.

—. "Rasskazy ob animatorakh". *Kinovedcheskie zapiski* 73 (2005): 204–211.

—. "Samoe 'detskoe' iskusstvo". *Iskusstvo kino* 7 (1982): 37–52.

—. "'Situatsiia u vas dostatochno obeshchaiushchaia' (stenogramma zaniatiia v masterskoi F. S. Khitruka na Vysshikh kursakh stsenaristov i rezhisserov 14 ianvaria 1987)". *Kinovedcheskie zapiski* 73 (2005): 123–125.

—. "Stepen' neveroiatnosti". *Iskusstvo kino* 4 (1993): 122–129.

—. "Sto vosem' vstrech". *Iskusstvo kino* 12 (1966): 49–54.

—. "Uchitel' i agitator". *Iskusstvo kino* 2 (1976): 68–70.

—. "Vospominaniia, razmyshleniia, issledovaniia, lektsii (Publikatsiia i predislovie Iu. Mikhailina)". *Kinovedcheskie zapiski* 73 (2005): 5–89.

Khitruk, Fedor, and Andrei Khrzhanovskii. "Besedy pri iasnoi lune". *Kinovedcheskie zapiski* 52 (2001): 59–97.

Khodataev, Nikolai. "Iskusstvo mul'tiplikatsii". *Mul'tiplikatsionnyi fil'm. Sbornik*. Moscow: Kinofotoizdat, 1936. 15–99.

—. "Ot kino-triuka k mul'tiplikatsionnoi komedii". *Sovetskii Ekran* 9 (1929): 8–9.

—. "'Pridia iz neizvestnosti, ia i ukhozhu v neizvestnost'": Nikolai Khodataev o prichinakh svoego ukhoda iz mul'tiplikatsii (Publikatsiia, predislovie i kommentarii I. R. Margolinoi)". *Kinovedcheskie zapiski* 52 (2001): 186–190.

—. "Zabavnoe iskusstvo". *Sovetskii Ekran* 31 (1928): 8–9.

"Khronika razvitiia animatsionnykh tekhnologii". *Kinovedcheskie zapiski* 52 (2001): 6–26.

Khryzhanovskii, Boris N. *Mul'tipanorama - 2. Sbornik stsenarii*. Kiev: Izdatel'stvo Mistetstvo, 1984.

Khrzhanovskii, Andrei. "A.S. Pushkin. Puteshestvie v Ararum vo vremia pokhoda 1829 g. Proektsiia na ekran". In *Problemy sinteza v khudozhestvennoi kul'ture*. Eds. Anatoly Prokhorov, B. Raushenbakh and Fedor Khitruk. Moscow: Nauka, 1985. 157–204.

—. "'Byvaiut strannye sblizheniia'". *Kinovedcheskie zapiski* 42 (1999): 165–173.

—. "Drugoe kino". *Iskusstvo kino* 6 (1986): 110–117.

—. "Esli vy sprosite menia". *Iskusstvo kino* 7 (1992): 95–103.

—. "Fedor Khitruk – Andrei Khrzhanovskii. Besedy pri iasnoi lune". *Kinovedcheskie zapiski* 52 (2001): 59–97.

—. "Fyodor Khitruk". *Soviet Film* 6 (1984): 36–38.

—. "Ia k Vam lechu vospominan'em. I s Vami snova ia. Osen'". In *Soiuzmul'tfil'm predstavliaet*. Ed. L.A. Karaev. Moskva: Soiuzniformkino, 1986. 53–55.

—. "Kinorezhissura kak predmet kinovedcheskogo analiza". *Kinovedcheskie zapiski* 41 (1999): 73–83.

—. "O teorii otnositel'nosti, vorone na snegu i drugikh veshchakh, o kotorykh polezno znat' rezhisseru". *Kinovedcheskie zapiski* 70 (2004): 259–279.

—. "The House that Jack Built". *Soviet Film* 12 (1985): 24–26.

—. "Vybrannye mesta iz shkoly iziashchnykh iskusstv". *Iskusstvo kino* 7 (1997): 57–71.

Khrzhanovskii, Andrei, and S.A. Filippov. "Iz vystuplenii na konferentsii". *Kinovedcheskie zapiski* 34 (1997): 121–130.

"Kinematograficheskii kot". *Ekran Kino-gazety* 2 (1925).

Kino detiam. Kino-molodezhi. Vol. 3. Moscow: Soiuzinformkino, 1989.

Kitson, Clare. "The Little Grey Wolf: Yuri Norstein and Tale of Tales". *Hrvatski filmski ljetopis* 31–32 (2002): 35–48.

—. *Yuri Norstein and Tale of Tales: An Animator's Journey*. Eastleigh: John Libbey; Bloomington: Indiana University Press: 2005.

Kiva, Nikolai. "Soiuzmul'tfil'm - nachalo puti". *Kinovedcheskie zapiski* 80 (2006): 153–173.

Klado, Ekaterina. "Luchshii iz mirov". In *Katalog-al'manakh. Otkrytyi*

Rossiiskii festival' animatsionnogo kino Tarusa 2001. Berezovaia Roshcha: Izdanie otkritiia Rossiiskogo festivalia animatsionnogo kino, 2001.

Klado, N. "Tarakanishche". *Iskusstvo kino* 4 (1964): 45–47.

Kleiman, Naum. "K publikatsii issledovaniia Sergeia Eizenshteina ob Uolte Disnee". In *Problemy sinteza v khudozhestvennoi kul'ture*. Eds. Anatoly Prokhorov, B. Raushenbakh and Fedor Khitruk. Moscow: Nauka, 1985. 205–208.

Kliaksa. Sovetskii mul'tiplikatsionnyi geroi. Moscow: Izdanie mezhrabpomfil'ma, 1934.

Klimentovich, N. Iu. "Chernoe-beloe kino". In *Soiuzmul'tfil'm predstavliaet*. Ed. L.A. Karaev. Moskva: Soiuzinformkino, 1986. 52.

—. "Iskusstvo mul'tiplikatsii". In *Ot s"esda k s"ezdu. Sovetskii kinematograf v odinnadtsatoi piatiletke*. Ed. L.A. Karasev. Moscow: Soiuzinformkino, 1985. 47–53.

—. *Na ekrane skazka*. Moscow: Soiuzinformkino, 1984.

Kol'tsova, Elizaveta. "Med, bezprizornye i cherviak". *Sovetskii ekran* 10 (1928).

Konchalovskaia, Nataliia. "Podlinno russkii". *Iskusstvo kino* 12 (1964): 17.

Kotenochkin, Viacheslav. "Dlia detei ob Olimpiade". *Iskusstvo kino* 4 (1980): 73–75.

—. "Uroki garmonii". *Iskusstvo kino* 6 (1980): 115.

Koval', Iurii. "Prizvanie mul'tiplikatsiia". *Sovetskii ekran* 3 (1984): 20.

Kovalenskaia, N. "Bratishkin ob ob"emnoi mul'tiplikatsii". *Sovetskii Ekran* 17 (1928): 10.

Kovalevskaia, I. "*Bremenskie muzykanty*. Pervyi mul'tiplikatsionnyi miuzikl nepridumannaia istoriia ego sozdaniia (Predislovie, kommentarii, sostavlenie biograficheskoi i fil'mograficheskoi spravok Georgiia Borodina)." *Kinograf* 20 (2009): 326–365.

—. "Puteshestvie v budushchee". *Iskusstvo kino* 10 (1962): 60–61.

Kovalov, Oleg. "'Soiuzmul'tfil'm' prasdnuet 50-letie so dnia osnovaniia". In *Kino i kontekst tom IV 1986–1988. Noveishaia istoriia otechestvennogo kino 1986–2000*. St. Petersburg: SEANS, 2002. 87–96.

Kozlovskii, Evgenii. "Mul'tfil'm. Kak eto delaetsia". *Smena* 12 (1979): 16–18.

Krakauer, Siegfried, *Theory of Film: The Redemption of Physical Reality*. Princeton, NJ: Princeton University Press, 1960.

"'Kratkaia istoriia'". *Iskusstvo kino* 1 (1959): 91–96.

Kristeva, Julia. *Desire in Language: A Semiotic Approach to Literature and Art*. Trans. Thomas Gora, Alice Jardine, and Leon S. Roudiez. New York: Columbia UP, 1980.

Krivulia, Nataliia G. *Labirinty animatsii: Issledovanie khudozhestvennogo obraza rossiiskikh animatsionnykh fil'mov vtoroi poloviny XX veka*. Moscow: Izdatel'skii Dom Graal', 2002.

—. "Udivitel'nye puteshestviia v prostranstve kul'tury, ili Intellektual'nye igry Andreia Khrzhanovskogo". *Kinovedcheskie zapiski* 92/93 (2009): 319–342.

Krivulia, Natal'ia, ed. Animatsiia kak fenomen kul'tury. Materialy pervoi vserossiiskoi nauchno-*prakticheskoi konferentsii*. Moscow: VGIK, 2006.

—. *Animatsiia kak fenomen kul'tury. Materialy vtoroi mezhdunarodnoi nauchno-prakticheskoi konferentsii*. Moscow: VGIK, 2006.

—. *Prostranstvo vozmozhnostei i dialog tsivilizatsii. Materialy III mezhdunarodnoi nauchno-prakticheskoi konferentsii "Animatsiia kak fenomen kul'tury"*. Moscow: VGIK, 2007.

—. *Animatsiia v epokhu innovatsionnykh transformatsii. Materialy III mezhdunarodnoi nauchno-prakticheskoi konferentsii "Animatsiia kak fenomen kul'tury"*. Moscow: VGIK, 2008.

Krylov, Andrei et al. (ed.). *N. Re-mi, B. Malakhovskii, V. Deni. Mastera sovetskoi karikatury. Stranitsy istorii sovetskoi satiricheskoi grafiki*. Moscow: Sovetskii Khudozhnik, 1985.

Kukulin, I, M. Lipovetskii and M. Maiofis. *Veselye chelovechki: Kul'turnye geroi sovetskogo detstva. Sb. Statei*. Moscow: Novoe Literaturnoe obozrenie, 2008.

Kurchevskaia, Marina. "Khudozhnik-postanovshchik". *Iskusstvo kino* 9 (1985): 59–61.

Kurchevskii, Vadim. *Izobrazitel'noe reshenie mul'tiplikatsionnogo fil'ma. O prirode groteska i metafory*. Moscow: VGIK, 1986.

—. "Ozhivshii mir khudozhnika". *Iskusstvo kino* 11 (1985): 60–63.

Kurlyandsky, Alexander. "Millions On Cartoons". *Soviet Film* 9 (1990): 38–39.

Kurs, Aleksandr. "Skazka o tsare Durandae. Kinostsenarii (mul'tiplikatsiia). (Publikatsiia A. Ia. Bernshteina)". *Kinovedcheskie zapiski* 52 (2001): 171–185.

Kushnirov, M. "Boevoi kinosbornik N°...". *Iskusstvo kino* 2 (1967): 15–17.

Kutsnutdinova, Roza. "Dom, kotoryi postroil Andrei". *Sovetskii ekran* 2 (1988): 6–8.

Kuz'ma, O. "Zadachi mul'tiplikatsii v kino". *Sovetskoe kino* 2–3 (1925): 56–60.

Kuznetsov, E., and V. Kuznetsova. *Tsekhanovskii*. Leningrad: Izdatel'stvo "Khudozhnik RSFSR", 1973.

Kuznetsova, E. "Prazdnik risovannogo fil'ma". *Iskusstvo kino* 1 (1958): 124–126.

Kuznetsova, V. "Mul'tiplikatsionnoe kino v Leningrade". In *Iz istorii Lenfil'ma. Stat'i, vospominaniia, dokumenty 1920-e gody. Vypusk 2*. Ed. N.S. Gornitskaia. Leningrad: Izdatel'stvo "Iskusstvo" Leningradskoe otdelenie, 1970. 200–202.

Lagina, Natal'ia. "Mul'tipliktsiia: lirika i epos". *Iskusstvo kino* 11 (1971): 82–87.

Lagorio, A. "Mul'tiplikatornaia s"emka". *Kino zhurnal ARK* 3 (1925): 9–11.

Lander, I., A. Petrov, and S. Kim. *Sny i real'nost' Aleksandra Petrova. Personal'naia vystavka v Muzee kino*. Moscow: Muzei Kino, 2002.

Larina, Iuliia. "Krasno-belo-goluboi ogonek". *Ogonek* December, 26 2005-January, 1 2006, http://www.ogoniok.com/4926/2/

Lazarev, P. "200 let nauchnoi raboty v Rossii – na ekrane". *Kino-zhurnal* 8 (1925): 13.

Leiborn, Kit. "Animatsionnaia kniga". *Kinovedcheskie zapiski* 73 (2005): 137–203.

Lekomtseva, M. "Nekotorye osobennosti semioticheskoi struktury mul'tiplikatsii". In *Problemy sinteza v khudozhestvennoi kul'ture*. Eds. Anatoly Prokhorov, B. Raushenbakh and Fedor Khitruk. Moscow: Nauka, 1985. 57–66.

Leyda, Jay. *Eisenstein on Disney*. Trans. Alan Upchurch. London: Methuen, 1988.

—. *Kino: a history of the Russian and Soviet film*. 1st Collier Books ed. New York: Collier Books, 1973.

Lissitzky, El. *For Two Squares*. Berlin: Skythen, 1922.

—. "The Topography of Typography". *Merzhefte* 4 (1923).

—. "Typographical Facts" (1925).

Lissitzky, El, and Vladimir Maiakovskii. *Dlia golosa*. Berlin: Gosizdat RSFSR, 1923.

Lotman, Iurii. "Fenomen kul'tury". In *Izbrannye stat'i v trekh tomakh*, vol. 1. Tallin: Aleksandra, 1992. 34–45.

—. "O iazyke mul'tiplikatsionnykh fil'mov". In *Ob iskusstve*. St. Petersburg: Iskusstvo, 1998. 671–674.

—. "The Semiosphere". Trans. Ann Shukman. In *Universe of the Mind: A Semiotic Theory of Culture*. London: I.B. Tauris & Co. Ltd., 1990. 123–214.

—. *Universe of the Mind: A Semiotic Theory of Culture*. London: I.B. Tauris & Co. Ltd., 1990.

—. "Vnutri mysliashchikh mirov". In *Semiosfera*. St. Petersburg: Iskusstvo-SPB, 2001. 150–390.

Lukinykh, Nataliia. "Animator bez raboty, mul'tfil'm bez kreativa, strana - bez oskara". In *Katalog-al'manakh. Otkrytyi Rossiiskii festival' animatsionnogo kino Tarusa 2001*. Berezovaia Roshcha: Izdanie otkrytogo rossiiskogo festivalia animatsionnogo kino, 2001. 113–117.

—. "Animatory vsekh stran, odushevliaites'!" In *Territoriia kino. Postsovetskoe desiatiletie. Kino stran SNG, Latvii, Litvy, Estonii*. Ed. Elena Stishova. Moscow: Pomatur, 2001. 348–369.

—. "Animatsiia novogo veka – traditsii, emotsiii, zagadki". *Kinoforum* 2 (2002): 26–30.

—. "Ei, skazka, kto v tereme zhivet?" *Iskusstvo kino* 6 (1996): 44–46.

—. "Kukly iz strany s vkusnym zapakhom". In *Katalog-al'manakh. Otkrytyi rossiiskii festival' animatsionnogo kino Suzdal' 2002*. Suzdal': Izdanie otkrytogo rossiiskogo festivalia animatsionnogo kino, 2002. 101–102.

—. "The master's *Greatcoat*: Will Yuri Norstein finish his new film?" *Soviet Film* 2 (1990): 38–39.

—. "Millenium i re-animatsiia. O geroiakh i tvortsakh novoi animatsii stran SNG i Baltii". In *Katalog-al'manakh. Otkrytyi rossiiskii festival' animatsionnogo kino Suzdal' 2002*. Suzdal': Izdanie otkrytogo rossiiskogo festivalia animatsionnogo kino, 2002. 95–97.

—. "Novoe puteshestvie iz Peterburga v Moskvu, ili 'Krok-2002' kak zerkalo prob i oshibok v mirovoi animatsii". In *Katalog-al'manakh. Otkrytyi rossiiskii festival' animatsionnogo kino Suzdal' 2003*. Suzdal': Izdanie otkrytogo rossiiskogo festivalia animatsionnogo kino, 2003. 112–119.

—. "Re-animatsiia animatsii". *Kinoforum* (2002): 41–48.

—. "Virtual'noe puteshestvie iz Peterburga v Moskvu". *Kinoforum* 1 (2003): 34–38.

—. "Zima nashikh nadezhd, ili Rossiiskie animatory pered novoi vstrechei v Taruse". In *Katalog-al'manakh. Otkrytyi Rossiiskii festival' animatsionnogo kino Tarusa 2000*. Berezovaia Roshcha: Izdanie otkrytogo rossiiskogo festivalia animatsionnogo kino, 2000. 111–115.

Léger, Fernand. "Zhivopis' i kino". *Sovetskii ekran* 37 (1927): 5.

MacFadyen, David. *Yellow Crocodiles and Blue Oranges: Russian Animated Film Since World War Two*. Montreal: McGill-Queen's University Press, 2005.

Macheret, Aleksandr, and Nina Glagoleva. *Sovetskie khudozhestvennye fil'my: Annotirovannyi katalog*. Vol. 1–4. Moscow: Iskusstvo, 1968.

Maevskii, E. "Neizbezhnost' fantomnogo mira (Kompiuter i dal'nie perspektivy kinematografa)". In *Mul'tiplikatsiia, animatograf, fantomatika*. Kiev: Izdanie Pervogo Vsesoiuznogo Festivalia mul'tiplikatsionnykh fil'mov "Krok-89", 1989. 5–14.

Maiakovskii, Vladimir V. *Izbrannye sochineniia v dvukh tomakh*, 2 vols. Moscow: Khudozhestvennaia literatura, 1981.

—. *Polnoe sobranie sochinenii: v trinadtsati tomakh*. 13 vols. Moscow: Gosudatstvennoe izdatelstvo khudozhestvennoi literatury, 1955–1961.

Maiorov, N. A. "A do voiny oni byli tsvetnymi". *Tekhnika i tekhnologii kino* 27 (2010): 18–22.

—. "Pervye v animatsii". *Mir tekhniki kino* 13 (2009): 39–48.

Maisetti, Massimo. *Chiodi, nodi, burattini. Cinema d'animazione in Estonia, Lettonia e Lituania*. Milano: ISCA, 1987.

—. *Dall'Icona al Film. Il cinema di animazione in Ucraina*. Milano: ISCA, 1984.

—. *I maestri di Mosca. Il cinema d'animazione russo dagli inizi ad oggi*. Milano: ISCA, 1988.

—. "Il cinema di animazione sovietico". *Letture* June-July 1989: 487–506.

—. *Iurij Norstein. Il poeta*. Milano: ISCA, 1988.

—. *Lilit e gli argonauti. Cinema di animazione in Armenia e Georgia*. Milano: ISCA, 1986.

—. "A lot of surprises". *Soviet Film* 2 (1989): 34–35.

—. *Mille e una fiaba dall'asia centrale. Il cinema d'animazione in Kazakhstan, Kirghizia, Tadgikistan, Turkmenia, Uzbekistan*. Milano: ISCA, 1985.

Makarova, Ania. "O Brat'iakh Pilotakh, okhotnikakh i probegaiushchikh sushchestvakh". *Harpers Bazaar* 11–12 (1996): 101–106.

Maksimov, Ivan. "'Kak v detskoi igre'". *Iskusstvo kino* 3 (1997): 73–75.

Maliantovich, Kirill. "Animatory 'Soiuzmul'tfil'ma'". *Kinovedcheskie zapiski* 81 (2007): 168–201.

—. "Iz zapisok starogo mul'tiplikatora (Predislovie i kommentarii G. Borodina)". *Kinograf* 11 (2002): 229–254.

—. "Kak borolis' s 'kosmopolitami' na 'Soiuzmul'tfil'me'". *Kinovedcheskie zapiski* 52 (2001): 191–197.

—. "Kak na 'Soiuzmul'tfil'me' poluchal Stalinskuiu premiiu". *Kinograf* 9 (2000): 168–174.

Maliukova, Larisa. "Figaro zdes'". *Iskusstvo kino* 6 (1996): 46–48.

—. "Fil'my, kotorye postroil Bronzit". *Iskusstvo kino* 9 (1999): 63–69.

—. "Igrushechnye istorii Marii Muat". *Iskusstvo kino* 6 (2003): 69–75.

—. "Kuda idem my s piatachkom". *Iskusstvo kino* 6 (1996): 29–35.

—. "Padal proshlogodnii sneg". In *Katalog. Otkrytie Rossiskogo Festivalia animatsionnogo kino*. Tarusa: Izdanie otkrytogo rossiiskogo festivalia animatsionnogo kino, 1997. 69–71.

—. "Razgovor poetov o kinotorgovle". *Iskusstvo kino* 6 (2003): 4–22.

—. "Zolushka 'Tarusa'". In *Katalog-al'manakh. Otkrytyi Rossiiskii festival' animatsionnogo kino Tarusa 1998*. Berezovaia Roshcha: Izdanie otkrytogo rossiiskogo festivalia animatsionnogo kino, 1998. 90–92.

—. "Zolushka, ili kartinki s vystavki". *Iskusstvo kino* 8 (2004): 96–103.

Margolina, Irina and Natal'ia Lozinskaia, eds. *Nashi mul'tfil'my. Litsa, kadry, eskizy, geroi, vospominaniia, interv'iu, stat'i, esse*. Moscow: Interros, 2006.

Mar'iamov, A. "Posle *Bani*". *Iskusstvo kino* 10 (1962): 55–60.

Martin, François. *Ladislav Starewitch: Magicien des ciné-marionnettes*. Paris: Afca, L'équipée, Forum des images, 2003.

Maskina, Natalia. "Tale of Good and Evil". *Soviet Film* 11 (1981): 24–25.

—. "We Hope It'll Be a Lucky Start". *Soviet Film* 3 (1989): 38.

Melkonyan, Dolores. "A Landscape with Junipers". *Soviet Film* 6 (1988): 34–35.

Mercier, Emilie. "Post-Analyse du film de M. Zechanovsky 1929". School of Applied arts, Gobelins, 1990.

Merkulov, Iu. "Koe-chto o Bratishkine". *Sovetskii Ekran* 49 (1928): 7.

—. "Mul'tiplikatsionnyi typazh". *Sovetskii ekran* 31 (1927): 6.

—. "O politsharzhakh". *Sovetskii Ekran* 17 (1927): 5.

—. "Ob"emnaia mul'tiplikatsiia". *Sovetskii Ekran* 28 (1927): 3.

"Metodicheskie ukazaniia k uchebnoi programme po distsipline 'Tekhnika odushevleniia'". *Kinovedcheskie zapiski* 73 (2005): 129–133.

Migunov, Evgenii. "Dezhkin: Kakoi on byl". In *Katalog-al'manakh. Otkrytyi Rossiiskii festival' animatsionnogo kino Tarusa 1999*. Berezovaia Roshcha: Izdanie otkrytogo rossiiskogo festivalia animatsionnogo kino, 1999. 121–127.

—. "Ia – kosmopolit? (Publikatsiia, predislovie i kommentarii G.N. Borodina)". *Kinovedcheskie zapiski* 52 (2001): 197–205.

—. "Iz vospominanii (Predislovie i publikatsiia G. Borodina)". *Kinograf* 8 (2000): 152–168.

—. "Iz vospominanii (Publikatsiia G. Borodina)". *Kinograf* 10 (2001): 138–158.

—. "Iz vospominanii (Publikatsiia G. Borodina)". *Kinograf* 18 (2007): 188–230.

—. "'Novatorom dostaetsia ne tol'ko po golove...' Zamechaniia o perestroike tvorcheskogo protsessa, 1959". *Kinovedcheskie zapiski* 80 (2006): 188–191.

—. "O Khitruke". In *Katalog-al'manakh. Suzdal' 2002*. Suzdal': Otkrytyi rossiiskii festival' animatsionnogo kino, 2002. 113–120.

—. "O L.I. Mil'chine: Fragmenty zapisok 'O, ob i pro'". In *Katalog-al'manakh. Otkrytyi Rossiiskii festival' animatsionnogo kino Tarusa 2000*. Berezovaia Roshcha: Izdanie otkrytogo rossiiskogo festivalia animatsionnogo kino, 2000. 125–128.

—. "O Romane Davydove: Fragmenti zapisok 'O, ob i pro'". In *Katalog-al'manakh. Otkrytyi Rossiiskii festival' anim. kino Tarusa 2001*. Berezovaia Roshcha: Izdanie otkrytogo rossiiskogo festivalia animatsionnogo kino, 2001. 133–135.

—. "O, ob i pro. Alma-Ata: Studencheskie gody (1941–1943) (Publikatsiia, predislovie i kommentarii G.N. Borodina)". *Kinovedcheskie zapiski* 62 (2003): 276–301.

—. "O, ob i pro. VGIK, 1939-i i drugie gody (Publikatsiia, predislovie i kommentarii G. N. Borodina)". *Kinovedcheskie zapiski* 68 (2004): 324–362.

—. "Ob uslovnosti (Fragment iz esse 'Gde zhivet Baba-Iaga?')". In *Katalog-al'manakh. Suzdal' 2003*. Suzdal': VIII otkrytyi rossiiskii festival' animatsionnogo kino, 2003. 120–135.

—. "Rabota v kukol'noi mul'tiplikatsii (Publikatsiia, predislovie i kommentarii G. Borodina)". *Kinovedcheskie zapiski* 73 (2005): 310–332.

—. "S tochki zreniia zhivogo pokoinika". In *Katalog-al'manakh. Otkrytyi Rossiiskii festival' animatsionnogo kino Tarusa 1999*. Berezovaia Roshcha: Izdanie otkrytogo rossiiskogo festivalia animatsionnogo kino, 1999. 109–112.

Mikhailov, V. "Nazim Tuliakhodzhaev". *Sovetskii ekran* 17 (1985): 17, 24.

Mikhin, B. "Khudozhnik-chudesnik". *Iskusstvo kino* 8 (1961): 119–126.

"Mirovaia animatsiia: luchshe animatsionnye fil'my i rezhissery". *Kinovedcheskie zapiski* 73 (2005): 213–215.

Moldavskii, Dmitrii. *S Maiakovskim v teatre i kino. Kniga o Sergee Iutkeviche*. Moscow: Vserossiiskoe teatral'noe obshchestvo (VTO), 1975.

Moritz, William. "The Spirit of Genius: Fedor Khitruk". *Animation World Magazine* March 1 (1999), http://www.awn.com/mag/issue3.12/3.12 pages/moritzkhitruk.php3

Muat, Mariia. "Pervaia stat'ia v zhizni ili Kak ia odnazhdy prochla vosem'desiat chetyre stsenariia". In *Katalog-al'manakh. Otkrytyi rossiiskii festival' animatsionnogo kino Suzdal' 2003*. Suzdal': Izdanie otkrytogo rossiiskogo festivalia animatsionnogo kino, 2003. 89–92.

"Mul'tiplikatornaia fil'ma". *Ekran kino-gazety* 7 (1925).

"Mul'tiplikatsiia segodnia". *Iskusstvo kino* 9 (1967): 65–71.

Mul'tiplikatsiia, animatograf, fantomatika. Kiev: Izdanie Pervogo Vsesoiuznogo Festivalia mul'tiplikatsionnykh fil'mov "Krok-89", 1989.

N., N. Iu. "Raznovidnosti mul'tiplikatsionnoi tekhniki". *Kino Front* 4 (1927): 23–25.

Nazarov, Eduard. "Dom na Kaliaevskoi". *Iskusstvo kino* 6 (1996): 40–43.

—. "Four Days in Shangai". *Soviet Film* 4 (1989): 39.

Nechai, O., and T. Ratnikov. *Osnovy kino-iskusstva*. Minsk: Vysheishaia shkola, 1978.

Neporozhnaia, Ol'ga. "Peizazh s Fellini". *Iskusstvo kino* 7 (1997): 76–80.

Nikitkina, Elena. "Challenging Stereotypes". *Soviet Film* 12 (1988): 34–35.

—. "Encounter with a classic". *Soviet Film* 10 (1988): 28–29.

—. "Having a Good Laugh at the Stereotypes". *Soviet Film* 5 (1989): 38.

—. "The Searches of Debutants, or Six-Armed Kele and a Landfish". *Soviet Film* 8 (1989): 38–39.

—. "Problema geroia v sovremennoi sovetskoi mul'tiplikatsii". Diss. VGIK, 1987.

—. "Soiuzmul'tfil'm pokazyvaet". *Sovetskii ekran* 4 (1984): 11.

—. "Sotsial'no-nravstvennaia problematika i novyi geroi v sovetskoi mul'tiplikatsii 70–80-x godov". In *Sovetskii mnogonatsional'nyi kinematograf na sovremennom etape. Sbornik nauchnykh trudov*. Moscow: VGIK, 1983. 61–72.

—. "The Third Return of the Prodigal Parrot". *Soviet Film* 4 (1989): 38.

—. "Unusual Adventures in the World of Knowledge". *Soviet Film* 12 (1979): 30–31.

Norshtein, Iurii. "Dvizhenie". *Iskusstvo kino* 4 (1989): 107–121.

—. "Dvizhenie". *Iskusstvo kino* 10 (1988): 103–116.

—. "From the Incredible to the Inspired". *Soviet Film* 4 (1987): 30–32.

—. "Igol'chatii ekran". *Iskusstvo kino* 4 (1993): 113–121.

—. *La genèse d'un film*. Paris: L'Association pour la Promotion des Arts a l'Hôtel de Ville de Paris, 2001.

—. "La genèse d'un film". *AnimeLand* July–August 2001: 32–34.

—. "Lektsii dlia slushatelei Vysshikh stsenarnykh i rezhisserskikh kursov Goskino SSSR. Lektsia 1". In *Animatograficheskie zapiski*. Vol. 1. Moscow: Animatograficheskii tsentr "Pilot", 1991. 18–31.

—. "Metafory". *Iskusstvo kino* 7 (1994): 109–118.

—. "Metafory". *Iskusstvo kino* 8 (1994): 92–104.

—. "Neskol'ko slov o Kerolain Lif". *Kinovedcheskie zapiski* 73 (2005): 212.

—. "'On vnes inoe ponimanie izobrazheniia'". *Kinovedcheskie zapiski* 73 (2005): 90–102.

—. "Ot stsenariia k fil'mu". *Iskusstvo kino* 12 (2001): 124–317.

—. "Priznanie masteru". *Iskusstvo kino* 8 (1987): 74–78.

—. "Sneg na trave". *Iskusstvo kino* 9 (1999): 102–110.

—. "Sneg na trave". *Iskusstvo kino* 10 (1999): 98–109.

—. "Sneg na trave". *Iskusstvo kino* 9 (2001): 118–135.

—. "Sneg na trave". *Iskusstvo kino* 11 (2001): 108–128.

—. "Sneg na trave". *Iskusstvo kino* 5 (2002): 74–93.

—. "Sneg na trave". *Iskusstvo kino* 8 (2002): 94–115.

—. "Sneg na trave". *Iskusstvo kino* 1 (2003): 127–143.

—. "Sneg na trave". *Iskusstvo kino* 2 (2003): 132–144.

—. "Sneg na trave". *Iskusstvo kino* 3 (2003): 109–125.

—. "Sneg na trave". *Iskusstvo kino* 7 (2003): 102–116.

—. "Sneg na trave". *Iskusstvo kino* 8 (2003): 94–107.

—. *Sneg na trave*. 2 vols. Moscow: Izdatel'stvo "Krasnaia ploshad'", 2008.

—. *Sneg na trave. Glavy iz knigi*. Moskva: VGIK, 2005.

—. "Tainy animatsii, ili kak delaetsia *Shinel'*". *Kinovedcheskie zapiski* 41 (1999): 106–125.

—. "Tuda, V zaoblachnuiu kel'iu". *Kinovedcheskie zapiski* 40 (1998): 173–182.

—. "V pote litsa". *Iskusstvo kino* 12 (2000): 31–35.

—. "Vse eto bylo by smeshno". *Iskusstvo kino* 10 (1991): 136–147.

—. "Vse skazki nachinaiutsa s odnazhdy". *Kino Stsenarii* 6 (2000): 130–157.

—. "Zanovo otyskat' prostotu". *Iskusstvo kino* 3 (1997): 76–79.

Norshtein, Iurii, and M. Iampol'skii. "Za vidimoi kartinkoi na ekrane". In *Problemy sinteza v khudozhestvennoi kul'ture*. Eds. Anatoly Prokhorov, B. Raushenbakh, and Fedor Khitruk. Moscow: Nauka, 1985. 149–154.

Norshtein, Iurii, and Francheska Iarbusova. *Skazka skazok*. Moscow: Izdatel'stvo Krasnaia Ploshchad', 2005.

Norshtein, Iurii, and Francheska Iarbusova. "Razgovor, kotorogo ne bylo". *Iskusstvo kino* 3 (1977): 52–69.

"Novaia mul'tiplikatsiia". *Sovetskii ekran* 50 (1927): 14.

Nusinova, Nataliia. "Chas volshebstva. V studii L. Starevicha". *Kinovedcheskie zapiski* 52 (2001): 264–266.

——. "Volshebnik iz Fontenè". *Kinovedcheskie zapiski* 52 (2001): 259–264.

"O zamysle fil'ma M. Tsekhanovskogo 'Pamiat' o Lenine'". In *Iz istorii Lenfil'ma. Stat'i, vospominaniia, dokumenty 1920-e gody. Vypusk 2*. Ed. N.S. Gornitskaia. Leningrad: Izdatel'stvo "Iskusstvo" Leningradskoe otdelenie, 1970. 212–214.

"Obsuzhdenie tvorcheskikh problem mul'tiplikatsionnogo kino". *Iskusstvo kino* 1 (1959): 28.

Olifirenko, Sergei. "'Moi kukly pokhozhi na menia'". *Iskusstvo kino* 3 (1997): 80–81.

Orlov, Aleksei. "An Un-mythical Myth". *Soviet Film* 7 (1990): 38–39.

——. "AniFreud. Freidistskaia simvolika v animatsionnom kino". *Kinovedcheskie zapiski* 52 (2001): 216–324.

——. "Animated Cartoons in Troitse-Sergiyeva Lavra". *Soviet Film* 8 (1990): 36.

——. *Animatograf i ego anima*. Biblioteka animatografica. Moscow: Impeto, 1995.

——. "Animatsiia tret'ego tysiacheletiia: Veianie tikhogo vetra. Mozaika iz vos'mi fil'mov v zhanre zametok i sobesedovanii". *Kinovedcheskie zapiski* 52 (2001): 27–48.

——. "Attraktivnost' kinoestetiki avangarda v ee klassicheskom ismerenii (Mul'tiplikatsiia Normana Mak-Larena)". In *Mul'tiplikatsiia, animatograf, fantomatika*. Kiev: Izdanie Pervogo Vsesoiuznogo Festivalia mul'tiplikatsionnykh fil'mov "Krok-89", 1989. 60–106.

——. "Comics: It's the First Step that is Difficult". *Soviet Film* 12 (1988): 34–35.

——. "Fantaziia na temu russkikh narodnykh skazok". In *Katalog-al'manakh. Otkrytyi Rossiiskii festival' animatsionnogo kino Tarusa 1999*. Berezovaia Roshcha: Izdanie otkrytogo rossiiskogo festivalia animatsionnogo kino, 1999.

——. "Lift-off: New Cartoon Studio 'Pilot'". *Soviet Film* 11 (1989): 38–39.

——. "Luchshaia v mire 'Skazka skazok'". In *Animatograf i ego anima*. Moskva: Impeto, 1995. 227–253.

——. "Manifest-2000: Tezisy o tekushchem momente. Analiz sostoianiia i perspektiv rossiiskoi animatsii". In *Katalog-al'manakh. Otkrytyi Rossiiskii festival' animatsionnogo kino Tarusa 2000*. Berezovaia Roshcha: Izdanie otkrytogo rossiiskogo festivalia animatsionnogo kino, 2000. 120–122.

——. *Metodicheskie rekomendatsii po kursu. Esteticheskie problemy sovremennoi mul'tiplikatsii*. Moscow: Gosudarstvennyi komitet SSSR po kinematografii. Kursy povysheniia kvalifikatsii tvorcheskikh i rukovodiashchikh rabotnikov kinematografii pri VGIKe, 1987.

——. "Mul'tiplikatsionnyi fil'm i psikhologiia podrostka". In *Kino detiam. Kino-molodezhi*. Vol. 3. Moscow: Soiuzinformkino, 1989. 28–35.

——. "Non-camera story". *Soviet Film* 11 (1990): 38–39.

——. "Stories, tales, myth". *Soviet Film* 12 (1987): 30–31.

——. "Tra Disney e Zagabria. Le peculiarità stilistiche nell'animazione dell'Est-Europa". In *Animania. 100 anni di esperimenti nel cinema d'animazione*. Ed. Bruno Di Marino. Pesaro: Editrice Il Castoro, 1998. 55–62.

——. "Tsaplia i zhuravl' Iuriia Noshteina. Polemicheskie zametki o khudozhestvennykhsredstvakh sozdaniia kharaktera personazha". In *Katalog-al'manakh. Otkrytyi rossiiskii festival' animatsionnogo kino. Suzdal'*, 2002. Berezovaia Roshcha: Izdanie otkrytogo rossiiskogo festivalia animatsionnogo kino, 2002. 103–110.

—. *Virtual'naia real'nost'*. Moscow: Biblioteka animatographica, 1998.

Oster, Grigorii. "Everything Unknown Is Terribly Interesting". *Soviet Film* 12 (1977): 44.

Pal'dis, Riina. "Chetyre fil'ma Priita Piarna". *Kinovedcheskie zapiski* 52 (2001): 244–258.

Paporova. "Chudo mul'tiplikatsii". *Kul'tura i zhizn'* 6 (1973): 24.

Paramanova, Kira. "Both Entertaining and Serious". *Soviet Film* 8 (1975): 13.

Pashchenko, Mstislav. "Pis'mo M.S. Pashchenko E.A. Gailan (Publikatsiia i predislovie P. Bagrova)". *Kinovedcheskie zapiski* 73 (2005): 255–256.

Pavlov, Boris. "Animation in the 'Russian Hollywood' of the 1920–1930s". *Animation Journal* 6.2 (1998): 16–27.

—. "Gibel' 'imperiia dobra' pod oblomkami 'imperii zla'". In *Katalog-al'manakh. Otkrytyi Rossiiskii festival' animatsionnogo kino Tarusa 1998*. Berezovaia Roshcha: Izdanie otkrytogo rossiiskogo festivalia animatsionnogo kino, 1998. 126–129.

Pek, Liudmila. "Novoe prochtenie skazki". *Iskusstvo kino* 10 (1970): 39–43.

"Perepiska N. P. Khodataeva i M.M. Tsekhanovskogo (Publikatsiia S. Kim, predislovie G. Borodina)". *Kinovedcheskie zapiski* 73 (2005): 235–237.

Perloff, Marjorie. *The Futurist Moment: Avant-Garde, Avant Guerre, and the Language of Rupture*. Chicago: University of Chicago Press, 1986.

Petrov, Aleksandr. "'Ia ne mogu skazat', chto stanovlius' umnee s kazhdym fil'mom'". *Kinovedcheskie zapiski* 52 (2001): 49–58.

Petrov, Aleksandr, and Mikhail Tumelia. "Nauka udivliat'". *Kinovedcheskie zapiski* 73 (2005): 103–122.

Petrovich, Ivan. *Ivanov-Vano. 110 let so dnia rozhdeniia*. Moscow: VGIK, 2010.

Petrushevskaia, Liudmila. "Director Yury Norstein". *Soviet Film* 7 (1986): 8–9, 11.

—. "*Shinel'*. Po povesti N.V. Gogolia". *Iskusstvo kino* 2 (1985): 81–88.

Petrushevskaia, Liudmila, and Iurii Norshtein. "Ot stsenariia k fil'mu. Stsenarii L. Petrushevskoi, pri uchastii Iu. Norshteina". *Iskusstvo kino* 2 (1985): 81–98.

Politicheskaia tema v mul'tiplikatsionnom kino. (Stenogramma dvustoronnego simpoziuma mul'tiplikatorov SSSR i GDR). Moscow: Soiuz kinematografistov SSSR, 1973.

Pontieri Hlavacek, Laura. "Russian Animated Films of the 1960s as a Reflection of the Thaw: Ambiguities and Violation of Boundaries in *Story of a Crime*". *Studies in Russian and Soviet Cinema* 3, no. 1 (2009): 53–70.

—. Review of *About Ivan the Fool* (*Pro Ivana Duraka*), directed by M. Aldashin, O. Uzhinov, 2005. *Kinokultura* 11 (2006). http://www.kinokultura.com/2006/11r-ivanfool.shtml

Popesku-Gopo, Ion. "Obshchnost' nashikh tselei". *Iskusstvo kino* 5 (1976): 50–51.

Pravda."Sumbur vmesto muzyki". *Pravda*, 28 January 1936.

"Privet druz'iam!" *Iskusstvo kino* 7 (1957): 9–16.

Programma kursa. Esteticheskie problemy sovremennoi mul'tiplikatsii. Moscow: Gosudarstvennii komitet SSSR po kinematografii. Kursy povysheniia kvalifikatsii tvorcheskikh i rukovodiashchikh rabotnikov kinematografii pri VGIKe, 1987.

Prokhorov, Anatoly. "Animatograph. A Vague Yet Outrageous Prospect". *Soviet Film* 6 (1990): 38–39.

—. "Evolutsiia animatografa: ot mul'tiplikatsii k 'fantomu svobody'". In *Mul'tiplikatsiia, animatograf, fantomatika*. Kiev: Izdanie Pervogo Vsesoiuznogo Festivalia mul'tiplikatsionnykh fil'mov "Krok-89", 1989. 31–59.

—. "Krushenie kinoimperii ili udar po liubimym mozgam". In *Mul'tiplikatsiia, animatograf, fantomatika*. Kiev: Izdanie Pervogo Vsesoiuznogo Festivalia mul'tiplikatsionnykh fil'mov "Krok-89", 1989. 115–121.

—. "O vyrazitel'noi podvizhnosti risunka". In *Problemy sinteza v khudozhestvennoi kul'ture*. Eds. Anatoly Prokhorov, B. Raushenbakh and Fedor Khitruk. Moscow: Nauka, 1985. 42–56.

—. "Vvedenie. Animatograf v kontekste ekrannoi kul'tury". In *Animatograficheskie zapiski*. Vol. 1. Moscow: Animatograficheskii tsentr "Pilot", 1991. 5–17.

Prokhorov, Anatoly, Fedor Khitruk, and B. Raushenbakh eds. *Problemy sinteza v khudozhestvennoi kul'ture*. Moscow: Nauka, 1985.

Prytkov, Iurii. "Mu i shutochki!" In *Katalog-al'manakh. Otkrytyi rossiiskii festival' animatsionnogo kino Suzdal' 2003*. Suzdal': Izdanie otkrytogo rossiiskogo festivalia animatsionnogo kino, 2003. 146–155.

Ptushko, A. "Detskaia fil'ma i mul'tiplikatsiia". *Sovetskii Ekran* 16 (1928): 4.

—. "K proizvodstvu mul'tiplikatsionnoi fil'my". *Kino i kul'tura* 2 (1929): 43–46.

—. *Mul'tiplikatsiia fil'my*. Moscow: Gosudarstvennoe izdatel'stvo khudozhestvennoi literatury, 1931.

—. "Ob"emnaia mul'tiplikatsiia". In *Mul'tiplikatsionnyi fil'm*. Moscow: Kinofotoizdat, 1936. 197–256.

Rachuk, M. *Tvoi bol'shoi drug*. Moscow: Molodaia gvardiia, 1965.

Rakitina, E. *Zhanrovoe mnogoobrazie i khudozhestvennii iazyk sovremennoi mul'tiplikatsii*. Kino i vremia. Informatsionno-metodicheskii sbornik. Vol. 1. Moscow: Soiuz Kinematografistov SSSR. Biuro propagandy sovetskogo kinoiskusstva, 1972.

Rappaport, A. "Pul'siruiushchee bytie (zametki o mul'tfil'makh-animatsiiakh Normana Mak-Larena)". In *Mul'tiplikatsiia, animatograf, fantomatika*. Kiev: Izdanie Pervogo Vsesoiuznogo Festivalia mul'tiplikatsionnykh fil'mov "Krok-89", 1989. 15–30.

—. "Pul'siruiushchee bytie: Zametki o mul'tifil'makh-animatsiiakh Normana Mak-Larena". *Kinovedcheskie zapiski* 52 (1989): 206–215.

—. "Tsentr i periferiia". In *Animatograficheskie zapiski*. Vol. 1. Moscow: Animatograficheskii tsentr "Pilot", 1991. 33–60.

—. "Zhest i prostranstvo v iskusstve mul'tiplikatsii". In *Problemy sinteza v khudozhestvennoi kul'ture*. Eds. Anatoly Prokhorov, B. Raushenbakh and Fedor Khitruk. Moscow: Nauka, 1985. 67–75.

Raushrova, Gelena. "Ekran rebiach'ikh grez". *Sotsialisticheskaia chekhoslovakia* 10 (1985): 16–17.

"Razbory i razmyshleniia. Shkola iziashchnogo iskusstva". *Iskusstvo kino* 6 (1996): 20–28.

Redovich, A. "Neskol'ko tezisov o zhiznepodobii". In *Mul'tiplikatsiia, animatograf, fantomatika*. Kiev: Izdanie Pervogo Vsesoiuznogo Festivalia mul'tiplikatsionnykh fil'mov "Krok-89", 1989. 1–4.

Romanenko, A. P., ed. *Kogda Luna vmeste s solntsem*. Moscow: TID Kontinent-Press, 2002.

Romanov, Al. "*Fitil'* – pravoflangovyi satiricheskogo tsekha". *Iskusstvo kino* 7 (1972): 40–44.

Roshchin, Nikolai. "V volshebnom tsarstve (pis'mo iz Parizha) (Publikatsiia i kommentarii N. I. Nusinovoi)". *Kinovedcheskie zapiski* 52 (2001): 267–270.

Roth-Ey, Kristin Joy. "Mass Media and the Remaking of Soviet Culture 1950s–1960s". Diss. Princeton University, 2003.

Ruland, Bob. "Kino-plakat v povestku dnia". *Kino-nedelia* 18 (1924): 7.

"Satiricheskii kinozhurnal *Diatel*'". *Iskusstvo kino* 9 (1959): 98.

Sazonov, Anatolii. *Izobrazitel'naia kompozitsiia i rezhisserskaia raskadrovka risovannogo fil'ma*. Moscow: Vsesoiuznyi gosudarstvennyi institut kinematografii nauchno-issledovatel'skii kabinet, 1960.

—-. "Izobrazitel'naia vzaimosviaz' personazha i dekoratsii v risovannom fil'me. Avtoreferat". Abstract. VGIK, 1953.

—-. *Personazh risovannogo fil'ma*. Moskva: VGIK, 1959.

Segel', Iakov. "Idem v skazku". *Iskusstvo kino* 1 (1970): 61–64.

Serebriakov, Nikolai, and A. Petrov. "Prizes for Soviet Cartoons". *Soviet Film* 9 (1977): 24.

Serebrovskii, V. "Sergei Alimov". In *Sovetskie khudozhniki teatra i kino*. Ed. V.N. Kuleshova. Vol. 77/78. Moscow: Sovetskii khudozhnik, 1980. 76–84.

Seregin, Sergei. "Mstislav Pashchenko. Fragmenty zaiavki na nesostoiavshiisia dokumental'nyi videofil'm". In *Katalog-al'manakh. Suzdal' 2002*. Suzdal': Otkrytyi rossiiskii festival' animatsionnogo kino, 2002. 139–140.

Seregin, Sergei and O. Potemkina. "Ostorozhno-detskii seans!" In *Kino detiam. Kino-molodezhi*. Vol. 3. Moscow: Soiuzinformkino, 1989. 10–14.

Shafranok, V.A. *Poniatie o kuklakh-akterakh i traditsionnye zabluzhdeniia*. Moskva: STELS, 2001.

Sharman, Leslie Felperin. "Down the White Road". *Sight & Sound* 37 (1994): 20–21.

"Sharzhi v kino". *Sovetskii ekran* 49 (1927): 14.

Shatunovskii, I. "Sto shagov 'Fitilia'". *Iskusstvo kino* 12 (1970): 71–80.

Shilova, Irina. *I moe kino: Piatidesiatye, shestidisiatye, semidesiatye*. Moscow: NIIK, Kinovedcheskie zapiski, 1993.

Shitova, V. "O svoem dele, o tovarishchakh, o sebe". *Iskusstvo kino* 4 (1977): 104–117.

Shorina, Nina. "Vmesto predisloviia". In *Kino detiam. Kino-molodezhi*. Vol. 3. Moscow: Soiuzinformkino, 1989. 14.

Shostakovich, Dmitrii. "Pis'ma D.D. Shostakovicha M.M. Tsekhanovskomu (Publikatsiia S. Kim, A. S. Deriabina, kommentarii A. S. Deriabina)". *Kinovedcheskie zapiski* 57 (2002): 360–361.

Shpalikov, Gennadii. "Gennadii Shpalikov: Nachalo (Predislovie, publikatsiia i kommentarii E. O. Dolgopiat)". *Kinovedcheskie zapiski* 61 (2002): 231–262.

Shteiner, Evgenii. *Avangard i postroenie novogo cheloveka: Iskusstvo sovetskoi detskoi knigi 1920-kh godov*. Moscow: Novoe literaturnoe obozrenie, 2002.

—. *See also* Steiner, Evgeny.

Shul'ga, Tat'iana. "Shestnadtsat' serii o sovokuplenii. (K voprosu ob obraze zaitsa v mul'tiplikatsionnom seriale *Nu, pogodi!*)". In *Animatograficheskie zapiski. Vypusk 1*. Moscow: Animatograficheskii tsentr "Pilot", 1991.

Shumiatskii, Boris Z. "A Cinema for the Millions (Extracts)". In *The Film Factory: Russian and Soviet Cinema in Documents 1896–1939*. Eds. Richard Taylor and Ian Christie. London: Routledge, 1988. 358–369.

—. *Kinematografiia millionov: opyt analiza*. Moscow: Kinofotoizdat, 1936.

Sidorenko, Mar'iana. "Mnogoseriinaia Bibliia". *Vechernaia Moskva* (1993): 6.

Silant'eva, T. "Sed'moe iskusstvo". *Tvorchestvo* 9 (1967): 15–17.

Sivokon', Evgenii. *Esli vy liubite mul'tiplikatsiiu*. Kiev: Mistetsvo, 1985.

Smirnova, N. "Igraiut kukly". *Iskusstvo kino* 2 (1961): 124–130.

Smolianov, Gennadii. *Anatomiia i sozdanie obraza personazha v animatsionnom fil'me*. Moscow: VGIK, 2005.

—. "Izobrazitel'noe reshenie personazha kukol'nogo fil'ma. Avtoreferat". Abstract. Goskino SSSR Vsesoiuznyi gosudarstvennyi ordena trudovogo krasnogo znameni institut kinematografii, 1984.

—. *Kukol'nyi personazh na s"emochnoi ploshchadke. Uchebnoe posobie*. Moscow: Goskino SSSR. Vsesoiuznyi gosudarstvennyi ordena trudovogo krasnogo znameni institut kinematografii, 1984.

Snesarev, Arkadii. "Miracles Happen Every Day. Visiting Soiuzmul'tfil'm". *Soviet Film* 4 (1974): 32–33.

"Soiuzmul'tfil'm at forty: 'The largest in Europe'". *Soviet Film* 2 (1977): 40–42.

"Soiuzmul'tfil'm otchityvaetsia". *Iskusstvo kino* 3 (1966): 52.

Sokolov, Ippolit. "'Plan velikikh rabot'". *Kino i zhizn'* 10 (1930): 5–6.

—. "Tekhnicheskaia baza Sovetskogo tonkino". *Kino i zhizn'* 12 (1930): 18–19.

Sokolova, Nataliia. "The Nutcracker". *Soviet Film* 2 (1974): 31–32.

—. "Po-leskovski". *Iskusstvo kino* 12 (1964): 16–17.

Solov'eva, Inna. "Strasti pod viazom i viaz". *Iskusstvo kino* 8 (1988): 23–31.

Starr, S. Fredrerick. *Red and Hot: The Fate of Jazz in the Soviet Union 1917–1980*. New York: Limelight Editions, 1985.

Steiner, Evgeny. *Stories for Little Comrades: Revolutionary Artists and the Making of Early Soviet Children's Books*. Seattle: University of Washington Press, 1999.

Stepantsev, Boris. "Mul'tiplikatsiia i zritel'". *Iskusstvo kino* 8 (1981): 85–99.

Stites, Richard. *Russian Popular Culture: Entertainment and Society since 1900*. Cambridge: Cambridge University Press, 1992.

"Stsenarii mul'tfil'ma (konspekt lektsii)". *Kinovedcheskie zapiski* 73 (2005): 134–136.

Suny, Ronald Grigor. *The Soviet Experiment: Russia, the USSR, and the Successor States*. New York: Oxford University Press, 1998.

Sviridova, Irina, ed. *Dmitrii Moor*. Moskva: Sovetskii khudozhnik, 1987.

Svobodin, A. "Soedinenie". *Iskusstvo kino* 10 (1984): 59–63.

Syrkina, F. "Rol' khudozhnika v izobrazitel'nom reshenii mul'tfil'ma". In *O khudozhnikakh teatra, kino i TV*. Ed. V.V. Vanslov. Leningrad: Khudozhnik RSFSR, 1984. 146–163.

—. "Rol' khudozhnika v izobrazitel'nom reshenii mul'tfil'ma". In *Sovetskiie khudozhniki teatra i kino*. Vol. 7. Moscow: Sovetskii khudozhnik, 1986. 170–185.

Tade, Eleonora. "Soyuzmultfilm Studio in 1975". *Soviet Film* 7 (1975): 32.

—. "Viacheslav Kotenochkin: neveroiatno interesnaia professiia". *Sovetskii fil'm* 8 (1975): 32.

Tanaka, Tomoko. "Psikhologicheskoe vremia v kinematografe Iuriia Norshteina". *Kinovedcheskie zapiski* 52 (2001): 235–243.

Tatarskii, Aleksandr. "Fil'my dlia tineidzherov (sekret attraktivnosti mul'tiplikatsii)". In *Kino detiam. Kino-molodezhi*. Vol. 3. Moscow: Soiuzinformkino, 1989. 18–21.

Tatarskii, Aleksandr, and Anatolii Prokhorov. "Sizifov trud". *Iskusstvo kino* 4 (1995): 61–64.

Taylor, Richard, and Ian Christie, eds. *The Film Factory: Russian and Soviet Cinema in Documents 1896–1939*. London and New York: Routledge, 1988.

Tessier, Max. "Le conte des contes". *Revue du Cinéma* 401 (1985): 34.

Thompson, Kristin. "Implications of the Cel Animation Technique". In *The Cinematic Apparatus*. Eds. T. De Lauretis and S. Heath. London: Macmillan, 1980. 106–120.

Thomson, Philip J. *The Grotesque*. The critical idiom, 24. London: Methuen, 1972.

Tiurin, Mikhail. *Katalog vystavki k 70-letiiu so dnia rozhdeniia Arkadiia Tiurina*. Moskva: Gosudarstvennyi literaturyi muzei, 2003.

Todorov, Tzvetan. *The Fantastic: A Structural Approach to a Literary Genre*. Cleveland: Press of Case Western Reserve University, 1973.

Troianovskaia, I. "Samye molodye kinematografisty strany" *Iskusstvo kino* 10 (1978): 84–90.

Troitsky, Artemy. *Back in the USSR: The True Story of Rock in Russia*. London and Boston: Faber and Faber, 1987.

Tsekhanovskaia, Vera. "Nachalo". In *Zhizn' o kino: Veterany o sebe i svoikh tovarishchakh*. Ed. O.T. Nesterovich. Vol. 2. Moscow: Iskusstvo, 1979. 252–267.

—. "O stsenarii M. Tsekhanovskogo 'Pamiat' o Lenine'". In *Iz istorii Lenfil'ma. Stat'i, vospominaniia, dokumenty 1920-e gody. Vypusk 2*. Ed. N.S. Gornitskaia. Leningrad: Izdatel'stvo "Iskusstvo" Leningradskoe otdelenie, 1970. 215–216.

Tsekhanovskii, Mikhail. "Dykhanie voli: Dnevniki Mikhaila Tsekhanovskogo (Publikatsiia Aleksandra Deriabina i Svety Kim)". *Kinovedcheskie zapiski* 54 (2001): 170–211.

—. "Dykhanie voli: Dnevniki Mikhaila Tsekhanovskogo (Publikatsiia Aleksandra Deriabina i Svety Kim)". *Kinovedcheskie zapiski* 55 (2001): 216–273.

—. "Dykhanie voli: Dnevniki Mikhaila Tsekhanovskogo". *Kinovedcheskie zapiski* 57 (2002): 292–350.

—. "Dykhanie voli: Dnevniki Mikhaila Tsekhanovskogo (Publikatsiia Aleksandra Deriabina i Svety Kim)". In *Katalog-al'manakh. Suzdal' 2002*.

Suzdal': Izdanie Otkrytogo Rossiiskogo Festivalia animatsionnogo kino, 2002. 128–138, 216–273.

—-. "Ermitazh: Kul'turfil'm v 2-kh chastiakh (Stsenarii) (Publikatsiia S.M. Ishevskoi, kommentarii A.S. Deriabina)". *Kinovedcheskie zapiski* 63 (2003): 62–74.

—-. "Kino i zhivopis'". *Proletarskoe Kino* 4 (1931): 5–7.

—-. "O zvukovoi risovannoi fil'me". *Kino i zhizn'* 34–35 (1930): 14–16.

—-. "Ot Murzilki k bol'shomu iskusstvu". *Sovetskoe kino* 10 (1934): 20–27.

—-. "Skazka o pope i o rabotnike ego Balde: Kinolubok". *Kinovedcheskie zapiski* 57 (2002): 351–359.

—-. "Spetsifika Tonfil'ma". *Proletarskoe Kino* 12 (1931): 12–19.

Tsivian, Yuri. "The Case of the Bioscope Beetle: Starewicz's Answer to Genetics". *Discourse: Theoretical studies in media and culture* 17 (1995): 119–125.

Tsizin, I. "Fil'my-skazki". *Iskusstvo kino* 11 (1959): 137–138.

—-. "Mir, sotvorennyi mul'tiplikatorom". *Iskusstvo kino* 3 (1959): 99–103.

"U nas v gostiakh". *Iskusstvo kino* 10 (1962): 69–80.

"Uchebnaia programma podgotovki rezhisserov-animatorov". *Kinovedcheskie zapiski* 73 (2005): 126–128.

Ulovich, V. "Mul'tiplikatsiia dlia detei". *Sovetskii ekran* 36 (1927): 5.

Uvarova, Irina. "Bozhdi i kukly v nashem dome". *Iskusstvo kino* 1 (1996): 45–46.

"V laboratorii kino". *Sovetskii ekran* 16 (1928): 11.

Vail', Petr and Aleksandr Genis. *60-e: Mir sovetskogo cheloveka*. Ann Arbor: Ardis, 1988.

Val'dman, E, N. Nosov, and I. Nosov. "Kontrabanda amerikanshchiny v sovetskoi mul'tiplikatsii". *Proletarskoe Kino* 5 (1932): 45–48.

Valenten, Al'bert. "Ugadok zapadnogo kino". *Sovetskii ekran* 9 (1928): 10.

Vartanov, An. "Don Kikhot oderzhivaet pobedu". *Iskusstvo kino* 1 (1986): 72–76.

—-. "Pust' dozd' budet laskovym". *Iskusstvo kino* 7 (1985): 69–71.

—-. "Sekret uspekha". *Iskusstvo kino* 12 (1975): 72–80.

—-. "Vdokhnovenie". *Iskusstvo kino* 11 (1982): 80–85.

—-. "Vernost'". *Iskusstvo kino* 1 (1985): 82–86.

—-. "Vozvrashchenie v skazku". *Iskusstvo kino* 2 (1977): 72–77.

Vasil'kova, Aleksandra. "Bez paradigmy". In *Katalog-al'manakh. Otkrytyi Rossiiskii festival' animatsionnogo kino Tarusa 2001*. Berezovaia Roshcha: Izdanie otkrytogo rossiiskogo festivalia animatsionnogo kino, 2001. 118–122.

—-. *Dusha i telo kukly. Priroda uslovnosti kukly v iskusstve XX veka: teatr, kino, televidenie*. Moscow: Agraf, 2003.

—-. "Pritiagatel'nosto pustoty". In *Katalog-al'manakh. Otkrytyi rossiiskii festival' animatsionnogo kino Suzdal' 2003*. Suzdal': Izdanie otkrytogo rossiiskogo festivalia animatsionnogo kino, 2003. 106–111.

—-. "Ryba interesnee grushi". In *Katalog-al'manakh. Otkrytyi Rossiiskii festival' animatsionnogo kino Tarusa 2000*. Berezovaia Roshcha: Izdanie otkrytogo rossiiskogo festivalia animatsionnogo kino, 2000. 116–119.

Venzher, Nataliia. "Mesto vstrechi – teleekran". In *Katalog-al'manakh. Otkrytyi Rossiiskii festival' animatsionnogo kino Tarusa 1999*. Berezovaia

Roshcha: Izdanie otkrytogo rossiiskogo festivalia animatsionnogo kino, 1999. 113–117.

—. *Mul'tfil'm vchera, segodnia i vsegda*. Moscow: Soiuzinformkino, 1979.

—. "Pirrova pobeda". In *Katalog-al'manakh. Suzdal' 2003*. Suzdal': VIII otkrytyi rossiiskii festival' animatsionnogo kino, 2003. 93–95.

—. "Pol'za ne v ushcherb udovol'stviiu". In *Kino detiam. Kino-molodezhi*. Vol. 3. Moscow: Soiuzinformkino, 1989. 35–38.

—, ed. *Rezhissery i khudozhniki sovetskogo mul'tiplikatsionnogo kino*. Moscow: Soiuzinformkino, Goskino SSSR, 1984.

—, ed. *Sotvorenie fil'ma ili neskol'ko interv'iu po sluzhebnym voprosam (O soiuzmul'tfil'me rasskazyvaiut dramaturgi, rezhissery, khudozhniki, kompozitory, aktery, operatory)*. Moscow: Soiuz kinematografistov SSSR, Vsesoiuznoe tvorchesko-proizvodstvennoe ob''edinenie "Kinotsentr", 1990.

—. "Tekhnologiia volshebstva". In *Problemy sinteza v khudozhestvennoi kul'ture*. Eds. Anatoly Prokhorov, B. Raushenbakh and Fedor Khitruk. Moscow: Nauka, 1985. 25–41.

—. "Tsentral'nye telekanaly Rossii: animatsionnoe meniu". In *Katalog-al'manakh. Otkrytyi Rossiiskii festival' animatsionnogo kino Tarusa 1998*. Berezovaia Roshcha: Izdanie otkrytogo rossiiskogo festivalia animatsionnogo kino, 1998. 112–116.

Vertov, Dziga. *Kino-eye: The writing of Dziga Vertov*. Ed. Annette Michelson. Berkeley: University of California Press, 1984.

Viktorov, A. "Mudraia skazka". *Iskusstvo kino* 1 (1966): 45–46.

Vimenet, Pascal. *Garri Bardine, six films courts*. Paris: Les enfants de cinéma, 2001.

Viskova, I., ed. *V. Lebedev*. Moscow: Sovetskii khudozhnik, 1990.

—. *Luchshie stranitsy sovetskoi satiricheskoi grafiki: Al'bom satiricheskikh risunkov. Vypusk I: 1917–1941*. Moscow: Sovetskii khudozhnik, 1988.

"Voinstvuiushchii kino-teatr". *Sovetskii ekran* 31 (1928): 3.

Volkov, Anatolyi. "Est' kontakt!" *Iskusstvo kino* 7 (1980): 65–70.

—. "Mul'tiplikatsia". In *Kino. Politika i liudi: 30-e gody*. Ed. L. Kh. Mamatova. Moscow: Materik, 1995.

—. *Mul'tiplikatsionnyi fil'm*. Moscow: Znanie, 1974.

—. "Neissiakaemaia fantaziia khudozhnika". *Iskusstvo kino* 2 (1975): 119–120.

—. "Novoe i privychnom". *Iskusstvo kino* 3 (1976): 76–80.

—. "Paradoksy animatsionnoi fantastiki". In *Mul'tiplikatsiia, animatograf, fantomatika*. Kiev: Izdanie Pervogo Vsesoiuznogo Festivalia mul'tiplikatsionnykh fil'mov "Krok-89", 1989. 107–114.

—. "Paradoksy, 'total'noi' mul'tiplikatsii". In *Problemy khudozhestvennoi spetsifiki kino. Sbornik nauchnykh trudov*. Ed. Z.G. Kutorga. Moscow: VNIIK, 1986. 200–207.

—. "Poiski novykh kontaktov". *Iskusstvo kino* 10 (1978): 117–123.

—. "Razvitiia iskusstva sovremennoi mul'tiplikatsii. Avtoreferat". Abstract. VGIK, 1971.

—. "S''est li volk zaitsa?" In *Ekran 74/75*. Eds. E. Bauman and G. Dolmatovskaia. Moscow: Iskusstvo, 1976. 130–135.

—. "Stanovlenie natsional'nykh shkol mul'tiplikatsii". In *Sovremennyi kinematograficheskii protsess. Sbornik nauchnykh trudov*. Ed. L. Kh. Mamatova. Moscow: Institut teorii i istorii kino, 1979. 108–123.

—. "Stilevye osobennosti sovremennogo mul'tiplikatsionnogo fil'ma". In *O khudozhnikakh teatra, kino i TV*. Ed. V.V. Vanslov. Leningrad: Khudozhnik RSFSR, 1984. 163–172.

Wells, Paul. "Case study: Tale of Tales". In *Understanding Animation*. London: Routledge, 1998. 93–104.

Wheeler Mjolsness, Lora. "Vertov's Soviet Toys: Commerce, Commercialization and Cartoons". *Studies in Russian and Soviet Cinema* 2, no. 3 (2008): 247–267.

Woll, Josephine. *Real Images: Soviet Cinema and the Thaw*. London: I.B. Tauris, 2000.

Yakovlev, Nikifor. "Portrait with Puppets and Drawings". *Soviet Film* 6 (1986): 29–30.

Yampolsky, Mikhail. "The Space of Animated Film: Khrzhanovsky's *I Am with You Again* and Norstein's *The Tale of Tales*". *Animating the Fantastic*. Spec. issue of *Afterimage* 13 (1987): 93–117.

Youngblood, Denise. *The Magic Mirror: Moviemaking in Russia 1908–1918*. Madison: The University of Winsconsin Press, 1999.

—. *Movies for the Masses: Popular cinema and Soviet society in the 1920s*. Cambridge: Cambridge University Press, 1992.

Zakrzhevskaia, L. "Mul'tiplikatsiia zhdet dramaturga". *Iskusstvo kino* 7 (1973): 86–96.

—. "Na poroge velikoi zhizni". *Iskusstvo kino* 3 (1971): 78–84.

—. "O skameikakh v Kopengagene i drugikh gorodakh". *Iskusstvo kino* 7 (1968): 48–50.

—. "Pravdivo, kak vymysel". *Iskusstvo kino* 11 (1981): 139–143.

—. "V poiske". *Iskusstvo kino* 12 (1978): 65–72.

—. *Vadim Kurchevskii*. Moscow: Soiuz kinematografistov SSSR. Vsesoiuznoe biuro propagandy kinoisskustva, 1987.

Zel'ma, Roza. "Sindrom Masiani". In *Katalog-al'manakh. Otkrytyi rossiiskii festival' animatsionnogo kino Suzdal' 2003*. Suzdal': Izdanie otkrytogo rossiiskogo festivalia animatsionnogo kino, 2003. 110–111.

—. "Ukhodit vek, ukhodit shkola". In *Katalog-al'manakh. Otkrytyi Rossiiskii festival' animatsionnogo kino Tarusa 2001*. Berezovaia Roshcha: Izdanie otkrytogo rossiiskogo festivalia animatsionnogo kino, 2001. 130–132.

Zhdan, V., ed. *Mul'tiplikatsionnye fil'my*. Moscow: Iskusstvo, 1969.

—, ed. *Risovannye i kukol'nye fil'my*. Moscow: Iskusstvo, 1969.

"Zhivopis', grafika, skul'ptura. Pust' ekran priblizit ikh k zriteliam!" *Iskusstvo kino* 9 (1959): 82–90.

Zil'ver, E., ed. *Mul'tiplikatsionnyi fil'm*. Moscow: Kinofotoizdat, 1936.

Zlotnik, Olga. "Winnie-the-Pooh". *Soviet Film* 2 (1973): 37.

Zorkaia, V. "V tsarstve slavnogo saltana". *Sovetskii ekran* 8 (1982): 11, 22.

Suggested readings on animation art and critical and historical works

Abramskii, I. "Mastera satiry". *Tvorchestvo* 2 (1963): 10–12.

Adams, James Luther. "The Grotesque and Our Future". In *The Grotesque in Art and Literature: Theological Reflections*. Grand Rapids, Michigan: William B. Eerdmans Publishing Company, 1997.

Bibliography

Andrew, Dudley, ed. *Image Dispute: Age of Photography*. Austin: University of Texas Press, 1997.

Anninskii, Lev. *Shestidesiatniki i my*. Moscow: Soiuz kinematografistov SSSR, 1991.

Arnheim, Rudolf. *Art and Visual Perception: A Psychology of the Creative Eye*. Berkeley: University of California Press, 1954.

—-. *Films as Art*. Berkeley: University of California Press, 1957.

Asenin, S. *Fantasticheskii kinomir Karela Zemana*. Moscow: Iskusstvo, 1979.

—-. *Irzhi Trnka-Taina kinokukly*. Moscow: Soiuz kinematografistov SSSR Vsesoiuznoe biuro propagandy kinoiskusstva, 1982.

Bakhtin, Mikhail. *The Dialogic Imagination: Four Essays*. University of Texas Press Slavic series no. 1. Ed. Michael Holquist. Austin: University of Texas Press, 1981.

Barthes, Roland. *The Responsibility of Forms: Critical Essays on Music, Art, and Representation*. 1st ed. New York: Hill and Wang, 1985.

Bazin, André. "The Evolution of the Language of Cinema". Trans. Hugh Gray. In *What is Cinema?* Vol. 1. Berkeley: University of California Press, 1967. 23–40.

—-. "Painting and Cinema". Trans. Hugh Gray. In *What is Cinema?* Vol. 1. Berkeley: University of California Press, 1967. 164–169.

—-. "The Virtues and Limitations of Montage". Trans. Hugh Gray. In *What is Cinema?* Vol. 1. Berkeley: University of California Press, 1967. 41–52.

—-. *What is Cinema?* Ed. Hugh Gray. 2 vols. Berkeley: University of California Press, 1967.

Beckerman, Howard. *Animation: the Whole Story*. New York: Allworth Press, 2003.

Beneshova, Mariia. "Mastera chekhoslovatskogo kukol'nogo fil'ma (Germina Tyrlova, Karel Zeman, Irzhi Trnka)". In *Voprosy kino iskusstva ezhegodnyi istoriko-teoreticheskii sbornik. Vypusk 5*. Moscow: Izdatel'stvo akademii nauk SSSR, 1961. 241–278.

Bogatyrev, Petr. *Cheshskii kukol'nyi i russkii narodnyi teatr*. Berlin-Peterburg: Izdatel'stvo Opoiaz, 1923.

—-. "Příspěvek ke vykoumání divadelních znaků". In *Svit loutkového divadla*. Ed. František Sokol. Prague: Albatros, 1987. 68–77.

Bordwell, David, and Kristin Thompson. *Film Art: An Introduction*. 7th ed. Boston: McGraw-Hill, 2004.

Canemaker, John, ed. *Storytelling in Animation: The Art of the Animated Image*. Vol. 2. Los Angeles: The American Film Institute, 1988.

Chegodaev, A. D. *Stranitsy istorii sovetskoi zhivopisi i sovetskoi grafiki*. Moscow: Izdatel'stvo sovetskii khudozhnik, 1984.

Cholodenko, Alan. "The Illusion of the Beginning: A Theory of Drawing and Animation". *Afterimage* 28.1 (2000): 9–12.

Deleuze, Gilles. *Cinema 1: The Movement-image*. Trans. Hugh Tomlinson and Barbara Habberjam. Minneapolis: University of Minnesota Press, 1986.

Eco, Umberto. *A Theory of Semiotics*. Bloomington: Indiana University Press, 1976.

Efimov, Boris. "Maiakovskii-khudozhnik". *Tvorchestvo* 7 (1963): 17–19.

Eggeling, Vol'fram. *Politika i kul'tura pri Khrushcheve i Brezhneve 1953–1970 gg.* Moscow: Airo-XX, 1999.

Eisenstein, Sergei. *Izbrannye proizvedeniia v shesti tomakh*. 6 vols. Moscow: Iskusstvo, 1964.

Finch, Christopher. *The Art of Disney from Mickey Mouse to the Magic Kingdoms.* New York: Harry N. Abrams, 1995.

Fomin, Valerii. *Kinematograf ottepeli: dokumenty i svidetel'stva.* Moscow: Materik, 1998.

Freud, Sigmund. "The Uncanny". In *Literary Theory: An Anthology*. Eds. Julie Rivkin and Michael Ryan. Malden, MA: Blackwell Publishing, 1998. 418–430.

Furniss, Maureen, ed. *Animation: Art & Industry*. New Barnet, Herts (UK): John Libbey, 2009; Distributed in North America by Indiana University Press.

Golovskoy, Val S., and John Rimberg. *Behind the Soviet Screen: The Motion-Picture Industry in the USSR 1972–1982*. Trans. Steven Hill. Ann Arbor: Ardis, 1986.

Gombrich, Ernst H. *Art and Illusion: A Study in the Psychology of Pictorial Representation*. Princeton: Princeton University Press, 1960.

—. *The Story of Art*. 11th ed. London: Phaidon Press, 1967.

Graffy, Julian. "Scant Sign of Thaw: Fear and Anxiety in the Representation of Foreigners in the Soviet Films of the Khrushchev Years". In *Russia and its Other(s) on Film: Screening Intercultural Dialogue*. Ed. Stephen Hutchings. NY: Palgrave Macmillan, 2008. 27–46.

Greenberg, Clement. *Clement Greenberg: the Collected Essays and Criticism*. Ed. John O'Brian. 4 vols. Chicago: University of Chicago Press, 1986.

Halas, John. *Art in Movement: New Directions in Animation*. London: Studio Vista London, 1970.

Halfin, Igal, ed. *Language and Revolution: Making Modern Political Identities*. London: Frank Cass, 2002.

Hames, Peter, ed. *Dark Alchemy: The Films of Jan Švankmajer*. Westport, Conn.: Praeger, 1995.

Harrison, Charles, and Paul Wood. *Art in Theory, 1900–2000: An Anthology of Changing Ideas*. 2nd ed. Oxford, UK: Blackwell, 2003.

Holquist, Michael. *Dialogism: Bakhtin and his World*. London: Routledge, 1990.

Ivanov, Viktor. "Chto nado znat' nachinaiushchemu plakatistu". *Tvorchestvo* 5 (1958): 19–20.

Kanevskii. "Sila smeshnogo". *Tvorchestvo* 2 (1957): 16–17.

Karanovich, Anatolii. "Rober Benaiun i ego kniga". *Iskusstvo kino* 12 (1964): 86–90.

Khalaminskii, Iu. "Puti razvitiia knizhnoi grafiki". *Tvorchestvo* 9 (1959): 1–5.

Koretskii, V. "Agitplakat-publitsistka segodniashchego dnia". *Tvorchestvo* 5 (1958): 14–15.

—. "Iazyk kinoplakata". *Iskusstvo kino* 6 (1958): 104–115.

Kotenshul'te, Daniel'. "¡Que viva Disney! Vospriatiie Disneia Eizenshteinom". *Kinovedcheskie zapiski* 52 (2001): 115–129.

Krakauer, Zigfrid. "*Dambo*: novyi fil'm Uolta Disneia". *Kinovedcheskie zapiski* 52 (2001): 129–131.

Kral, Petr. "Questions à Jan Svankmajer". *Positif* 297.Nov (1985): 38–44.

Krivulia, Natal'ia. *Ozhivshie teni. Volshebnogo fonaria.* Krasnodar: Izdatel'stvo Ametist, 2006.

—-. *V zerkale vremeni. Animatsiia dvukh Amerik (nemoi period).* Moscow: Izdatel'stvo Ametist, 2007.

Kuz'min, N. "Russkii lubok". *Tvorchestvo* 2 (1959): 21–23.

Kuznecov, Erast. *L'illustrazione del libro per bambini e l'avanguardia russa.* Florence: Cantini, 1991.

Lawton, Anna. *The Red Screen: Politics, Society, Art in Soviet Cinema.* London: Routledge, 1992.

Leslie, Esther. *Hollywood Flatlands: Animation, Critical Theory and the Avant-Garde.* London: Verso, 2002.

Liehm, Mira and Antonin J. *The Most Important Art: Soviet and East European Film After 1945.* Berkeley: U of CA P, 1977.

Liubushkina, Liubov'. "Goskino: 1938–2000. Iz ofitsial'noi khroniki". *Kinograf* 16 (2005): 156–157.

Lotman, Iurii. *Izbrannye stat'i: v trekh tomakh.* 3 vols. Tallinn: Aleksandra, 1992.

—-. "Khudozhestvennaia priroda russkikh narodnykh kartinok". In *Materialy nauchnoi konferentsii (1975): Narodnaia graviura i fol'klor v Rossii XVII-XIX vv. (k 150-letiiu so dnia rozhdeniia D. A. Rovinskogo).* Ed. I. E. Danilova. Moscow: Sovetskii khudozhnik, 1976. 247–267.

—-. "Kukly v sisteme kul'tury". In *Ob iskusstve.* St. Petersburg: Iskusstvo, 1998. 645–649.

—-. *Ob iskusstve.* St. Petersburg: Iskusstvo-SPB, 1998.

—-. *Semiotics of Cinema.* Trans. Mark Suino. Ann Arbor: University of Michigan Press, 1976.

—-. "Semiotika kino i problemy kinoestetiki". In *Ob iskusstve.* St. Petersburg: Iskusstvo, 1998. 288–372.

—-. "Struktura khudozhestvennogo teksta". In *Ob iskusstve.* St. Petersburg: Iskusstvo, 1998. 13–285.

Lunacharskii, A.V. *Russkaia literatura.* Moscow: Gosudarstvennoe izdatel'stvo khudozhestvennoi literatury, 1947.

Maltin, Leonard. *The Disney Films.* 4th ed. New York: Disney Editions, 2000.

Margolit, Evgenii. "Kinematograf 'ottepeli': K portretu fenomena". *Kinovedcheskie zupiski* 61 (2002): 195–230.

Matejka, Ladislav, and I. R. Titunik. *Semiotics of art: Prague School contributions.* Cambridge, Mass.: MIT Press, 1976.

Mukařovský, Jan. *Aesthetic Function, Norm and Value as Social Facts.* Ann Arbor: University of Michigan Press, 1970.

—-. "Art as Semiotic Fact". In *Semiotics of art: Prague School contributions.* Eds. Ladislav Matejka and I. R. Titunik. Cambridge, Mass.: MIT Press, 1976. 3–10.

Nikitina, S. "Ob obshchikh siuzhetakh v fol'klore i narodnom izobrazitel'nom iskusstve". *Materialy nauchnoi konferentsii (1975): Narodnaia graviura i fol'klor v Rossii XVII-XIX vv. (k 150-letiiu so dnia rozhdeniia D. A. Rovinskogo).* Ed. I. E. Danilova. Moscow: Sovetskii khudozhnik, 1976. 320–369.

O'Pray, Michael. "The Animated Film". In *The Oxford Guide to Film*

Studies. Eds. J. Hill and Church Gibson. New York: Oxford University Press, 1998. 434–439.

—-. "Surrealism, Fantasy and the Grotesque: The Cinema of Jan Švankmajer". In *Fantasy and the Cinema.* Ed. James Donald. London: BFI, 1989. 253–268.

Panofsky, Erwin. *Perspective as Symbolic Form.* New York: Zone Books, 1997.

Petrov, Petre. "The Freeze of Historicity in Thaw Cinema". *KinoKultura* 8 (April 2005). http://www.kinokultura.com/articles/apr05-petrov.html

Pilling, Jayne. *A Reader in Animation Studies.* London: J. Libbey, 1997.

Poš, Jan, Howard Beckerman, and Jeffrey Wechsler. *Krátký film: the Art of Czechoslovak Animation.* New Brunswick, N.J.: The Jane Voorhees Zimmerli Art Museum, Rutgers, 1991.

Prokhorov, Alexander. "The Adolescent and the Child in the Cinema of the Thaw". *Studies in Russian and Soviet Cinema* 1.2 (2007): 115–129.

—-. "Inherited Discourse: Paradigms of Stalinist Culture in Literature and Cinema of the Thaw". Diss. University of Pittsburg, 2002.

—-. *Unasledovannyi diskurs: paradigmy stalinskoi kultury v literature i kinematografe "ottepeli".* Sankt-Peterburg: Akademicheskii proekt, 2007.

Prokhorov, Alexander, ed. *Springtime for Soviet Cinema: Re/Viewing the 1960s.* Pittsburgh: Pittsburgh Russian Film Symposium, 2001.

Propp, Vladimir. *Morphology of the Folktale.* Bloomington: Research Center, Indiana University, 1958.

—-. and Anatoly Liberman. *Theory and History of Folklore.* Theory and history of literature. Vol. 5. Minneapolis: University of Minnesota Press, 1984.

Prorokov, B. "Uroki Moora". *Tvorchestvo* 1 (1959): 18–19.

Rivkin, Julie, and Michael Ryan, eds. *Literary Theory: An Anthology.* 2nd ed. Malden, MA: Blackwell Publishing, 2004.

Robinson, Chris, J. *Between Genius and Utter Illiteracy: A Story of Estonian Animation.* Eastleigh (UK): John Libbey, 2006. Distributed in North America by Indiana University Press. First published 2003 by Varrak.

Rosen, Philip, ed. *A Film Theory Reader: Narrative, Apparatus, Ideology.* New York: Columbia University Press, 1986.

Russet, Roger, and Cecile Starr. *Experimental Animation: Origins of a New Art.* New York: Da Capo Press, 1976.

Samu, Charles. "Zagreb and the Art of Animation". *The Film Study-Guide* 1.1 (1973): 1–4.

Semenova, T. "Gde zhe satira?" *Tvorchestvo* 1 (1962): 8–10.

Shafraniuk, Vladimir. *Poniatie o kuklakh-akterakh i traditsionnye zabluzhdeniia (Obshchie osobennosti, opredelenie, nekotorye posledstviia).* Moscow: Stels, 2001.

Small, Edward, S., and Eugene Levinson. "Toward a Theory of Animation". *The Velvet Light Trap* Review of Cinema N. 24 (1989): 67–74.

Sokol, František, ed. *Svìt loutkového divadla.* Prague: Albatros, 1987.

Stephenson, Ralph. *The Animated Film.* London: Tantivy Press, 1973.

Taylor, Richard. *Inside the Film Factory: New Approaches to Russian and Soviet Cinema.* London: Routledge, 1994.

Taylor, Richard, ed. *The Eisenstein Reader.* London: British Film Institute, 1998.

Tolstykh, Valentin et al. "Khudozhnik i vlast'". *Iskusstvo kino* 5 (1989): 22–47.

Troianovskii, Vitalii. *Kinematograf ottepeli: k 100-letiiu mirovogo kino*. Moscow: Materik, 1996.

Tsivian, Yuri. "K istorii sviazei teatra i kino v russkoi kul'ture nachala XX v. ('istochnik' i 'mimikriia')". In *Problemy sinteza v khudozhestvennoi kul'ture*. Eds. Anatoly Prokhorov, B. Raushenbakh and Fedor Khitruk. Moscow: Nauka, 1985. 100–113.

Tsyrlin, I. "Sovetskii kinoplakat". *Tvorchestvo* 7 (1958): 15–18.

Tynianov, Iurii. *Arkhaisty i novatory*. Leningrad: Priboi, 1929.

Vail', Petr and Aleksandr Genis. "60-e: sovetskoe kino i stil' epokhi. Razmyshleniia i kommentarii". *Close-Up: Istoriko-teoreticheskii seminar vo VGIKe: Lektsii 1996–1998 gody*. Ed. Aleksandr Troshin. Moskva: VGIK, 1999. 230–233.

Wells, Paul. "Animation: Forms and Meanings". In *An Introduction to Film Studies*. Ed. Jill Nelmes. London: Routledge, 1996. 213–238.

—-. "Body Consciousness in the Films of Jan Svankmajer". In *A Reader in Animation Studies*. Ed. Jayne Pilling. London: J. Libbey, 1997. 177–194.

—-. *Understanding Animation*. London: Routledge, 1998.

Youngblood, Denise. *Soviet Cinema in the Silent Era, 1918–1935*. Austin: University of Texas Press, 1991. First published 1985 by UMI Research Press.

Zhegalova, S. "O stilisticheskom edinstve lubochnykh kartinok i severnykh rospisei po derevu XVII-XVIII veka". In *Materialy nauchnoi konferentsii (1975): Narodnaia graviura i fol'klor v Rossii XVII-XIX vv. (k 150-letiiu so dnia rozhdeniia D. A. Rovinskogo)*. Ed. I.E. Danilova. Moscow: Sovetskii khudozhnik, 1976. 131–139.

Zich, Otakar. "Loutkové divadlo". In *Svĕt loutkového divadla*. Ed. František Sokol. Prague: Albatros, 1987. 24–38.

Filmography

Soviet animated films 1910–1979[227]

25th – The First Day (*25-oe-pervyi den'*). Dir. Iurii Norshtein. Soiuzmul'tfil'm, 1968.

38 Parrots (*38 Popugaev*). Dir. Ivan Ufimtsev. Soiuzmul'tfil'm, 1976–1991.

A Box with a Secret (*Shkatulka s sekretom*). Dir. Vladimir Ugarov. Soiuzmul'tfil'm, 1976.

A Commonplace Story (*Banal'naia istoriia*). Dir. Iosif Boiarskii. Soiuzmul'tfil'm, 1962.

A Dangerous Prank (*Opasnaia shalost'*). Dir. Evgenii Raikovskii. Soiuzmul'tfil'm, 1954.

A Fire is Burning in the Yaranga (*V iarange gorit ogon'*). Dir. Ol'ga Khodataeva. Soiuzmul'tfil'm, 1956.

A Forest Story (*Lesnaia istoriia*). Dir. Aleksandr Ivanov. Soiuzmul'tfil'm, 1956.

A Gift for the Weakest One (*Podarok dlia samogo slabogo*). Dir. Leonid Kaiukov. Soiuzmul'tfil'm, 1978.

A Heavenly Creation (*Nebesnoe sozdanie*). Dir. Sergei Obraztsov and Georgii Natanson. Soiuzmul'tfil'm, 1956.

A House for Leopard (*Dom dlia leoparda*). Dir. Anatolii Reznikov. Ekran, 1979.

A Lake in the Desert (*Ozero v pustyne*). Dir. Nazim Tuliakhodzhaev. Uzbekfil'm, 1979.

A Light Wind (*Veterok*). Dir. Nikolai Serebriakov. Soiuzmul'tfil'm, 1972.

A Million in the Bag (*Million v meshke*). Dir. Dmitrii Babichenko. Soiuzmul'tfil'm, 1956.

A Miraculous Day (*Den' chudesnyi*). Dir. Andrei Khrzhanovskii. Soiuzmul'tfil'm, 1975.

A Noisy Voyage (*Shumnoe plavanie*). Dir. Vladimir Suteev. Soiuzmul'tfil'm, 1937.

A Robbery Like… (*Ograblenie po…*). Dir. Efim Gamburg. Soiuzmul'tfil'm, 1978.

A Sack Full of Apples (*Meshok iablok*). Dir. Vitol'd Bordzilovskii. Soiuzmul'tfil'm, 1974.

A Spring Tale (*Vesennaia skazka*). Dir. Viktor Gromov. Soiuzmul'tfil'm, 1949.

A Strange Voice (*Chuzhoi golos*). Dir. Ivan Ivanov-Vano. Soiuzmul'tfil'm, 1949.

A Sweet Tale (*Sladkaia skazka*). Dir. Vladimir Degtiarev. Soiuzmul'tfil'm, 1970.

---

[227] The films listed here are either animated films specifically discussed, or films that are relevant to this study. I included some notable Soviet animated films from the 1970s in order to convey a sense of how Soviet animation progressed after the period covered in this book.

A Tale of Laziness (*Skazka pro len'*). Dir. Iurii Prytkov. Soiuzmul'tfil'm, 1976.
A Terrible Tale (*Strashnaia istoriia*). Dir. Galina Barinova. Soiuzmul'tfil'm, 1979.
A Winter Tale (*Zimniaia skazka*). Dir. Ivan Ivanov-Vano. Soiuzmul'tfil'm, 1945.
About a Giant who Was Afraid of Needles (*Pro begemota, kotoryi boialsia privivok*). Dir. Leonid Amal'rik. Soiuzmul'tfil'm, 1966.
About a Puppy (*Pro shchenka*). Dir. Boris Ablynin. Soiuzmul'tfil'm, 1979.
About an Evil Stepmother (*Pro zluiu machekhu*). Dir. Valentina Brumberg and Zinaida Brumberg. Soiuzmul'tfil'm, 1966. (Gosfil'mofond)
About the Cranky Little Frog – Merry Go Round No. 4 (*Pro chudaka liagushonka – Veselaia karusel' N. 4*). Dir. Vladimir Ugarov. Soiuzmul'tifil'm, 1972.
Absent-minded Giovanni – Merry Go Round No. 1 (*Rasseiannyi Dzhovanni – Veselaia karusel' N. 1*). Dir. Anatolii Petrov. Soiuzmul'tfil'm, 1969.
The Adventures of Baron Munchausen (*Prikliucheniia barona Miunkhauzena*). Dir. Anatolii Karanovich. Soiuzmul'tfil'm, 1967.
The Adventures of Bolvashka (*Prikliucheniia Bolvashki*). Dir. Iurii Zheliabuzhskii. Mezhrabpom-Rus', 1927. (Gosfil'mofond)
Adventures of Bratishkin (*Prikliucheniia Bratishkina*). Dir. Iurii Merkulov, A. Barshch. Gosvoenkino, 1929. No longer available.
The Adventures of Buratino (*Prikliucheniia Buratino*). Dir. Ivan Ivanov-Vano and Dmitrii Babichenko. Soiuzmul'tfil'm, 1959.
The Adventures of Captain Vrungel, 1–13 (*Prikliucheniia kapitana Vrungelia, 1–13*). Dir. David Cherkasskii. Kievnauchfil'm, 1976–1979.
The Adventures of Chichikov: Manilov (*Pokhozhdeniia Chichikova: Manilov*). Dir. Boris Stepantsev. Soiuzmul'tfil'm, 1974.
The Adventures of Chichikov: Nozdrev (*Pokhozhdeniia Chichikova: Nozdrev*). Dir. Vladimir Danilevich and Boris Stepantsev. Soiuzmul'tfil'm, 1974.
The Adventures of Comma and Period (*Prikliucheniia zapiatoi i tochki*). Dir. Nikolai Fedorov. Soiuzmul'tfil'm, 1965.
The Adventures of Do-it-yourselfer (*Prikliucheniia Samodelkina*). Dir. Vakhtang Bakhtadze. Soiuzmul'tfil'm, 1957.
The Adventures of Leopold the Cat, 1–10 (*Prikliucheniia kota Leopol'da, 1–10*). Dir. Anatolii Reznikov. Ekran, 1975–1987.
The Adventures of Munchausen (*Pokhozhdeniia Miunkhgauzena*). Dir. Daniil Cherkes. Mezhrabpomfil'm, 1929. (Gosfil'mofond)
The Adventures of Munchausen (*Prikliucheniia Miunkhgauzena*). Dir. Anatolii Solin and Natan Lerner. Ekran, 1973–1974.
The Adventures of Murzilka (*Prikliucheniia Murzilki*). Dir. Boris Stepantsev and Evgenii Raikovskii. Soiuzmul'tfil'm, 1956.
The Adventures of the Red Neckties (*Prikliucheniia krasnykh galstukov*). Dir. Vladimir Pekar' and Vladimir Popov. Soiuzmul'tfil'm, 1971.
Alarm Clock (*Budil'nik*). Dir. Lev Mil'chin. Soiuzmul'tfil'm, 1967.
Ali Baba and the Forty Bandits (*Ali-baba i sorok razboinikov*). Dir. Grigorii Lomidze. Soiuzmul'tfil'm, 1959.
All About the Cossacks (*Vse o kazakakh*). Dir. Vladimir Dakhno. Kievnauchfil'm, 1967–1995.
Allowed and Not Allowed (*Mozhno i nel'zia*). Dir. Lev Mil'chin. Soiuzmul'tfil'm, 1964.

All-Union Boiler Room (*Vsesoiuznaia kochegarka*). Dir. Daniil Cherkes, 1930. (Gosfil'mofond)

An Event at the Stadium (*Sluchai na stadione*). Dir. Aleksandr Ptushko. Sovkino (3-ia f-ka Sovkino), 1928. (Gosfil'mofond)

An Incarnated Dream (*Voploshchennaia mechta*). Dir. Nikolai Fedorov. Soiuzmul'tfil'm, 1957.

An Incident with an Artist (*Sluchai s khudozhnikom*). Dir. Grigorii Kozlov. Soiuzmul'tfil'm, 1962. (Gosfil'mofond)

An Unusual Match (*Neobyknovennyi match*). Dir. Boris Dezhkin and Mstislav Pashchenko. Soiuzmul'tfil'm, 1955.

Anansi the Little Spider and the Magic Wand (*Pauchok Anansi i volshebnaia palochka*). Dir. Ideia Garanina and Marianna Novogrudskaia. Ekran, 1973.

And I am with you again (*I s Vami snova ia*). Dir. Andrei Khrzhanovskii. Soiuzmul'tfil'm, 1980.

And My Mother will Forgive Me (*I mama menia prostit*). Dir. Anatolii Petrov. Soiuzmul'tfil'm, 1975.

And Suddenly it Came About (*A vdrug poluchitsia*). Dir. Ivan Ufimtsev. 1978.

And We, too, to the Olympiad (*I my na Olimpiadu*). Dir. Vladimir Suteev. Soiuzmul'tfil'm, 1940. (Gosfil'mofond)

Animated Crocodile No. 1 (*Mul'tiplikatsionnyi krokodil N.1*). Dir. Vladimir Pekar', Vladimir Popov and Lev Pozdneev. Soiuzmul'tfil'm, 1960. (Gosfil'mofond)

Animated Crocodile No. 2 (*Mul'tiplikatsionnyi krokodil N.2*). Dir. Mikhail Botov and Grigorii Kozlov. Soiuzmul'tfil'm, 1960. (Gosfil'mofond)

Animated Crocodile No. 3 (*Mul'tiplikatsionnyi krokodil N.3*). Dir. Dmitrii Babichenko. Soiuzmul'tfil'm, 1961. (Gosfil'mofond)

Animated Crocodile No. 4 (*Mul'tiplikatsionnyi krokodil N.4*). Dir. Dmitrii Babichenko. Soiuzmul'tfil'm, 1961. (Gosfil'mofond)

Animated Crocodile No. 5 (*Mul'tiplikatsionnyi krokodil N. 5*). Dir. Vladimir Pekar' and Vladimir Popov. Soiuzmul'tfil'm, 1961. (Gosfil'mofond)

Animated Crocodile No. 6 (*Mul'tiplikatsionnyi krokodil N. 6*). Dir Mikhail Botov and Grigorii Kozlov. Soiuzmul'tfil'm, 1961. (Gosfil'mofond)

The Annoying Musician and Other Little Jokes (*Nadoedlivyi muzykant i drugie shutki-maliutki*). Dir. Rein Raamat. Tallinnfil'm, 1972.

Another Bad Mark (*Opiat' dvoika*). Dir. Evgenii Raikovskii and Boris Stepantsev. Soiuzmul'tfil'm, 1957.

Antoshka – Merry Go Round No. 1 (*Antoshka – Veselaia karusel' N. 1*). Dir. Leonid Nosyrev. Soiuzmul'tfil'm, 1969.

Argonauts (*Argonavty*). Dir. Aleksandra Snezhko-Blotskaia. Soiuzmul'tfil'm, 1971.

Around 3:15 (*Rovno v tri piatnadtsat'*). Dir. Evgenii Migunov and Boris Dezhkin. Soiuzmul'tfil'm, 1959.

The Arrow Flies into the Tale (*Strela uletaet v skazku*). Dir. Leonid Amal'rik. Soiuzmul'tfil'm, 1954.

At the Back Desk (*Na zadnei parte*). Dir. Vladimir Ugarov. Soiuzmul'tfil'm, 1978–85.

Attention, Wolves! (*Vnimanie, volki!*) Dir. Efim Gamburg. Soiuzmul'tfil'm, 1970.

Aurora (*Avrora*). Dir. Roman Kachanov. Soiuzmul'tfil'm, 1973.

Autumn (*Osen'*). Dir. Andrei Khrzhanovskii. Soiuzmul'tfil'm, 1982.

Ave Maria (*Ave Mariia*). Dir. Ivan Ivanov-Vano and Vladimir Danilevich. Soiuzmul'tfil'm, 1972.

Baba Iaga Objects! (*Baba-Iaga protiv!*). Dir. Vladimir Pekar'. Soiuzmul'tfil'm, 1979–1980.

The Baby Frog Searches for His Father (*Liagushonok ishchet papu*). Dir. Roman Kachanov. Soiuzmul'tfil'm, 1964.

The Ballad of the Table (*Ballada o stole*). Dir. Roman Davydov and Mikhail Kalinin. Soiuzmul'tfil'm, 1956. (Gosfil'mofond)

Ballerina Aboard a Ship (*Balerina na korable*). Dir. Lev Atamanov. Soiuzmul'tfil'm, 1969.

Barankin, be a man! (*Barankin, bud' chelovekom!*). Dir. Aleksandra Snezhko-Blotskaia. Soiuzmul'tfil'm, 1963.

Barmalei. Dir. Leonid Amal'rik and Vladimir Polkovnikov. Soiuzmul'tfil'm, 1941.

The Bath or *The Sauna* (*Bania*). Dir. Anatolii Karanovich and Sergei Iutkevich. Soiuzmul'tfil'm, 1962. (Gosfil'mofond)

The Battle of Kerzhenets (*Secha pri Kerzhentse*). Dir. Iurii Norshtein and Ivan Ivanov-Vano. Soiuzmul'tfil'm, 1971.

The Beautiful Liukanida, or the Battle Between Stag Beetles and Long-horn Beetles (*Prekrasnaia Liukanida, ili voina rogachei i usachei*). Dir. Vladislav Starevich. 1910.

The Bench (*Skameika*). Dir. Lev Atamanov. Soiuzmul'tfil'm, 1967.

Big-Ears and His Friends 1–5 (*Ushastik i ego druz'ia 1–5*). Dir. Ol'ga Rozovskaia. Ekran, 1979–1982.

Birthday (*Den' rozhdeniia*). Dir. Valentina Brumberg and Zinaida Brumberg. Soiuzmul'tfil'm, 1959.

Black and White (*Blek end uait*). Dir. Leonid Amal'rik and Ivan Ivanov-Vano. Mezhrabpomfil'm, 1932. (Gosfil'mofond)

Blue Meteorite – Merry Go Round No. 3 (*Goluboi meteorit – Veselaia karusel' N. 3*). Dir. Anatolii Petrov. Soiuzmul'tfil'm, 1971.

The Blue Puppy (*Goluboi shchenok*). Dir. Efim Gamburg. Soiuzmul'tfil'm, 1976.

The Boastful Little Ant (*Murav'ishka-khvastunishka*). Dir. Vladimir Polkovnikov. Soiuzmul'tfil'm, 1961.

Bobik Visits Barbos (*Bobik v gostiakh u Barbosa*). Dir. Vladimir Popov. Soiuzmul'tfil'm, 1977.

Bonifatius's Holidays (*Kanikuly Bonifatsiia*). Dir. Fedor Khitruk. Soiuzmul'tfil'm, 1965.

Boris Savinkov – Story of a Disappointment (*Boris Savinkov – Istoriia odnogo razocharovaniia*). Dir. Aleksandr Bushkin, Ivan Beliakov, 1924. (Gosfil'mofond)

The Bouquet (*Buket*). Dir. Lev Atamanov. Soiuzmul'tfil'm, 1966.

The Boy from Neapolis (*Mal'chik iz Neapolia*). Dir. Ivan Aksenchuk. Soiuzmul'tfil'm, 1958.

Bratishkin Competes (*Bratishkin sorevnuetsia*). Dir. V. Tvardovskii. Soiuzkino (Leningrad), 1930. No longer available.

The Brave Fawn (*Khrabryi olenenok*). Dir. Ol'ga Khodataeva and Leonid Aristov. Soiuzmul'tfil'm, 1957.

The Brave Inspector Mamochkin (*Bravyi inspektor Mamochkin*). Dir. Garri Bardin. Soiuzmul'tfil'm, 1977.

Brave Pak (*Khrabryi Pak*). Dir. Evgenii Raikovskii and Vladimir Degtiarev. Soiuzmul'tfil'm, 1953.

Brave Robin Hood (*Otvazhnyi Robin Gud*). Dir. Anatolii Karanovich. Soiuzmul'tfil'm, 1970.

Braveheart (*Serdtse khrabretsa*). Dir. Boris Dezhkin and Gennadii Filippov. Soiuzmul'tfil'm, 1951.

Bread Manufacturing (*Khlebozagotovki*). Dir. Nikolai Khodataev, 1930. (Gosfil'mofond)

Break No. 1 (*Peremenka N. 1*). Dir. Efim Gamburg. Soiuzmul'tfil'm, 1976.

The Bremen Musicians (*Bremenskie muzykanty*). Dir. Inessa Kovalevskaia. Soiuzmul'tfil'm, 1969.

The Brothers Liu (*Brat'ia Liu*). Dir. Dmitrii Babichenko. Soiuzmul'tfil'm, 1953.

Butterfly (*Babochka*). Dir. Andrei Khrzhanovskii. Soiuzmul'tfil'm, 1972.

The Butterfly and the Tiger – Merry Go Round No. 10 (*Babochka i tigr – Veselaia karusel' N. 10*). Dir. Vladimir Ugarov. Soiuzmul'tfil'm, 1978.

Buzz-buzz-buzz (*Zhu-zhu-zhu*). Dir. Lev Mil'chin. Soiuzmul'tfil'm, 1966.

The Calico Street (*Sittsevaia ulitsa*). Dir. Petr Nosov. Soiuzmul'tfil'm, 1964.

The Cameraman's Revenge (*Mest' kinooperatora*). Dir. Vladislav Starevich. 1911.

The Canterville Ghost (*Kentervil'skoe prividenie*). Dir. Valentina Brumberg and Zinaida Brumberg. Soiuzmul'tfil'm, 1970.

The Capricious Princess (*Kapriznaia printsessa*). Dir. Valentina Brumberg and Zinaida Brumberg. Soiuzmul'tfil'm, 1969.

Cat by the Name of Gav 1–4 (*Kotenok po imeni Gav 1–4*). Dir. Lev Atamanov. Soiuzmul'tfil'm, 1976–1980.

Cat in Boots (*Kot v sapogakh*). Dir. Valentina Brumberg and Zinaida Brumberg. Soiuzmul'tfil'm, 1938. (Gosfil'mofond)

Cat in Boots (*Kot v sapogakh*). Dir. Zinaida Brumberg and Valentina Brumberg. Soiuzmul'tfi'm, 1968.

The Cat who Went About by Himself (*Kot, kotoryi gulial sam po sebe*). Dir. Aleksandra Snezhko-Blotskaia. Soiuzmul'tfil'm, 1968.

The Cat's House (*Koshkin dom*). Dir. Leonid Amal'rik. Soiuzmul'tfil'm, 1958.

Champion (*Chempion*). Dir. Aleksandr Ivanov. Soiuzmul'tfil'm, 1948.

The Champion Willy-Nilly (*Chempion ponevole*). Dir. Viktor Smirnov. Mul'tstudiia GUKF, 1934. (Gosfil'mofond)

Cheburashka. Dir. Roman Kachanov. Soiuzmul'tfil'm, 1971.

Check Your Watch (*Prover'te vashi chasy*). Dir. Ivan Aksenchuk. Soiuzmul'tfil'm, 1963. (Gosfil'mofond)

The Cheerful Musicians (*Veselye muzykanty*). Dir. Aleksandr Ptushko. Mosfil'm, 1936.

Children of the Sun (*Ditia solntsa*). Dir. Aleksandr Ivanov. Soiuzmul'tfil'm, 1957.

Children's Album (*Detskii al'bom*). Dir. Inessa Kovalevskaia. Soiuzmul'tfil'm, 1976.

Chin Up! (*Vyshe golovu!*) Dir. Lev Atamanov. Soiuzmul'tfil'm, 1972.

China in Flames (*Hands off of China!*) (*Kitai v ogne – Ruki proch' ot Kitaia!*).

221

Dir. Zenon Komissarenko, Iurii Merkulov, and Nikolai Khodataev. GTK, Kino-Moskva, 1925. (Gosfil'mofond)

Chipollino. Dir. Boris Dezhkin. Soiuzmul'tfilm', 1961.

Cinemacircus (Kinotsirk). Dir. Leonid Amal'rik and Ol'ga Khodataeva. Soiuzmul'tfil'm, 1942.

Circus (Tsirk). Dir. Aleksandr Sinitsyn. Lenfil'm, 1940. (Gosfil'mofond)

The Closet (Shkaf). Dir. Andrei Khrzhanovskii. Soiuzmul'tfil'm, 1970.

Clown – Merry Go Round No. 9 (Kloun – Veselaia karusel' N. 9). Dir. Leonid Kaiukov. Soiuzmul'tfil'm, 1977.

The Comedian (Komediant). Dir. Anatolii Karanovich. Soiuzmul'tfil'm, 1968.

Contact (Kontakt). Dir. Vladimir Tarasov. Soiuzmul'tfil'm, 1978.

The Coocoo and the Rooster (Kukushka i petukh). Dir. Ivan Aksenchuk. Soiuzmul'tfil'm, 1953.

The Coocoo and the Starling (Kukushka i skvorets). Dir. Vladimir Polkovnikov and Leonid Amal'rik. Soiuzmul'tfil'm, 1949.

Crane Feathers (Zhuravlinye pera). Dir. Ideia Garanina. Soiuzmul'tfil'm, 1977.

The Crow and the Fox, the Cuckoo and the Cock (Vorona i lisitsa, kukushka i petukh). Dir. Ivan Aksenchuk. Soiuzmul'tfil'm, 1953.

The Daring and Brave Man (Khrabrets-udalets). Dir. Roman Davydov. Soiuzmul'tfil'm, 1976.

Dem'ian's Fuddle (Durman Dem'iana). Dir. Aleksandr Bushkin, 1925. (Gosfil'mofond)

The Devastation – Merry Go Round No. 3 (Razgrom – Veselaia karusel' N. 3). Dir. Vladimir Ugarov. Soiuzmul'tfil'm, 1971.

The Disappeared Letter (Propavshaia gramota). Dir. Valentina Brumberg and Zinaida Brumberg. Soiuzmul'tfil'm, 1945.

Disarming: a Political Caricature (Razoruzhaiutsia. Polit-sharzh). Dir. Aleksandr Ivanov, n.d. Soiuzkino. (Gosfil'mofond)

The Disobedient Kitten (Neposlushnyi kotenok). Dir. Mstislav Pashchenko. Soiuzmul'tfil'm, 1953.

Dobrynia Nikitich the Epic Hero (Dobrynia Nikitich). Dir. Vladimir Degtiarev. Soiuzmul'tfil'm, 1965.

Does-Too-Little and Does Too Much (Nedodel i peredel). Dir. Gennadii Sokol'skii. Soiuzmul'tfil'm, 1979.

Do-it-yourselfer in Space (Samodelkin v kosmose). Dir. Vakhtang Bakhtadze. Gruziia-fil'm, 1971.

Drawing in the Sand (Risunok na peske). Dir. Anatolii Karanovich. Soiuzmul'tfil'm, 1969.

The Duckling who Couldn't Play Football (Utenok, kotoryi ne umel igrat' v futbol). Dir. Vitol'd Bordzilovskii. Soiuzmul'tfil'm, 1972.

Dzhiabzha. Dir. Mstislav Pashchenko. Lenfil'm, 1938.

The Eaglet (Orlenok). Dir. Vitol'd Bordzilovskii. Soiuzmul'tfil'm, 1968.

Elegy (Elegiia). Dir. Nataliia Bodiul. Moldova-fil'm, 1975.

The Elephant and the Ant (Slon i muravei). Dir. Boris Dezhkin. Soiuzmul'tfil'm, 1948.

Emergency Assistance (Skoraia pomoshch'). Dir. Lamis Bredis. Soiuzmul'tfil'm, 1949.

The Enchanted Boy (*Zakoldovannyi mal'chik*). Dir. Vladimir Polkovnikov and Aleksandra Snezhko-Blotskaia. Soiuzmul'tfil'm, 1955.

The End of the Black Swamp (*Konets chernoi topi*). Dir. Vladimir Degtiarev. Soiuzmul'tfil'm, 1960.

Ericaceous Honey (*Vereskovyi med*). Dir. Irina Gurvich. Kievnauchfil'm, 1974.

Exercises for a Tail (*Zariadka dlia khvosta*). Dir. Ivan Ufimtsev. 1979.

Fables in Faces – Merry Go Round No. 5 (*Nebylitsy v litsakh – Veselaia karusel' N. 5*). Dir. Gennadii Sokol'skii. Soiuzmul'tfil'm, 1973.

Fables – Merry Go Round No. 2 (*Nebylitsy – Veselaia karusel' N. 2*). Dir. Rasa Strautmane. Soiuzmul'tfil'm, 1970.

Familiar Faces (*Znakomye litsa*). Dir. Faina Epifanova. Soiuzmul'tfil'm, 1966.

Fantik – A Primitive Story (*Fantik – Pervobytnaia istoriia*). Dir. Efim Gamburg. Soiuzmul'tfil'm, 1975.

The Fascist Boot Won't Trample the Soil of Our Motherland (*Ne toptat' fashistskomu sapogu nashei rodiny*). Dir. Aleksandr Ivanov and Ivan Ivanov-Vano. Soiuzmul'tfil'm, 1941. (Gosfil'mofond)

Favorite Heroes (*Liubimye geroi*). Dir. Dmitrii Babichenko. Soiuzmul'tfil'm, 1940.

Fear Has Wide Eyes (*U strakha glaza veliki*). Dir. Ol'ga Khodataeva and Petr Nosov. Soiuzmul'tfil'm, 1946.

Fedia Zaitsev. Dir. Valentina Brumberg and Zinaida Brumberg. Soiuzmul'tfil'm, 1948.

Fedor the Hunter (*Okhotnik Fedor*). Dir. Aleksandr Ivanov. Soiuzmul'tfil'm, 1938. (Gosfil'mofond)

Film, Film, Film (*Fil'm, fil'm, fil'm*). Dir. Fedor Khitruk. Soiuzmul'tfil'm, 1968.

The Field (*Pole*). Dir. Rein Raamat. Tallinnfil'm, 1978.

Fire (*Ogon'*). Dir. Valentina Brumberg and Zinaida Brumberg. Soiuzmul'tfil'm, 1971.

The Firebird (*Zhar-ptitsa*). Dir. Rein Raamat. Tallinfil'm, 1974.

The Firefly – Merry Go Round No. 10 (*Svetliachok – Veselaia karusel' N. 10*). Dir. Anatolii Petrov. Soiuzmul'tfil'm, 1978.

Firefly No. 2 (*Svetliachok N. 2*). Dir. Petr Nosov. Soiuzmul'tfil'm, 1962.

The Flight (*Polet*). Dir. Rein Raamat. Tallinnfil'm, 1973.

Flight to the Moon (*Polet na lunu*). Dir. Valentina Brumberg and Zinaida Brumberg. Soiuzmul'tfil'm, 1953.

The First Lesson (*Pervyi urok*). Dir. Lamis Bredis. Soiuzmul'tfil'm, 1948.

The Flower with Seven Colors (*Tsvetik-semitsvetik*). Dir. Mikhail Tsekhanovskii. Soiuzmul'tfil'm, 1948.

The Fly Tsokotukha (*Mukha-tsokotukha*). Dir. Boris Dezhkin. Soiuzmul'tfil'm, 1960.

The Flying Proletarian (*Letaiushchii proletarii*). Dir. Iosif Boiarskii. Soiuzmul'tfil'm, 1962.

The Flying Ship (*Letuchii korabl'*). Dir. Garri Bardin. Soiuzmul'tfil'm, 1979.

Football Stars (*Futbol'nye zvezdy*). Dir. Boris Dezhkin. Soiuzmul'tfil'm, 1974.

For a Snap – Merry Go Round No. 9 (*Za shchelchok – Veselaia karusel' N. 9*). Dir. Leonid Kaiukov. Soiuzmul'tfil'm, 1977.

For Adults Only (*Tol'ko dlia vzroslykh*). Dir. Efim Gamburg. Soiuzmul'tfil'm, 1971.

For You, Moscow! (*Tebe, Moskva!*) Dir. Grigorii Lomidze. Soiuzmul'tfil'm, 1947. (Gosfil'mofond)

The Forest Chronicle (*Lesnaia khronika*). Dir. Petr Nosov. Soiuzmul'tfil'm, 1970.

The Forest Concert (*Lesnoi kontsert*). Dir. Ivan Ivanov-Vano. Soiuzmul'tfil'm, 1953.

Forest Travelers (*Lesnye puteshestvenniki*). Dir. Mstislav Pashchenko. Soiuzmul'tfil'm, 1951.

Forward, Time! (*Vpered, vremia!*) Dir. Vladimir Tarasov. Soiuzmul'tfil'm, 1977. (Films by Jove, Inc.)

Four from the Same Yard (*Chetvero s odnogo dvora*). Dir. Inessa Kovalevskaia. Soiuzmul'tfil'm, 1967.

The Fox and the Grapes (*Lisa i vinograd*). Dir. Viacheslav Levandovskii. Mosfil'm, 1936.

The Fox and the Hare (*Lisa i zaiats*). Dir. Iurii Norshtein. Soiuzmul'tfil'm, 1973.

The Fox and the Wolf (*Lisa i volk*). Dir. Nikolai Nosov. Soiuzmul'tfil'm, 1958.

The Fox Builder (*Lisa-stroitel'*). Dir. Panteleimon Sazonov. Soiuzmul'tfil'm, 1950.

The Fox, the Beaver, and Others (*Lisa, Bober i drugie*). Dir. Mikhail Tsekhanovskii. Soiuzmul'tfil'm, 1960.

Frantishek. Dir. Vadim Kurchevskii. Soiuzmul'tfil'm, 1967.

The Princess-Frog (*Tsarevna-liagushka*). Dir. Mikhail Tsekhanovskii. Soiuzmul'tfil'm, 1954.

The Frog Traveler (*Liagushka-puteshestvennitsa*). Dir. Aleksandr Trusov and Viacheslav Kotenochkin. Soiuzmul'tfil'm, 1965.

Fulfilment of Wishes (*Ispolnenie zhelanii*). Dir. Valentina Brumberg and Zinaida Brumberg. Soiuzmul'tfil'm, 1957.

Funtik and Cucumbers (*Funtik i ogurtsy*). Dir. Leonid Aristov. Soiuzmul'tfil'm, 1961.

Geese-Swans (*Gusi-lebedi*). Dir. Aleksandr Ivanov. Soiuzmul'tfil'm, 1949.

Gena the Crocodile (*Krokodil Gena*). Dir. Roman Kachanov. Soiuzmul'tfil'm, 1969.

The Giraffe and the Glasses (*Zhirafa i ochki*). Dir. Galina Barinova. Soiuzmul'tfil'm, 1978.

The Girl and the Elephant (*Devochka i slon*). Dir. Leonid Amal'rik. Soiuzmul'tfil'm, 1969.

The Girl in the Circus (*Devochka v tsirke*). Dir. Valentina Brumberg and Zinaida Brumberg. Soiuzmul'tfil'm, 1950.

The Girl in the Jungle (*Devochka v dzhungliakh*). Dir. Vera Tsekhanovskaia. Soiuzmul'tfil'm, 1956.

Give Back Rex (*Vernite Reksa*). Dir. Vladimir Pekar' and Vladimir Popov. Soiuzmul'tfil'm, 1975.

The Glass Harmonica (*Stekliannaia garmonika*). Dir. Andrei Khrzhanovskii. Soiuzmul'tfil'm, 1968.

Glory to You, Celestial Brothers! (*Slava vam, nebesnye brat'ia!*) Dir. Roman Davydov and Ivan Aksenchuk. Soiuzmul'tfil'm, 1961. (Gosfil'mofond)

The Goat Musician (*Kozel-muzykant*). Dir. Boris Dezhkin. Soiuzmul'tfil'm, 1954.

The Golden Antelope (*Zolotaia antilopa*). Dir. Lev Atamanov. Soiuzmul'tfil'm, 1954.

The Golden Egg (*Zolotoe iaichko*). Dir. Ippolit Lazarchuk. Soiuzmul'tfil'm, 1963.

The Golden Plume (*Zolotoe peryshko*). Dir. Ol'ga Khodataeva and Leonid Aristov. Soiuzmul'tfil'm, 1960.

Go There – I Don't Know Where (*Podi tuda – ne znaiu kuda*). Dir. Ivan Ivanov-Vano and Vladimir Danilevich. Soiuzmul'tfil'm, 1966.

Golden Foreheads (*Zolochennye lby*). Dir. Nikolai Serebriakov. Soiuzmul'tfil'm, 1971.

Grandpa and Grandchild (*Dedushka i vnuchek*). Dir. Aleksandr Ivanov. Soiuzmul'tfil'm, 1950.

Grandmother's Kid: a Tale for Grown-Ups (*Babyshkin kozlik. Skazka dlia vzroslykh*). Dir. Leonid Amal'rik. Soiuzmul'tfil'm, 1963.

Grandmother's Umbrella (*Babushkin zontik*). Dir. Lev Mil'chin. Soiuzmul'tfil'm, 1969.

The Grasshopper and the Ant (*Strekoza i muravei*). Dir. Nikolai Fedorov. Soiuzmul'tfil'm, 1961.

The Great Cold (*Velikie Kholoda*). Dir. Nikolai Serebriakov. Soiuzmul'tfil'm, 1969.

The Greatest Friend (*Samyi bol'shoi drug*). Dir. Petr Nosov. Soiuzmul'tfil'm, 1966.

Great Troubles (*Bol'shie nepriiatnosti*). Dir. Valentina Brumberg and Zinaida Brumberg. Soiuzmul'tfil'm, 1961.

The Guess (*Dogada*). Dir. Stanislav Sokolov. Soiuzmul'tfil'm, 1977.

Habanero (*Khabanera*). Dir. Sergei Obraztsov and A. Mazur. Soiuzdetfil'm, 1938. (Gosfil'mofond)

The Hare Tailor (*Zaiats-portnoi*). Dir. Zinaida Brumberg and Valentina Brumberg. Soiuzmul'tfil'm, 1937. (Gosfil'mofond)

The Helper Stick (*Palka-vyruchalka*). Dir. Zinaida Brumberg and Valentina Brumberg. Soiuzmul'tfil'm, 1956.

He Surpassed (*Prevzoshel*). Dir. Vladimir Mudzhiri. Tbiliskaia kinostudiia, 1942.

Heart (*Serdtse*). Dir. Boris Stepantsev. Soizumul'tfil'm, 1971. (Gosfil'mofond)

Hedgehog in the Fog (*Ezhik v tumane*). Dir. Iurii Norshtein. Soiuzmul'tfil'm, 1975.

Hello, Friends (*Privet druz'iam*). Dir. Dmitrii Babichenko, Boris Dezhkin and Mstislav Pashchenko. Soiuzmul'tfil'm, 1957. (Gosfil'mofond)

Hello, Martyshka (*Privet Martyshke*). Dir. Ivan Ufimtsev. 1978.

The Heron and the Crane (*Tsaplia i zhuravl'*). Dir. Iurii Norshtein. Soiuzmul'tfil'm, 1974.

The Hippopotamus – Kaleidescope No. 68 (*Begemot – Kaleidoskop N. 68*). Dir. Anatolii Petrov. Soiuzmul'tfil'm, 1968.

Hothead Hare (*Zaika-zaznaika*). Dir. Boris Ablynin. Soiuzmul'tfil'm, 1976.

The Hot Stone (*Goriachii kamen'*). Dir. Perch Sarkisian. Soiuzmul'tfil'm, 1965.

The Hour Before the Rendezvous (*Za chas do svidaniia*). Dir. Valentina Brumberg and Zinaida Brumberg. Soiuzmul'tfil'm, 1965.

The House that Jack Built (*Dom, kotoryi postroil Dzhek*). Dir. Andrei Khrzhanovskii. Soiuzmul'tfil'm, 1976.

How a Duckling Musician Became a Football Player (*Kak utenok-muzykant stal futbolistom*). Dir. Vitol'd Bordzilovskii. Soiuzmul'tfil'm, 1978.

How Masha Fought with a Pillow (*Kak Masha possorilas' s podushkoi*). Dir. Lev Mil'chin. Soiuzmul'tfil'm, 1977.

How One Man Fed Two Generals (*Kak odin muzhik dvukh generalov prokormil*). Dir. Vladimir Danilevich and Ivan Ivanov-Vano. Soiuzmul'tfil'm, 1965.

How the Fox Tried to Catch the Hare (*Kak lisa zajtsa dogoniala*). Dir. Anatolii Solin. Soiuzmul'tfil'm, 1979.

How the Kid Saved the World (*Kak kozlik zemliu derzhal*). Dir. Vladimir Polkovnikov. Soiuzmul'tfil'm, 1974.

How the Little Lion and the Turtle Sang a Song (*Kak l'venok i cherepakha peli pesniu*). Dir. Inessa Kovalevskaia. Soiuzmul'tfil'm, 1974.

How They Built a House for a Kitten (*Kak kotenku postroili dom*). Dir. Roman Kachanov. Soiuzmul'tfil'm, 1963.

How to Get Big (*Kak stat' bol'shim*). Dir. Vladimir Degtiarev. Soiuzmul'tfil'm, 1967.

How Vasia Terkin Went to Be Recruited (*Kak Vasia Terkin prizyvat'sia shel*). Dir. Vitalii Siumkin and Pavel Shmidt. Soiuzmul'tfil'm, 1941. (Gosfil'mofond)

The Huge Cockroach (*Tarakanishche*). Dir. Aleksandr Ivanov. Moskovskaia Fabrika Sovkino, 1927. No longer available.

The Huge Cockroach (*Tarakanishche*). Dir. Vladimir Polkovnikov. Soiuzmul'tfil'm, 1963.

Humorous Stories (*Iumoreski*). Dir. Dziga Vertov. Goskino (Kul'tkino), 1924. No longer available.

Humorous Stories 1–3 (*Iumoreski 1–3*). Dir. Valentin Karavaev. Soiuzmul'tfil'm, 1973–74.

The Hunchbacked Horse (*Konek-gorbunok*). Dir. Ivan Ivanov-Vano. Soiuzmul'tfil'm, (orig. 1947 no longer available), remake 1975.

The Hunt (*Okhota*). Dir. Eduard Nazarov. Soiuzmul'tfil'm, 1979.

The Hunting Rifle (*Okhotnich'e ruzh'e*). Dir. Roman Davydov and Panteleimon Sazonov. Soiuzmul'tfil'm, 1948.

I Draw the Sun (*Ia narisuiu solntse*). Dir. Vadim Kurchevskii. Soiuzmul'tfil'm, 1970.

I Drew the Little Man (*Chelovechka narisoval ia*). Dir. Valentina Brumberg and Zinaida Brumberg. Soiuzmul'tfil'm, 1960.

I fly to you in a memory (*Ia k Vam lechu vospominaniem*). Dir. Andrei Khrzhanovskii. Soiuzmul'tfil'm, 1977.

I Give You a Star (*Dariu tebe zvezdu*). Dir. Fedor Khitruk. Soiuzmul'tfil'm, 1974.

I Remember (*Ia vspominaiu*). Dir. Lev Atamanov. Soiuzmul'tfil'm, 1975.

I Want to Be Brave (*Khochu byt' otvazhnym*). Dir. Vadim Kurchevskii and Nikolai Serebriakov. Soiuzmul'tfil'm, 1963.

I'm Waiting for the Bird (*Ia zhdu ptentsa*). Dir. Nikolai Serebriakov. Soiuzmul'tfil'm, 1966.

If You Don't Like It, Don't Listen (*Ne liubo – ne slushai*). Dir. Leonid Nosyrev. Soiuzmul'tfil'm, 1977.

Ikar and the Sages (*Ikar i mudretsy*). Dir. Fedor Khitruk. Soiuzmul'tfil'm, 1976.

In a Certain Kingdom (*V nekotorom tsarstve*). Dir. Ivan Ivanov-Vano. Soiuzmul'tfil'm, 1957.

In the Arena for the First Time (*Vpervye na arene*). Dir. Vladimir Pekar' and Vladimir Popov. Soiuzmul'tfil'm, 1961.

In the Heart of the Forest (*V lesnoi chashche*). Dir. Aleksandr Ivanov. Soiuzmul'tfil'm, 1954.

In the Land of Unlearned Lessons (*V strane nevyuchennykh urokov*). Dir. Iurii Prytkov. Soiuzmul'tfil'm, 1969.

In the Port (*V portu*). Dir. Inessa Kovalevskaia. Soiuzmul'tfil'm, 1975.

In the Snout of the Second International – fragment (*V mordu vtoromy internatsionalu – fragment*). Dir. Aleksandr Bushkin. Goskino (Kul'tkino), 1924. (Gosfil'mofond)

In the Thirtieth Century (*V tridesiatom veke*). Dir. Vladimir Samsonov. Soiuzmul'tfil'm, 1972.

In the World of Fables (*V mire basen*). Dir. Andrei Khrzhanovskii. Soiuzmul'tfil'm, 1973.

Interplanetary Revolution (*Mezhplanetnaia revoliutsiia*). Dir. Zenon Komissarenko, Iurii Merkulov and Nikolai Khodataev. GTK (Gos.Tekh.Kino), Mezhrabpom-Rus', 1924. (Gosfil'mofond)

Is This Film about You? – Merry Go Round No. 5 (*Ne pro tebia li etoi fil'm? – Veselaia karusel' N. 5*). Dir. Vladimir Ugarov. Soiuzmul'tfil'm, 1973.

The Island of Mistakes (*Ostrov oshibok*). Dir. Valentina Brumberg and Zinaida Brumberg. Soiuzmul'tfil'm, 1955.

The Island (*Ostrov*). Dir. Fedor Khitruk. Soiuzmul'tfil'm, 1973.

It Happened in Winter (*Sluchilos' eto zimoi*). Dir. Vladimir Pekar'. Soiuzmul'tfil'm, 1968.

It's in Our Power (*Eto v nashikh silakh*). Dir. Lev Atamanov. Soiuzmul'tfil'm, 1970.

It's Not about Me (*Eto ne pro menia*). Dir. Boris Dezhkin. Soiuzmul'tfil'm, 1966.

Ivan Ivanych Got Sick (*Ivan Ivanych zabolel*). Dir. Vera Tsekhanovskaia and Aleksandr Trusov. Soiuzmul'tfil'm, 1966.

Ivas'. Dir. Ivan Ivanov-Vano. Soiuzmul'tfil'm, 1940. (Gosfil'mofond)

Jokes (*Shutki*). Dir. Lev Atamanov. Soiuzmul'tfil'm, 1963.

The Jolly Old Fellow (*Veselyi starichok – Veselaia karusel' N. 4*). Dir. Anatolii Petrov. Soiuzmul'tfil'm, 1972.

Journal of Political Satire No. 2 (*Zhurnal politsatiry N. 2*). Dir. Ivan Ivanov-Vano and Ol'ga Khodataeva. Soiuzmul'tfil'm, 1941. (Gosfil'mofond)

Just You Wait! – Merry Go Round No. 1 (*Nu, pogodi! – Veselaia karusel' N. 1*). Dir. Gennadii Sokol'skii. Soiuzmul'tfil'm, 1969.

Just You Wait! (*Nu pogodi!*) Dir. Viacheslav Kotenochkin. Soiuzmul'tfil'm, 1969–1993.

Karlson Returned (*Karlson vernulsia*). Dir. Boris Stepantsev. Soiuzmul'tfil'm, 1970.

Kashtanka. Dir. Mikhail Tsekhanovskii. Soiuzmul'tfil'm, 1952.

The Key (*Kliuch*). Dir. Lev Atamanov. Soiuzmul'tfil'm, 1961.

The Kid (*Kozlenok*). Dir. Roman Davydov. Soiuzmul'tfil'm, 1961.

The Kid who Counted to Ten (*Kozlenok, kotoryi schital do desiati*). Dir. Vladimir Degtiarev. Soiuzmul'tfil'm, 1968.

Kikos. Dir. Robert Saakiants. Armenfil'm, 1979.

Kino-krokodil N. 5. Dir. Aleksandr Evmenenko, Petr Nosov, Nikolai Nosov, V. Trotsenko and V. Bochkarev. Moskovskaia fabrika Soiuzkino, 1932. (Gosfil'mofond)

Know-Nothing (*Neznaika*). Dir. Aleksandr Bogoliubov, Iurii Trofimov, Kirill Maliantovich, Iurii Klepatskti, David Sulakauri, V. Golikov. Gosteleradio SSSR, 1971–1973.

Know-Nothing in the Sunny City (*Neznaika v solnechnom gorode*). Dir. Nina Shorina and P. Murashov. Ekran, Gosteleradio, 1976–1977.

Know-Nothing Studies (*Neznaika uchitsia*). Dir. Petr Nosov. Soiuzmul'tfil'm, 1961.

Kolia, Olia, and Arkhimed (*Kolia, Olia i Arkhimed*). Dir. Iurii Prytkov. Soiuzmul'tfil'm, 1972.

Kotofei Kotofeevich. Dir. Ivan Ivanov-Vano. Soiuzmul'tfil'm, 1937.

Labyrinth (*Labirint*). Dir. Aleksandra Snezhko-Blotskaia. Soiuzmul'tfil'm, 1971.

The Land where You Live (*Krai, v kotorom ty zhivesh'*). Dir. Efim Gamburg. Soiuzmul'tfil'm, 1972.

The Lefthander (*Levsha*). Dir. Ivan Ivanov-Vano and Vladimir Danilevich. Soiuzmul'tfil'm, 1964.

The Legend of Grig (*Legenda o Grige*). Dir. Vadim Kurchevskii. Soiuzmul'tfil'm, 1967.

Legends of the Peruan Indians (*Legendy peruanskikh indeitsev*). Dir. Vladimir Pekar'. Soiuzmul'tfil'm, 1978.

The Lesson is No Use (*Urok ne vprok*). Dir. Valentin Karavaev. Soiuzmul'tfil'm, 1971.

Let's Bring The Cinema to the Countryside! (*Kino v derevniu!*). Dir. Aleksandr Ptushko, I. Nikitchenko. Sovkino (Kul'turfil'm), 1930. No longer available.

The Letter (*Pis'mo*). Dir. Roman Kachanov. Soiuzmul'tfil'm, 1970.

The Life and Sufferings of Ivan Semenov (*Zhizn' i stradaniia Ivana Semenova*). Dir. Vadim Kurchevskii and Nikolai Serebriakov. Soiuzmul'tfil'm, 1964.

Limpopo River (*Limpopo*). Dir. Leonid Amal'rik and Vladimir Polkovnikov. Soiuzmul'tfil'm, 1939. (Gosfil'mofond)

The Little Bear (*Medvezhonok*). Dir. Petr Nosov, Aleksandr Evmenenko and Ol'ga Khodataeva. Soiuzmul'tfil'm, 1940. (Gosfil'mofond)

The Little Bear on the Road (*Medvezhonok na doroge*). Dir. Rasa Strautmane. Soiuzmul'tfil'm, 1964.

The Little Boy and Karlson (*Malysh i Karlson*). Dir. Boris Stepantsev. Soiuzmul'tfil'm, 1968.

The Little Elephant (*Slonenok*). Dir. Efim Gamburg. Soiuzmul'tfil'm, 1967.

The Little Elephant (*Slonenok*). Dir. V. Shchekalin. Soiuzmul'tfil'm, 1936.

The Little Golden Key (*Zolotoi kliuchik*). Dir. Aleksandr Ptushko. Mosfil'm, 1939.

The Little Grey Neck (*Seraia sheika*). Dir. Leonid Amal'rik. Soiuzmul'tfil'm, 1948.

The Little Hippo – Merry Go Round No. 7 (*Begemotik – Veselaia karusel' N. 7*). Dir. Eduard Nazarov. Soiuzmul'tfil'm, 1975.

The Little Icebreaker (*Katerok*). Dir. Inessa Kovalevskaia. Soiuzmul'tfil'm, 1970.

The Little Organ (*Organchik*). Dir. Nikolai Khodataev. Moskinokombinat, 1934. (Gosfil'mofond)

The Little Round Bun (*Kolobok*). Dir. Vladimir Suteev. Soiuzmul'tfil'm, 1936. (Gosfil'mofond)

The Little Scarlet Flower (*Alen'kii tsvetochek*). Dir. Lev Atamanov. Soiuzmul'tfil'm, 1952.

The Little Ship (*Korablik*). Dir. Leonid Amal'rik. Soiuzmul'tfil'm, 1956.

The Little Train from Romashkov (*Parovozik iz Romashkova*). Dir. Vladimir Degtiarev. Soiuzmul'tfil'm, 1967.

The Lively Market Garden (*Veselyi ogorod*). Dir. Vladimir Suteev. Soiuzmul'tfil'm, 1947.

Look Out! A Pike! (*Ostorozhno, shchuka!*) Dir. Ivan Ufimtsev and Mikhail Kamenetskii. Soiuzmul'tfil'm, 1968.

Looking at the Gleam of the Polar Sunset (*Gliadia na luch poliarnogo zakata*). Dir. Sergei Obraztsov and A. Mazur. Soiuzdetfil'm, 1938. (Gosfil'mofond)

Losharik. Dir. Ivan Ufimtsev. Soiuzmul'tfil'm, 1971.

Lucanus Cervus. Dir. Vladislav Starevich, 1910.

MacDonald's Career (*Kar'era Makdonal'da*). Dir. Aleksandr Bushkin. Goskino (Kul'tkino), 1925.

The Magic Ring (*Volshebnoe kol'tso*). Dir. Leonid Nosyrev. Soiuzmul'tfil'm, 1979.

The Magic Store (*Volshebnyi magazin*). Dir. Leonid Amal'rik and V. Polkovnikov. Soiuzmul'tfil'm, 1953.

The Magician Bakhram's Inheritance (*Nasledstvo volshebnika Bakhrama*). Dir. Roman Kachanov. Soiuzmul'tfil'm, 1975.

The Main Star (*Glavnyi zvezdnyi*). Dir. Roman Davydov. Soiuzmul'tfil'm, 1966.

The Man in the Frame (*Chelovek v ramke*). Dir. Fedor Khitruk. Soiuzmul'tfil'm, 1966.

The Market – Fragment from The Tale of the Pope and his Worker Balda (*Bazar*, fragment from *Skazka o pope i rabotnike ego Balda*). Dir. Mikhail Tsekhanovskii. Leningradskaia fabrika Sovkino, 1936. (Gosfil'mofond)

Marusia's Carousel (*Marusina karusel'*). Dir. Natan Lerner. Ekran, 1967.

Mashen'ka and the Bear (*Mashen'ka i medved'*). Dir. Roman Kachanov. Soiuzmul'tfil'm, 1960.

Mashen'ka's Concert (*Mashen'kin kontsert*). Dir. Mstislav Pashchenko. Soiuzmul'tfil'm, 1949.

The Master from Clamsy (*Master iz Klamsi*). Dir. Vadim Kurchevskii. Soiuzmul'tfil'm, 1972.

Master of Daily Life (*Vlastelin byta*). Dir. Aleksandr Ptushko. Soiuzkino, 1932.

Maugli. Dir. Roman Davydov. Soiuzmul'tfil'm, 1967–1971.

Maugli. Dir. Roman Davydov. Soiuzmul'tfil'm, 1973.

Mechanics of the Brain (Mekhanika golovnogo mozga). Dir. Vsevolod Pudovkin, animation sequences by Iurii Merkulov, 1926. (Gosfil'mofond)

The Mermaid (Rusalochka). Dir. Ivan Aksenchuk. Soiuzmul'tfil'm, 1968.

The Meteor in the Ring (Meteor na ringe). Dir. Boris Dezhkin. Soiuzmul'tfil'm, 1970.

Militant Pages (Boevye stranitsy). Dir. Dmitrii Babichenko. Soiuzmul'tfil'm, 1939. (Gosfil'mofond)

Millionaire (Millioner). Dir. Vitol'd Bordzilovskii and Iurii Prytkov. Soiuzmul'tfil'm, 1963. (Films by Jove, Inc.)

Miracle – Merry Go Round No. 5 (Chudo – Veselaia karusel' N. 5). Dir. Anatolii Petrov. Soiuzmul'tfil'm, 1973.

The Miracle Maker (Chudesnitsa). Dir. Aleksandr Ivanov. Soiuzmul'tfil'm, 1957.

The Miracle Mill (Chudo-mel'nitsa). Dir. Ol'ga Khodataeva. Soiuzmul'tfil'm, 1950.

Miracles in a Sieve (Chudesa v reshete). Dir. Andrei Khrzhanovskii. Soiuzmul'tfil'm, 1978.

Miracles in the Middle of the Day (Chudesa sredi bela dnia). Dir. Mikhail Kamenetskii. Soiuzmul'tfil'm, 1978.

The Miraculous Bell (Chudesnyi Kolokol'chik). Dir. Zinaida Brumberg and Valentina Brumberg. Soiuzmul'tfil'm, 1949.

The Miraculous Garden (Chudesnyi sad). Dir. Aleksandra Snezhko-Blotskaia. Soiuzmul'tfil'm, 1962.

The Miraculous Well (Chudesnyi kolodets). Dir. Vladimir Degtiarev. Soizmul'tfil'm, 1956.

The Mirror of Time (Zerkalo vremeni). Dir. Vladimir Tarasov. Soiuzmul'tfil'm, 1976.

Mister Twister (Mister Tvister). Dir. Anatolii Karanovich. Soiuzmul'tfil'm, 1963. (Gosfil'mofond)

Mister Wolf (Mister Uolk). Dir. Viktor Gromov. Soiuzmul'tfil'm, 1949. (Gosfil'mofond)

The Mitten (Varezhka). Dir. Roman Kachanov. Soiuzmul'tfil'm, 1967.

Moidodyr. Dir. Maria Benderskaia. Mezhrabpomfil'm, 1927. No longer available.

Moidodyr. Dir. Ivan Ivanov-Vano. Soiuzmul'tfil'm, 1939. (Gosfil'mofond)

Moidodyr. Dir. Ivan Ivanov-Vano. Soiuzmul'tfil'm, 1954.

Mosaic – Merry Go Round No. 1 (Mozaika – Veselaia karusel' N. 1). Dir. Galina Barinova. Soiuzmul'tfil'm, 1969.

The Most, Most, Most, Most (Samyi, samyi, samyi, samyi). Dir. Vasilii Livanov. Soiuzmul'tfil'm, 1966.

The Mountain Master (Gornyi master). Dir. Inessa Kovalevskaia. Soiuzmul'tfil'm, 1978.

The Mountain of Dinosaurs (Gora Dinozavrov). Dir. Rasa Strautmane. Soiuzmul'tfil'm, 1967.

The Muddle – Merry Go Round No. 6 (Putanitsa – Veselaia karusel' N. 6). Dir. Galina Barinova. Soiuzmul'tfil'm, 1974.

Mumi-Troll and the Comet (*Mumi-Troll' i kometa*). Dir. Aida Ziablikova and Nina Shorina. Ekran, 1978.

Murzilka and the Giant (*Murzilka i velikan*). Dir. Petr Nosov. Soiuzmul'tfil'm, 1960.

Murzilka on the Sputnik (*Murzilka na sputnike*). Dir. Evgenii Raikovskii and Boris Stepantsev. Soiuzmul'tfil'm, 1960.

The Musicians from Nemukhino (*Nemukhinskie muzykanty*). Dir. Vadim Kurchevskii. Soiuzmul'tfil'm, 1973.

My Green Crocodile (*Moi zelenyi krokodil*). Dir. Vadim Kurchevskii. Soiuzmul'tifil'm, 1966.

Narcissus (*Nartsiss*). Dir. Vakhtang Bakhtadze. Gruziia-Fil'm, 1964.

Neither to God Nor to the Devil (*Ni bogu ni chertu*). Dir. Vadim Kurchevskii and Nikolai Serebriakov. Soiuzmul'tfil'm, 1965. (Gosfil'mofond)

New Great Troubles (*Novye bol'shie nepriiatnosti*). Dir. Valentina Brumberg and Zinaida Brumberg. Soiuzmul'tfil'm, 1973.

New Gulliver (*Novyi Gulliver*). Dir. Aleksandr Ptushko. Mosfil'm, 1935.

New Year's Eve (*Novogodniaia noch'*). Dir. Ol'ga Khodataeva and Petr Nosov. Soiuzmul'tfil'm, 1948.

New Year's Journey (*Novogodnee puteshestvie*). Dir. Petr Nosov. Soiuzmul'tfil'm, 1959.

Night Alarm – Bratishkin In The Barrack (*Nochnaia trevoga – Bratishkin v kazarme*). Dir. Iurii Merkulov, A. Barshch. Gosvoenkino, 1928. No longer available.

The Night Before Christmas (*Noch' pered rozhdestvom*). Dir. Vladislav Starevich. 1913.

The Night Before Christmas (*Noch' pered rozhdestvom*). Dir. Valentina Brumberg and Zinaida Brumberg. Soiuzmul'tfil'm, 1951.

The Nutcracker (*Shchelkunchik*). Dir. Boris Stepantsev. Soiuzmul'tfil'm, 1973.

Oak-Uprooter (*Validub*). Dir. Dmitrii Babichenko. Soiuzmul'tfil'm, 1952.

Octopuses (*Os'minozhki*). Dir. Rasa Strautmane. Ekran, 1976.

Old Acquaintances (*Starye znakomye*). Dir. Mstislav Pashchenko and Boris Dezhkin. Soiuzmul'tfil'm, 1956.

The Old Man and the Crane (*Starik i zhuravl'*). Dir. Roman Kachanov, Anatolii Karanovich. Soizmul'tfil'm, 1958.

Old Precepts (*Starye zavety*). Dir. Efim Gamburg. Soiuzmul'tfil'm, 1968.

The Old Toy (*Staraia igrushka*) Dir. Vladimir Samsonov. Soiuzmul'tfil'm, 1971.

On the Forest Stage (*Na lesnoi estrade*). Dir. Ivan Aksenchuk. Soiuzmul'tfil'm, 1954.

On the Material of Political Caricatures – A Cinematic Poster (*Po materialam politicheskikh karikatur. Kino-plakat*). Dir. Iurii Merkulov, n.d. Moskovskaia Fabrika Sovkino.

On the Origin of Species (*Proiskhozhdenie vida*). Dir. Efim Gamburg. Soiuzmul'tfil'm, 1966.

On the Trail of the Bremen Musicians (*Po sledam Bremenskikh muzykantov*). Dir. Vasilii Livanov. Soiuzmul'tfil'm, 1973.

One Among Many (*Odna iz mnogikh*). Dir. Nikolai Khodataev. Mezhrabpom-Rus', 1927. (Gosfil'mofond)

One, Two, Together! (*Raz-dva, druzhno!*). Dir. Vladimir Polkovnikov. Soiuzmul'tfil'm, 1967.
One Hundred Adventures (*Sto prikliuchenii*). Dir. Aleksandr Ptushko. Sovkino (Tret'ia fabrika), 1929. No longer available.
Operator Kyps in the Land of Mushrooms (*Operator Kyps v strane gribov*). Dir. Kheino Pars. Tallinfil'm, 1964.
Orange – Merry Go Round No. 8. (*Apel'sin – Veselaia karusel' N. 8*). Dir. Galina Barinova. Soiuzmul'tfil'm, 1976.
The Orange Throat (*Oranzhevoe gorlyshko*). Dir. Vladimir Polkovnikov. Soiuzmul'tfil'm, 1954.
Othello-67 (*Otello-67*). Dir. Fedor Khitruk. Soiuzmul'tfil'm, 1967.
Ott in Space (*Ott' v kosmose*). Dir. El'bert Tuganov. Tallinfil'm, 1961.
Our Answer to Chamberlain (*Nash otvet Chemberlenu*). Dir. Iurii Merkulov. Moskovskaia fabrika Sovkino, 1927. (Gosfil'mofond)
Our caricatures (*Nashi karikatury - kinoplakat*). Dir. Iurii Merkulov, n.d.
Our Sun (*Nashe solntse*). Dir. Ivan Aksenchuk. Soiuzmul'tfil'm, 1957. (Gosfil'mofond)
Overseas Reporter (*Zaokeanskii reporter*). Dir. Grigorii Lomidze. Soiuzmul'tfil'm, 1961. (Gosfil'mofond)
The Painted Fox (*Krashenyi lis*). Dir. Aleksandr Ivanov. Soiuzmul'tfil'm, 1953.
Paint Thieves (*Pokhititeli krasok*). Dir. Lev Atamanov. Soiuzmul'tfil'm, 1959.
The Parcel – Merry Go Round No. 10 (*Posylka – Veselaia karusel' N. 10*). Dir. Galina Barinova. Soiuzmul'tfil'm, 1978.
The Passions of Spies (*Shpionskie strasti*). Dir. Efim Gamburg. Soiuzmul'tfil'm, 1967.
Peace to You and Your Home (*Mir domu tvoemu*). Dir. Viktor Nikitin and Igor' Nikolaev. Soiuzmul'tfil'm, 1962. (Gosfil'mofond)
Peer Gynt (*Per Giunt*). Dir. Vadim Kurchevskii. Soiumul'tfil'm, 1979.
The Pen and the Blot – Lively Hunters (*Karandash i Kliaksa – veselye okhotniki*). Dir. Evgenii Migunov. Soiuzmul'tfil'm, 1954.
Perseus (*Persei*). Dir. Aleksandra Snezhko-Blotskaia. Soiuzmul'tfil'm, 1973.
Petia and Little Red Riding Hood (*Petia i krasnaia shapochka*). Dir. Boris Stepantsev and Evgenii Raikovskii. Soiuzmul'tfil'm, 1958.
Petia and the Wolf (*Petia i volk*). Dir. Anatolii Karanovich. Soiuzmul'tfil'm, 1958.
Phedora's Grief (*Fedorino gore*). Dir. Nataliia Chervinskaia. Soiuzmul'tfil'm, 1974.
Pik the Little Mouse (*Myshonok pik*). Dir. Gennadii Sokol'skii. Soiuzmul'tfil'm, 1978.
The Pioneer's Violin (*Skripka Pionera*). Dir. Boris Stepantsev. Soiuzmul'tfil'm, 1971. (Gosfil'mofond)
The Plasticine Hedgehog (*Plastilinovyi ezhik*). Dir. Vladimir Danilevich. Soiuzmul'tfil'm, 1969.
Plus Electrification (*Plius elektrifikatsiia*). Dir. Ivan Aksenchuk. Soiuzmul'tfil'm, 1972.
Political Revue, Based on the Drawings of Deni (*Politicheskoe obozrenie po*

risunkam Deni). Dir. Iurii Merkulov and Daniil Cherkes, n.d. (Gosfil'mofond)

Polygon (*Poligon*). Dir. Anatolii Petrov. Soiuzmul'tfil'm, 1977.

The Pony Runs in a Circle (*Poni begaet po krugu*). Dir. Lev Atamanov. Soiuzmul'tfil'm, 1974.

Poor Liza (*Bednaia Liza*). Dir. Ideia Garanina. Soiuzmul'tfil'm, 1978.

The Portrait (*Portret*). Dir. Roman Kachanov. Soiuzmul'tfil'm, 1965. (Gosfil'mofond)

The Post (*Pochta*). Dir. Mikhail Tsekhanovskii. Leningradskaia fabrika Sovkino, 1929. (Gosfil'mofond)

The Post (*Pochta*). Dir. Mikhail Tsekhanovskii. Soiuzmul'tfil'm, 1964. (Gosfil'mofond)

The Priest and the Nanny-Goat (*Pop i koza*). Dir. Lev Atamanov. Armenkino, 1941.

The Princess and the Cannibal (*Printsessa i liudoed – Veselaia karusel' N. 9*). Dir. Eduard Nazarov. Soiuzmul'tfil'm, 1977.

Prodelkin at School (*Prodelkin v shkole*). Dir. Anatolii Petrov, Gennadii Sokol'skii and Vladimir Ugarov. Soiuzmul'tfil'm, 1974.

Prometheus (*Prometei*). Dir. Aleksandra Snezhko-Blotskaia. Soiuzmul'tfil'm, 1974.

Prophets and Teachings (*Proroki i uroki*). Dir. Viacheslav Kotenochkin. Soiuzmul'tfil'm, 1967.

The Proud Little Ship (*Gordyi korablik*). Dir. Vitol'd Bordzilovskii. Soiuzmul'tfil'm, 1966.

Puck! Puck! (*Shaibu! Shaibu!*). Dir. Boris Dezhkin. Soiuzmul'tfil'm, 1964.

The Puppets Have the Word (*Slovo imeiut kukly*). Dir. Anatolii Karanovich. Soiuzmul'tfil'm, 1957. (Gosfil'mofond)

The Quartet (*Kvartet*). Dir. Aleksandr Ivanov. Soiuzmul'tfil'm, 1947.

The Quiet Meadow (*Tikhaia poliana*). Dir. Boris Dezhkin and Gennadii Filippov. Soiuzmul'tfil'm, 1946.

The Quiet Pier (*Tikhaia pristan'*). Dir. Anatolii Karanovich. Soiuzmul'tfil'm, 1957.

Rain (*Dozhd'*). Dir. Leonid Nosyrev. Soiuzmul'tfil'm, 1978.

Ratibor's Childhood (*Detstvo Ratibora*). Dir. Roman Davydov. Soiuzmul'tfil'm, 1973.

Read and Take a Drive to Paris and China (*Prochti i kutai v Parizh i kitai*). Dir. Anatolii Karanovich. Soiuzmul'tfil'm, 1960. (Gosfil'mofond)

Redhaired, Redhaired, Freckled – Merry Go Round No. 3 (*Ryzhii, ryzhii, konopatyi – Veselaia karusel' N. 3*). Dir. Leonid Nosyrev. Soiuzmul'tfil'm, 1971.

Rejuvenating Apples (*Molodil'nye iabloki*). Dir. Ivan Aksenchuk. Soiuzmul'tfil'm, 1974.

The Rematch (*Match-revansh*). Dir. Boris Dezhkin. Soiuzmul'tfil'm, 1968.

Return from Olympus (*Vozvrashchenie s Olimpa*). Dir. Aleksandra Snezhko-Blotskaia. Soiuzmul'tfil'm, 1969.

The Rifleman (*Strelok*). Dir. Rein Raamat. Tallinnfil'm, 1976.

Rikki-Tikki-Tavi. Dir. Aleksandra Snezhko-Blotskaia. Soiuzmul'tfil'm, 1965.

The Rooster and the Colors (*Petukh i kraski*). Dir. Boris Stepantsev. Soiuzmul'tfil'm, 1964.

Sadko the Rich (*Sadko Bogatyi*). Dir. Vadim Kurchevskii. Soiuzmul'tfil'm, 1975.

Samodelkin – Sportsman (*Samodelkin-sportsmen*). Dir. Vakhtang Bakhtadze. Gruziia-Fil'm, 1963.

The Samoed Boy (*Samoedskii mal'chik*). Dir. Nikolai Khodataev, Ol'ga Khodataeva, Valentina Brumberg, and Zinaida Brumberg. Sovkino, 1928. (Gosfil'mofond)

Sarmiko. Dir. Ol'ga Khodataeva and Evgenii Raikovskii. Soiuzmul'tfil'm, 1952.

The Secret of Child-Rearing (*Sekret vospitaniia*). Dir. Grigorii Lomidze. Soiuzmul'tfil'm, 1960.

The Secret of the Baked Cricket (*Taina zapechnogo sverchka*). Dir. Vadim Kurchevskii. Soiuzmul'tfil'm, 1977.

Sen'ka the African (*Krokodil Krokodilovich*) (*Sen'ka Afrikanets – Krokodil Krokodilovich*). Dir. Ivan Ivanov-Vano, Iurii Merkulov, and Daniil Cherkes. Mezhrabpom-Rus', 1927. (Gosfil'mofond)

Seven Giants: a Cinematic Poster (*Sem' gigantov. Kino-plakat*). Dir. Aleksandr Ivanov, Nikolai Voinov, and Panteleimon Sazonov, n.d. Soiuzkino. (Gosfil'mofond)

Shapokliak. Dir. Roman Kachanov. Soiuzmul'tfil'm, 1974.

Shareholders (*Aktsionery*). Dir. Roman Davydov. Soiuzmul'tfil'm, 1963.

The Shepherdess and the Chimney Sweep (*Pastushka i trubochist*). Dir. Lev Atamanov. Soiuzmul'tfil'm, 1965.

The Shooting Gallery (*Tir*). Dir. Vladimir Tarasov. Soiuzmul'tfil'm, 1979.

The Signature is Illegible (*Podpis' nerazborchiva*). Dir. Aleksandr Ivanov. Soiuzmul'tfil'm, 1954.

The Silent Hamster – Merry Go Round No. 4 (*Khomiak-molchun – Veselaia karusel' N. 4*). Dir. Leonid Nosyrev. Soiuzmul'tfil'm, 1972.

Silver Rain (*Serebrianyi dozhd'*). Dir. Viacheslav Levandovskii. Mosfil'm, 1937. (Gosfil'mofond)

Sindbad the Sailor (*Sindbad-Morekhod*). Dir. Valentina Brumberg and Zinaida Brumberg. Soiuzmul'tfil'm, 1944.

Sister Alenushka and Brother Ivanushka (*Sestritsa Alenushka i bratets Ivanushka*). Dir. Ol'ga Khodataeva. Soiuzmul'tfil'm, 1953.

Six Ivans – Six Captains (*Shest' Ivanov – shest' kapitanov*). Dir. Anatolii Karanovich. Soiuzmul'tfil'm, 1967.

The Skating Rink (*Katok*). Dir. Iurii Zheliabuzhskii. Mezhrabpom-Rus', 1927.

The Snow Queen (*Snezhnaia koroleva*). Dir. Lev Atamanov. Soiuzmul'tfil'm, 1957.

The Snow-Maiden (*Snegurochka*). Dir. Ivan Ivanov-Vano and Aleksandra Snezhko-Blotskaia. Soiuzmul'tfil'm, 1952.

The Sober Sparrow: A Tale for Adults (*Nep'iushchii vorobei*). Dir. Leonid Amal'rik. Soiuzmul'tfil'm, 1960.

The Song Flies Around the World (*Pesnia letit po svetu*). Dir. Anatolii Karanovich. Soiuzmul'tfil'm, 1965. (Gosfil'mofond)

The Song of Chapaev (*Pesnia o Chapaeve*). Dir. Ol'ga Khodataeva and Petr Nosov. Soiuzmul'tfil'm, 1944. (Gosfil'mofond)

Filmography

Song of Friendship (*Pesnia o druzhbe*). Dir. Ivan Ivanov-Vano and Mikhail Botov. Soiuzmul'tfil'm, 1957. (Gosfil'mofond)

Song of Friendship (*Pesnia o druzhbe*). Dir. Efim Gamburg and Otto Zakher. Soiuzmul'tfil'm, 1973. (Gosfil'mofond)

Song of Happiness (*Pesenka radosti*). Dir. Mstislav Pashchenko. Soiuzmul'tfil'm, 1946.

Songs of the Inflamed Years (*Pesni ognennykh let*). Dir. Inessa Kovalevskaia. Soiuzmul'tfil'm, 1971. (Gosfil'mofond)

The Song of the Falcon (*Pesnia o sokole*). Dir. Boris Stepantsev. Soiuzmul'tfil'm, 1967.

The Song of the Little Mouse (*Pesenka myshonka*). Dir. Iurii Prytkov. Soiuzmul'tfil'm, 1967.

The Song of the Young Drummer (*Pesnia o iunom barabanshchike*). Dir. Viacheslav Kotenochkin. Soiuzmul'tfil'm, 1972.

Soon It Will Rain (*Skoro budet dozhd'*). Dir. Vladimir Polkovnikov. Soiuzmul'tfil'm, 1959.

Soviet Toys (*Sovetskie igrushki*). Dir. Dziga Vertov. Goskino, 1924.

Sportland (*Sportlandiia*). Dir. Aleksandr Ivanov. Soiuzmul'tfil'm, 1958.

Spring Melodies (*Vesennie melodii*). Dir. Dmitrii Babichenko. Soiuzmul'tfil'm, 1946.

Stepa the Sailor (*Stepa-moriak*). Dir. Valentina Brumberg and Zinaida Brumberg. Soiuzmul'tfil'm, 1955.

Stolen Sun (*Kradenoe solntse*). Dir. Ivan Ivanov-Vano and Ol'ga Khodataeva. Soiuzmul'tfil'm, 1943.

Stories about Space (*Novelly o kosmose*). Dir. Lev Atamanov. Soiuzmul'tfil'm, 1973.

The Stork (*Aist*). Dir. Ivan Aksenchuk. Soiuzmul'tfil'm, 1956.

Story of a Crime (*Istoriia odnogo prestupleniia*). Dir. Fedor Khitruk. Soiuzmul'tfil'm, 1962.

Strange Traces (*Chuzhie sledy*). Dir. Vitol'd Bordzilovskii. Soiuzmul'tfil'm, 1971.

The Straw Bull-Calf (*Solomennyi bychok*). Dir. Ol'ga Khodataeva. Soiuzmul'tfil'm, 1954.

The Stupid Horse – Merry Go Round No. 7 (*Glupaia loshad' – Veselaia karusel' N. 7*). Dir. Galina Barinova. Soiuzmul'tfil'm, 1975.

Taiga Friends (*Taezhnye druz'ia*). Dir. Aleksandr Ivanov. Soiuzmul'tfil'm, 1939. (Gosfil'mofond)

Taiga Tale (*Taezhnaia skazka*). Dir. Ol'ga Khodataeva. Soiuzmul'tfil'm, 1951.

Tails (*Khvosty*). Dir. Vladimir Polkovnikov. Soiuzmul'tfil'm, 1966.

Tale by Tale: Peter the Joyful Liar (*Skazka za skazkoi. Peter – veselyi obmanshchik*). Dir. Vladimir Pekar' and Vladimir Popov. Soiuzmul'tfil'm, Pannonia (Hungary), 1974.

The Tale is Told (*Skazka skazyvaetsia*). Dir. Ivan Aksenchuk. Soiuzmul'tfil'm, 1970.

Tale of a Lively Time (*Skazka o zhivom vremeni*). Dir. Nikolai Serebriakov. Soiuzmul'tfil'm, 1970. (Gosfil'mofond)

Tale of a Soldier (*Skazka o soldate*). Dir. Valentina Brumberg and Zinaida Brumberg. Soiuzmul'tfil'm, 1948.

The Tale of Chapaev (*Skaz o Chapaeve*). Dir. Mikhail Tsekhanovskii. Soiuzmul'tfil'm, 1958. (Gosfil'mofond)

The Tale of Tales (*Skazka skazok*). Dir. Iurii Norshtein. Soiuzmul'tfil'm, 1979.

The Tale of the Boy-Kibal'chish (*Skazka o mal'chishe-kibal'chishe*). Dir. Aleksandra Snezhko-Brotskaia. Soiuzmul'fil'm, 1958.

The Tale of the Courageous Hare (*Skazka pro khrabrogo zaitsa*). Dir. Nina Pavlovskaia. Sverdlovskaia Kinostudiia, 1978.

The Tale of the Dead Princess and the Seven Bogatyrs (*Skazka o mertvoi tsarevne i o semi bogatyriakh*). Dir. Ivan Ivanov-Vano. Soiuzmul'tfil'm, 1951.

The Tale of the Fisherman and the Fish (*Skazka o rybake i rybke*). Dir. Mikhail Tsekhanovskii. Soiuzmul'tfil'm, 1950.

The Tale of the Little Gold Rooster (*Skazka o zolotom petushke*). Dir. Aleksandra Snezhko-Blotskaia. Soiuzmul'tfil'm, 1967.

The Tale of the Little Round Bun (*Skazka pro kolobok*). Dir. Nataliia Chervinskaia. Soiuzmul'tfil'm, 1969.

The Tale of the Old Oak (*Skazka starogo duba*). Dir. Ol'ga Khodataeva. Soiuzmul'tfil'm, 1949.

The Tale of the Pope and his Worker Balda (*Skazka o pope i rabotnike ego Balde*). Dir. Panteleimon Sazonov. Soiuzmul'tfil'm, 1940.

The Tale of the Pope and his Worker Balda (*Skazka o pope i rabotnike ego Balde*). Dir. Inessa Kovalevskaia. Soiuzmul'tfil'm, 1973.

The Tale of the Straw Bull-Calf (*Skazka o solomnnom bychke*, Viacheslav Levandovskii). Odesskaia Fabrika VUFKU, 1927. No longer available.

The Tale of the Stupid Little Mouse (*Skazka o glupom myshonke*). Dir. Mikhail Tsekhanovskii. Lenfil'm (Sankt Peterburgskaia kinostudiia - FUP), 1940.

The Tale of the White Bull-Calf (*Skazka pro belogo bychka*). Dir. Vladimir Suteev and Lev Atamanov. Mezhrabpomfil'm, 1933. (Gosfil'mofond)

The Tale of Tsar Durandai (*Skazka o tsare Durandae*). Dir. Valentina Brumberg, Zinaida Brumberg and Ivan Ivanov-Vano. Mezhrabpomfil'm, 1934. (Gosfil'mofond)

The Tale of Tsar Saltan (*Skazka o tsare Saltane*). Dir. Valentina Brumberg, Zinaida Brumberg, and T. Basmanova. Soiuzmul'tfil'm, 1943. (Gosfil'mofond)

Talent (*Talant*). Dir. El'bert Tuganov. Tallinfil'm, 1963.

Talent and Admirers (*Talant i poklonniki*). Dir. Boris Dezhkin. Soiuzmul'tfil'm, 1978.

The Tangle (*Klubok*). Dir. Nikolai Serebriakov. Soiuzmul'tfil'm, 1968.

Taniusha, Tiavka, Top, and Niusha (*Taniusha, Tiavka, Top i Niusha*). Dir. Viktor Gromov. Soiuzmul'tfil'm, 1954.

Telephone (*Telefon*). Dir. Mikhail Tsekhanovskii. Soiuzmul'tfil'm, 1944.

The Terrible Vengeance (*Strashnaia mest'*). Dir. Vladislav Starevich. 1912.

Terrible Vavila and Auntie Arina (*Groznyi Vavila i tetka Arina*). Dir. Nikolai Khodataev and Ol'ga Khodataeva. Mezhrabpom-Rus', Tsentrosoiuz, 1928.

There Is No Happiness in the Hat (*Ne v shliape schast'e*). Dir. Nikolai Serebriakov. Soiuzmul'tfil'm, 1968.

There Once Lived Koziavin (*Zhil-byl Koziavin*). Dir. Andrei Khrzhanovskii. Soiuzmul'tfil'm, 1966.

The Thief (*Vor*). Dir. Aleksandr Ivanov. Moskinokombinat, 1934. (Gosfil'mofond)

Three Bags of Cunning (*Tri meshka khitrosti*). Dir. Petr Nosov and Ol'ga Khodataeva. Soiuzmul'tfil'm, 1954.

Three Bananas (*Tri banana*). Dir. Mikhail Botov. Soiuzmul'tfil'm, 1971.

The Three Fat Men (*Tri tolstiaka*). Dir. Valentina Brumberg and Zinaida Brumberg. Soiuzmul'tfil'm, 1963.

Three Girlfriends (*Tri podrugi*). Dir. Pavel Shmidt. Lenfil'm, 1941.

Three Woodcutters (*Tri drovoseka*). Dir. Leonid Amal'rik. Soiuzmul'tfil'm, 1959.

Thumbelina (*Diuimovochka*). Dir. Leonid Amal'rik. Soiuzmul'tfil'm, 1964.

Thumbling (*Mal'chik s pal'chik*). Dir. Ol'ga Khodataeva. Soiuzmul'tfil'm, 1938. (Gosfil'mofond)

Thumbling (*Mal'chik s pal'chik*). Dir. Roman Davydov. Soiuzmul'tfil'm, 1977.

The Time Machine (*Mashinka vremeni*). Dir. Valentina Brumberg and Zinaida Brumberg. Soiuzmul'tfil'm, 1967.

Times of Year (*Vremena goda*). Dir. Ivan Ivanov-Vano. Soiuzmul'tfil'm, 1969.

Timoshkin's Fir-Tree (*Timoshkina elka*). Dir. Vladimir Degtiarev. Soiuzmul'tfil'm, 1966.

The Tin – Merry Go Round No. 8 (*Konservnaia banka – Veselaia karusel' N. 8*). Dir. Garri Bardin. Soiuzmul'tfil'm, 1976.

The Titmouse (*Sinitsa*). Dir. Mstislav Pashchenko and Aleksandr Ivanov. Soiuzmul'tfil'm, 1944.

To the Sixth Worldwide (*Shestomu vsemirnomu*). Dir. Evgenii Migunov. Soiuzmul'tfil'm, 1957.

Today: a Live Map (*Segodnia. Zhivaia karta*). Dir. Dziga Vertov. Goskino, 1923. (Gosfil'mofond)

Tomorrow Will be Tomorrow (*Zavtra budet zavtra*). Dir. Ivan Ufimtsev. 1979.

Toothbrush the Queen (*Koroleva – zubnaia shchetka*). Dir. Nikolai Fedorov. Soiuzmul'tfil'm, 1962.

Toptyzhka. Dir. Fedor Khitruk. Soiuzmul'tfil'm, 1964.

The Tower Room (*Teremok*). Dir. Ol'ga Khodataeva. Soiuzmul'tfil'm, 1945.

The Tower Room (*Terem-teremok*). Dir. Leonid Amal'rik. Soiuzmul'tfil'm, 1971.

Traces on the Asphalt (*Sledy na asfal'te*). Dir. Viacheslav Kotenochkin and Vladimir Danilov. Soiuzmul'tfil'm, 1964.

The Tracker (*Sledopyt*). Dir. Petr Nosov. Soiuzmul'tfil'm, 1963.

The Train of Memories (*Poezd pamiati*). Dir. Nikolai Serebriakov. Soiuzmul'tfil'm, 1975. (Gosfil'mofond)

The Trio from Prostokvashino (*Troe iz prostokvashino*). Dir. Vladimir Popov. Soiuzmul'tfil'm, 1978.

Twelve Months (*Dvenadtsat' mesiatsev*). Dir. Ivan Ivanov-Vano. Soiuzmul'tfil'm, 1956.

The Two Greedy Bear-Cubs (*Dva zhadnykh medvezhonka*). Dir. Vladimir Degtiarev. Soiuzmul'tfil'm, 1954.

Two Jolly Geese – Merry Go Round No. 2 (*Dva veselykh gusia – Veselaia karusel' N. 2*). Dir. Leonid Nosyrev. Soiuzmul'tfil'm, 1970.

Umka. Dir. Vladimir Popov and Vladimir Pekar'. Soiuzmul'tfil'm, 1969.
Umka Looks for a Friend (*Umka ishchet druga*). Dir. Vladimir Popov and Vladimir Pekar'. Soiuzmul'tfil'm, 1970.
Uncle Au 1–3 (*Diadiushka Au 1–3*). Dir. M. Buzinova and I. Douksha. Soiuztelefil'm, 1979.
Uncle Misha (*Diadia Misha*). Dir. Iurii Prytkov. Soiuzmul'tfil'm, 1970.
Uncle Stepa (*Diadia Stepa*). Dir. Lamis Bredis and Vladimir Suteev. Soiuzmul'tfil'm, 1938. (Gosfil'mofond)
Uncle Stepa – Police Officer (*Diadia Stepa – militsioner*). Dir. Ivan Aksenchuk. Soiuzmul'tfil'm, 1964.
Vania Datskii. Dir. Nikolai Serebriakov. Soiuzmul'tfil'm, 1974.
Vasilek. Dir. Stella Aristakesova. Soiuzmul'tfil'm, 1973.
Vasilii's Treatment – Merry Go Round No. 6 (*Lechenie Vasiliia – Veselaia karusel' N. 6*). Dir. Vladimir Morozov. Soiuzmul'tfil'm, 1974.
Vasilisa the Beautiful (*Vasilisa Prekrasnaia*). Dir. Vladimir Pekar'. Soiuzmul'tfil'm, 1977.
The Very First – Merry Go Round No. 2 (*Samyi pervyi – Veselaia karusel' N. 2*). Dir. Anatolii Petrov. Soiuzmul'tfil'm, 1970.
Victorious Destination (*Pobednyi marshrut*). Dir. Dmitrii Babichenko and Leonid Amal'rik. Soiuzmul'tfil'm, 1939. (Gosfil'mofond)
The Villain with a Label (*Zlodeika s nakleikoi*). Dir. Boris Stepantsev and Vsevolod Shcherbakov. Soiuzmul'tfil'm, 1954. (Gosfil'mofond)
Vintik-Shpintik. Dir. Vladislav Tvardovskii. Sovkino (Leningrad), 1927. No longer available.
Vintik and Shpuntik – Cheerful Masters (*Vintik i shpuntik – veselye mastera*). Dir. Petr Nosov. Soiuzmul'tfil'm, 1960.
Visiting the Summer (*V gostiakh u leta*). Dir. Boris Dezhkin. Soiuzmul'tfil'm, 1972.
Vovka in a Far-Away Kingdom (*Vovka v trideviatom tsarstve*). Dir. Boris Stepantsev. Soiuzmul'tfil'm, 1965.
Vovka the Trainer (*Vovka-trener*). Dir. Anatolii Reznikov. Ekran, 1979.
Vultures (*Sterviatniki*). Dir. Panteleimon Sazonov. Soiuzmul'tfil'm, 1941.
The Walnut Switch (*Orekhovyi prutik*). Dir. Ivan Aksenchuk. Soiuzmul'tfil'm, 1955.
Warlike Beavers (*Voinstvennye bobry*). Dir. Dmitrii Babichenko. Soiuzmul'tfil'm, 1939. (Gosfil'mofond)
We are Looking for a Blot (*My ishchem Kliaksu*). Dir. Vladimir Polkovnikov. Soiuzmul'tfil'm, 1969.
We Are With You, Cuba! (*My s toboi, Kuba! - kinoplakat*) Dir. Iurii Merkulov, n.d.
We Beat, We're Beating, and We Will Beat (*Bili, b'em i budem bit'*). Dir. Dmitrii. Babichenko. Soiuzmul'tfil'm, 1941. (Gosfil'mofond)
We Follow the Sun (*My za solnyshkom idem*). Dir. Vladimir Degtiarev. Soiuzmul'tfil'm, 1958.
We'll Be Vigilant (*Budem zorki*). Dir. Nikolai Khodataev. Mezhrabpom-Rus', 1926. (Gosfil'mofond)
The Well (*Kolodets*). Dir. Rein Raamat. Tallinfil'm, 1972.
Well-Known Pictures (*Znakomye kartinki*). Dir. Evgenii Migunov. Soiuzmul'tfil'm, 1957. (Gosfil'mofond)

The Whale and the Cat (Kit i kot). Dir. Irina Gurvich. Kievnauchfil'm, 1969.

What is Good and What is Bad (Chto takoe khorosho i chto takoe plokho). Dir. Efim Gamburg. Soiuzmul'tfil'm, 1969.

What the 13th Party Congress Said about Cooperatives (Chto skazal XIII s"ezd partii o kooperatsii). [Dir. Aleksandr Bushkin and Aleksandr Ivanov], 1924. (Gosfil'mofond)

When Goebbels Doesn't Lie (Kogda Gebbel's ne vret). Dir. S. Fedorchenko. Goskinprom Gruzii, 1944. (Gosfil'mofond)

When the Fir-trees Light Up (Kogda zazhigaiutsia elki). Dir. Mstislav Pashchenko. Soiuzmul'tfil'm, 1950.

Who is Grazing in the Meadow? – Merry Go Round No. 5 (Kto pasetsia na lugu? – Veselaia karusel' N. 5). Dir. Galina Barinova. Soiuzmul'tfil'm, 1973.

Who Said Meow? (Kto skazal miau?) Dir. Vladimir Degtiarev. Soiuzmul'tfil'm, 1962.

Who to be? (Kem byt'?). Dir. Dmitrii Babichenko. Soiuzmul'tfil'm, 1948.

Who to be? (Kem byt'?). Dir. Anatolii Karanovich. Soiuzmul'tfil'm, 1973.

Who's First? (Kto pervyi?). Dir. Boris Dezhkin. Soiuzmul'tfil'm, 1950.

Who's the Strongest? (Kto samyi sil'nyi?) Dir. Vladimir Degtiarev. Soizumul'tfil'm, 1961.

Whose Pinecones are Those in the Woods? (Ch'i v lesu shishki?). Dir. Ivan Ufimtsev and Mikhail Kamenetskii. Soiuzmul'tfil'm, 1965.

Why Does the Lion Have a Big Mane? – Merry Go Round No. 8 (Pochemu u l'va bol'shaia griva? – Veselaia karusel' N. 8.) Dir. Natal'ia Orlova and Nataliia Bogomolova. Soiuzmul'tfil'm, 1976.

Wild Swans (Dikie lebedi). Dir. Mikhail Tsekhanovskii. Soiuzmul'tfil'm, 1962.

The Wily Fox: The Cunning Fox, The Masquerade (Proidokha: khitraia lisitsa, maskarad lisa). Dir. Vladimir Mudzhiri. Goskinprom Gruzii, 1937. (Gosfil'mofond).

The Window (Okno). Dir. Boris Stepantsev. Soiuzmul'tfil'm, 1966.

Windows of Satire (Okna satiry). Dir. Teodor Bunimovich. Soiuzmul'tfil'm, 1961.

Winnie the Pooh (Vinni-pukh). Dir. Fedor Khitruk and Gennadii Sokol'skii. Soiuzmul'tfil'm, 1969.

Winnie the Pooh and the Day of Worries (Vinni-pukh i den' zabot). Dir. Fedor Khitruk and Gennadii Sokol'skii. Soiuzmul'tfil'm, 1972.

Winnie the Pooh Goes on a Visit (Vinni-Pukh idet v gosti). Dir. Fedor Khitruk. Soiuzmul'tfil'm, 1971.

The Wise Gudgeon (Premudryi peskar'). Dir. Valentin Karavaev. Soiuzmul'tfil'm, 1979.

The Wizard of the Emerald City 1 (Volshebnik izumrudnogo goroda 1). Dir. Kirill Maliantovich. Ekran, 1973.

The Wolf and Seven Kids (Volk i semero kozliat). Dir. Petr Nosov. Soiuzmul'tfil'm, 1957.

The Wolf and Seven Kids Redux (Volk i semero kozliat na novyi lad). Dir. Leonid Aristov. Ekran, 1975.

The Yellow Stork (Zheltyi aist). Dir. Lev Atamanov. Soiuzmul'tfil'm, 1950.

You'll See, It Will Come to No Good! A Political Cartoon (Smotrite, kak by chego ne vyshlo! Polit-sharzh). Dir. Aleksandr Ivanov, n.d. (Gosfil'mofond)

Your Health! (Vashe zdorov'e!). Dir. Ivan Aksenchuk. Soiuzmul'tfil'm, 1965. (Gosfil'mofond)

The Youth of Friedrich Engels (Iunosha Fridrikh Engel's). Dir. Vadim Kurchevskii, Fedor Khitruk, Klaus Georgi, and Katia Georgi. Soiuzmul'tfil'm, DEFA-film, 1970. (Gosfil'mofond)

Zai and Chik (Zai i chik). Dir. Ivan Aksenchuk. Soiuzmul'tfil'm, 1952.

Films and TV programs on Soviet animation

Animation from A to Z (Animatsiia ot A do IA). Dir. Irina Margolina and M. P. Liakhovetskii. RenTV, 1997.

Fedor Khitruk: Animator by Profession (Fedor Khitruk: Professia – Animator). Dir. Sergei Seregin. Shkola-studiia animatsionnogo kino SHAR, 1999.

Mikhail Tsekhanovskii: Dramatic Graphics (Mikhail Tsekhanovskii: Dramaticheskaia grafika). Dir. Sergei Seregin. Kinokompaniia MASTER-FIL'M, Shkola studiia animatsionnogo kino SHAR, 1996.

The Miracle Factory (Fabrika chudes). Dir. Aleksei Vakhrushev. 2005–2006.

Russian Magic (Magia Russica). Dir. Yonathan Zur and Masha Zur. Films by Jove, Inc., 2004.

The Spirit of Genius. Dir. Otto Alder. Tag/Traum, 1998.

World animated films cited

A Drop Too Many (O sklenicku víc). Dir. B. Pojar. Czechoslovakia, 1954.

Anémic Cinéma. Dir. Marcel Duchamp. France, 1926.

Babadou's Voyage (Le voyage de Badabou). Dir. Henri Gruel. France, 1955.

Bambi. Dir. David Hand. Walt Disney, USA, 1942.

Diagonal Symphony (Symphonie diagonale). Dir. Viking Eggeling. Germany, 1924.

Dreams of Toyland. Dir. Arthur Melbourne Cooper. UK, 1908.

The Enchanted Drawing. Dir. James Stuart Blackton, USA, 1900.

Gertie the Dinosaur. Dir. Winsor McCay. USA, 1914.

Gypsies and Butterflies (Gitanos et papillons). Dir. Henri Gruel. France, 1954.

The Hand (Ruka). Dir. Jiří Trnka. Czechoslovakia, 1965.

Humorous Phases of Funny Faces. Dir. J. Stuart Blackton. USA, 1906.

Illusions and Sounds, Attempt and Breakthrough: From the History of Drawn Music (Illiuzii i zvuki, popytka, proryva: iz istorii risovannoi muzyki). Dir. Il'ia Lainer et al. Khudozhestvennoe veshchanie lad, 1996.

Little Nemo. Dir. Winsor McCay. USA, 1911.

The Old Mill. Dir. Walt Disney. USA, 1937.

Opus I. Dir. Walter Ruttmann. Germany, 1921.

Opus II. Dir. Walter Ruttmann. Germany, 1921.

Opus III. Dir. Walter Ruttmann. Germany, 1924.

Out of the Inkwell. Dir. David Fleischer. USA, 1938.

Rhythm 21 (Rhythmus 21). Dir. Hans Richter. Germany, 1921.

Rhythm 23 (Rhythmus 23). Dir. Hans Richter. Germany, 1923.

Snow White and the Seven Dwarfs. Dir. Walt Disney. USA, 1937.

The Story of a Mosquito. Dir. Winsor McCay. USA, 1912.

Index

Note: Page references for illustrations are in *italics*; note numbers are introduced with an "n".

1918 in Petrograd	176	*The Villain with a Label*	63-64
25th - The First Day	176-178, *179*	*Story of a Crime*	100, 110, 110n163, 111, 118
		The Mountain of Dinosaurs	123
A		*The Man in the Frame*	133, 136
About Ivan the Fool	174	*Glass Harmonica*	163-165
About Two Squares	26	ASIFA	81
absenteeism	64, 109	*At the Dining Hall*	65n104
Actress, The	49n74	Atamanov, Lev	36, 44-45, 47, 79n128, 80, 122
Adorno, Theodor W.	147	*Attention Birds*	46n70
Adventures of Bolvashka, The	19-20	authorial animation, definition	82
Adventures of Bratishkin	20n41	*Autumn*	147
Adventures of Munchausen, The	17	avant-garde	1, 22, 26-28, 35, 48, 176-179
advertising	5, 9-11, 23, 77-78, 114	*Ave Maria*	179
self-advertising	9, 20	Avraamov, Arsenii	32-33
Aelita	11, 19		
agit-films (agitki)	11-13, 19, 36, 61-64	**B**	
agit-mul'tfil'm	61-64	Babel', Isaac	52
agitprop films See *agit-films*		*Babi Yar*	54-55
Akhmadulina, Bella	53	Babichenko, Dmitrii	42, 43, 65n105, 72
Akhmatova, Anna	52, 144	*Badabou's Journey*	80
Aksenchuk, Ivan	46n70, 47, 58, 58n91, 64, 66	Baikal-Amur Mainline (BAM)	74
Al'tman, Natan	144, 178	Bakhtin, Mikhail	71, 100, 108, 152
alcoholism	10, 15, 61-65, 69, 74	concretization	108, 108n161
Aleksandr Nevskii	42	Baklin, Nikolai	14-15
Aleksandrov ensemble	43	*Ball of Wool, The*	171
Aleksandrov, Grigorii	29, 48	*Ballad of the Table*	65, 69
Alekseev, Aleksandr	80	BAM See Baikal-Amur Mainline	
Alimov, Sergei	84, 99, 105-108, 114, 124-125, 172	*Bambi*	47, 173
		bard songs	70
See also *Story of a Crime*; *Man in the Frame*		See also Okudzhava	
All-Union Conference on Comedy	39	*Barmalei*	44
All-Union State Institute of Cinematography See VGIK		Batchelor, Joy	80
		Bath, The	69
Amal'rik, Leonid	30, 36, 41, 41n65, 42-43, 45-46, 49n76, 64,	*Battle of Kerzhenets, The*	178-180
American animation	1, 6, 8, 38-40, 76-79, 86, 169	*Beautiful Liukanida, or the Battle Between Stag Beetles and Long-horn Beetles, The*	5n3
See also Disney style		*Behind the Footlights*	49n74
An Event at the Stadium	20, *21*	Beliakov, Ivan	9-10
An Incarnated Dream	66n106	*Bench, The*	79n128, 122
And I am with You Again	147	Benderskaia, Maria	16n32
And My Mother Will Forgive Me	74	Berg, Alban	80
And We, Too, to the Olympiad	43	Bergson, Henri	117, 139
Anémic Cinéma	27-28	"Bewitched Place, The"	46
animated caricature	7-8, *8*, 86	*Bezbozhnik* (later called *Bezbozhnik u stanka*)	7
See also lightning sketches		Bidstrup, Herluf	79, 79n128, 122
Animated Crocodile (MUK)	67, 68, 73, 85n	Bilibin, Ivan	45, 174n213
Annenkov, Iurii	178	*Black and White*	30, 36
Antonov, Leonid	53	Blackton, James Stuart	8, 86
approval procedure	75-76	Bogoslovskii, Nikita	164
See also artistic council meeting		*Bonifatius's Holidays*	84, 174
Arcimboldo, Giuseppe	150, *151*	*Boris Savinkov: Story of a Disappointment*	10
Arrow Flies into the Tale, The	49n76	Bosch, Hieronymus	150, *150*, 154
artistic council meeting	3, 61, 75-76		

241

Bosustow, Stephen	80	effect	86, 96, 109, 111, 115-118, 122, 137-139
Botticelli, Sandro	129-130, 151	strips	6-7
Boym, Svetlana	101	See also laughter	
Braque, Georges	178	Communist Party	10, 42, 51-56, 83-84, 121
Bratishkin	18, 20, 20n41	See also Twentieth Party Congress;	
Bratishkin Competes	20n41	Twenty-First Party Congress	
Bray-Hurd Patent Company	39	Twenty-Second Party Congress	
Bray, John Randolph *See* Bray-Hurd Patent Company		Conference on Cinema Affairs (1928), Party	12
Bredis, Lamis	44	Congress of Soviet Writers	
Bremen Musicians, The	172	First	38, 46
Brezhnev, Leonid	70, 74, 122, 163, 167	Second	52
Brodsky, Joseph	60n, 166	Congress of the Union of	
Bruegel, Pieter (the Elder)	150, *151*	Cinematographers, Fifth	167
Brumberg, Valentina and Zinaida	11, 16-17,	concise style *See* laconic language	
	36, 42, 45-48, 49n76,	Constructivists	21, 26, 37, 176
	57n, 73, 81-98, 104, 175	Cooper, Althur Melbourne	5
Brumel', Valerii	58	*Courageous Men*	49n74
Buratino	19, 22	Crafton, Donald	8, 18, 40
bureaucrats	65, 69, 71, 77, 85, 124-148	cut-outs *See* flat marionette	
Bushkin, Aleksandr	9-10		
Buzilka	18	**D**	
byt	21, 83	Daniel', Iulii	121, 144
		Defense of Petrograd, The	176, *179*
C		Deineka, Aleksandr	176, 178, *179*
Cameraman's Revenge, The	6	dekulakization *See* collectivization	
Cancer Ward	54	Dem'ian's Fuddle	10
capitalism	9-12, 36-37, 49, 73, 166	Deni (Denisov, Victor)	7-9
caricature	1-2, 6-12, 18, 35-36, 41-44,	Deshevov, Vladimir	23
	77, 79, 106, 122, 176-177	*Diagonal Symphony*	26
See also animated caricature		*Diamond Arm*	85n
cel technique	18-19, 22-23, 39-40, 62, 64, 76, 82, 115	*Disappeared Letter, The*	46
censorship	37, 85, 124, 137,	Disney style	2, 38-41, 45-46, 49, 62,
	144, 146, 148, 166-167		76, 78-79, 81-83, 85-86,
See also shelved, banned works			98, 105-106, 148, 172-174
Central Committee Plenum	52	and method of production	2, 38-40, 76
Chagall, Mark	160, 162, 178	and political implication	38, 40-41, 46, 49, 76, 148
chalk talks *See* lightning sketches		rejection of	2, 38, 41, 62, 78-79, 81-83,
Chaplin, Charlie	*13*, 17, 137		85, 98, 105-106, 172-174
Charushin, Evgenii	172	*Disobedient Kitten, The*	46n70
Cheburashka	170, 170n207	Doré, Gustave	17
Cheburashka Goes to School	170n207	*Dragon-Fly and the Ant, The*	46
Check your Watch	64	drawings of sound	32-34
Chekhonin, Sergei	177, *179*	*Dreams of Toyland*	5
Cheremnykh, Mikhail	7, 11	*Drop Too Much, A*	63
Cherkes, Daniil	8, 11, 16-17, 19, 37	*Drunk Hare, The*	46n70
Chief Directorate of Film and Photo *See* GUFK		*druzhiny*	83, 102n151
Children's Album	172	Duchamp, Marcel	26-28
children's drawings	48, 80, 82, 85, 89, 97	Dudintsev, Vladimir	53
China in Flames	11	Dunaevskii, Isaak	70
Chipollino	122		
CHIZH (journal)	172	**E**	
Chukovskii, Kornei	16, 23, 43, 86-87	*Eaglet, The*	178
Cigarette Girl from Moscow, The	19	Echeistov, Georgii	37
Cinemacircus	42	educational films	1, 6-7, 61-65, 67-68, 111-112
Circus	43	for children	16-17, 38, 45,
Civil War	12, 42, 66, 178		46n70, 49, 55-56, 59-61, 104, 123
Clark, Katerina	46, 71	scientific films	14-15
Cold War	2, 73	*See also kul'turnost'*	
Cole, Emile	16	Eggeling, Viking	26
collectivization	37	Ehrenburg, Il'ia	52, 54, 144
Collegiate Registrar, The (or *The Station Master*)	19	Eisenstein, Sergei	24, 29, 42, 49, 81,
comic			106, 108, 126-127, 136,
actors	68-69		*138*, 172-173, 173n211
gags	16, 38, 109, 169	*ekler See* rotoscope	

Index

electrification 15, 66
Elephant and the Pug, The 44
elite audience, art for 61, 147, 164, 167
Elizarov, Georgii 43
Éluard, Paul 178
Enchanted Boy, The 47
Enchanted Drawing, The 8
End of the Black Swamp, The 59, 71
Erdman, Nikolai 48, 111n166, 167
Erevan 14, 44
estrada   See variety theatre
estrangement 96, 116
"Evenings Outside Moscow" 70-71, 140
Evgenii Onegin 115-116
Evtushenko, Evgenii 53-55, 144
EZH (journal) 172

F

Fairbanks, Douglas 17
fantastic, the 149
Fascist Boot Won't Trample the Soil of Our Motherland 43
Father Frost 49n74
Favorite Heroes 43
Favorskii, Vladimir 37, 178
Fears 55
Fedia Zaitsev 48-49, 104
Felix the Cat 17, 40
Film Festival, First International 38
Film, Film, Film 85, 122, 136-138, *138*
Filmtechnik 34
Filonov, Pavel 80, 178
First Circle, The 54
Fischinger, Oskar 34
Fitil': An All-Union Satirical Cinema Journal 68, 122
flat marionettes (cut-outs) 18-19, 23, 33, 40, 73, 80-81, 106, 115, 117n170, 144, 146, 156, 173-175, 179
Fleischer, Max 17
Flight to the Moon 57n
Flower with Seven Colors, The 48n73
Fly-Tsokotukha 44
Flying Proletarian, The 57, 175
Folklore and folk-art 45-47, 60, 157, 163, 173-174, 173n211
   See also *lubok*
For the Voice 26
formalism 22, 35, 38, 53
Formula for Revolution, The 178
Fox and the Grapes, The 20
Fox and the Hare, The 180
Fox-Builder, The 46n70
Frantishek 171
freedom
   of expression 2, 40, 51-55, 121-123, 128, 144-147
   religious 59, 146
   See also *Glass Harmonica*
full animation 76-78
   See also limited animation
Futurists 26

G

Gagarin, Iurii 57-58
Gamburg, Efim 73, 122
Garin, Erast 167
Gena the Crocodile 170, 170n207
Gerasimov, Sergei 147, 163
Glass and China Industry 15
Glass Harmonica, The 54, 123, 146-167, *149-165*
Glory to You, Celestial Brothers! 58
Go There – I Don't Know Where 174
Gogol', Nikolai 46, 144, 147
Golden Antelope, The 47
Golden Foreheads 174
Gorbachev, Mikhail 54
Gorky, Maxim 46, 49, 171
Gosizdat 172
Goskino 8-10, 15, 56, 62-63, 74, 76, 165-166
   Kul'tkino 8-10, 15
Goskinprom Gruzii, studio (Georgia) 14, 43
Goya y Lucientes, Francisco Jose de 150, *150*
Grasshopper and the Ant, The 6
Great Cold, The 171
Great Troubles 48, 73, 81-99, *90-99*
Greenberg, Clement 107
Grimault, Paul 80
grotesque 11, 18, 21, 35, 77, 79, 149-156, *153-155*, 164
Gruel, Henri 80
GUFK (Chief Directorate of Film and Photo) 38, 38n56
Gumilev, Nikolai 80
Gypsies and Butterflies 80

H

Halas, John 80
Hand, The *133-134*, 134
Happiness is not in the Hat 171
Haupe, Włodzimierz 80
He Surpassed 42
Heart 64
Hedgehog in the Fog 180
Heirs of Stalin 54
Hello Friends 65n105, 72
heroes
   Byronic hero 140
   Children heroes 74-75, 104, 178
   cosmonauts 56-58, 70
   new heroes 56, 58, 71, 101-102, 104
   of folk-tale 60
   socialist realist hero 56, 102, 104
   Soviet war heroes 66, 178-180
Heron and the Crane, The 180
heteroglossia 71
Hoffmann, E.T.A. 153, 172
Honegger, Arthur 30-31
Hour Before the Rendezvous, The 84, 85n
How Avdotia Became Literate 11
How One Man Fed Two Generals 174
How the Little Lion and the Turtle Sang a Song 172
How Vasia Terkin Went to Be Recruited 42
Hubley, John 80
Huge Cockroach, The
   directed by Aleksandr Ivanov 16n32
   directed by V. Polkovnikov 86-87
Humorous Stories 10

243

Humorous Phases of Funny Faces	8, 86	Khitruk	65, 71, 82-84, 98-119, 122-141, 170n207, 172, 174
Hunchbacked Horse, The	47		
Hungary, uprising	53	Khlebnikov, Velimir	26
Hurd, Earl *See* Bray-Hurd Patent Company		Khodasevich, Valentin	167
Huxley, Aldous	80	Khodataev, Nikolai	8n10, 11-12, 16-18, 36-37, 39, 41
I		Khodataeva, Ol'ga	11, 16-17, 42, 104
I Am Twenty (Il'ich's Gate)	53-54, 121, 146	Khrushchev Thaw	2, 51-55, 65, 88-89, 101, 109, 111, 113, 121, 147
I Drew the Little Man	48		
I Fly to You in Memory	147	and animation	1, 50, 55-75, 122-123
I Walk around Moscow	146	*See also* communist party; individual versus collective; *khrushchevki* (*khrushchoby*); "secret speech"; Twentieth Party Congress; Twenty-Second Party Congress	
I'm Waiting for the Bird	171, 174		
Iankovskii, Boris	32		
Il'f and Petrov	52		
Il'ich's Gate *See I Am Twenty*		Khrushchev, Nikita *See* Khrushchev's Thaw	
Il'inskii, Igor'	69	*khrushchevki* (*khrushchoby*)	109-110
Image, Jean	80	Khrzhanovskii, Andrei	54, 65, 123-124, 139-167
In the Land of Puppets	20	Khutsiev, Marlen	53-54, 121
In the Land of the Dolls	43	*Kidnapping, Caucasian Style*	85n
In the Snout of the Second International	10	Kiev	44
individual versus collective	64, 82-83, 89, 100-105, 108, 112-115, 123, 179	*Kino-Krokodil*	67
		Kino-Pravda	8-9
International Congress of Animation (Cannes)	80	*kinofabriki*	14
International Days of the Animated Films	81	*Kinonedelia*	9
Interplanetary Revolution	11	*kinoplakaty* *See* poster, animated	
intertextuality	149, 149n, 155	*kinozhurnal* (cinematic journal)	67-68, 122
intertitles	25-26, 63	*Kiss of Mary Pickford, The*	13, *13*
Iskusstvo Kino	66	*Kliaksa*	18
Island, The	85	Koko the Clown	17
Island of Mistakes, The	49n76	*kolkhoz* (and *kolkhoznik*)	41, 60, 71
Iunost'	121	*Kolobok*	41
Ivan the Terrible	136, *138*	Komarov, Sergei	13
Ivanov-Vano, Ivan	11, 15-17, 19, 30, 34, 36, 39, 42-45, 47, 57, 65n105, 72, 80-81, 171, 173-175, 179-180	Komissarenko, Zenon	11-12, 12n19
		Komsomol	45, 74, 87, 89, 121
		Korchagin, Pavel	74
		Kovalevskaia, Inessa	172
Ivanov, Aleksandr	10, 16n32, 17n34, 42-43, 46n70, 58n91, 59-60, 65, 66n106	Krakauer, Siegfried	105
		Kristl, Vlado	78
Ivas	43	*Krokodil* (Chukovskii's story)	16
Ivashko and Baba-Iaga	46	*Krokodil* (satirical journal)	7, 66, 73, 77, 88, 109
Izvolov, Nikolai	32	*See also Animated Crocodile*; *Kino-Krokodil*	
J		Kruchenykh, Aleksei	26
jazz	41, 72, 87-88, 140	Krylov, Ivan	44-45, 46n70, 123
Johnson, Priscilla	54	Krylov, Porfirii *See* Kukryniksy	
Journal of Political Satire, The	67	Kukryniksy	79
Just You Wait	169-170	*kul'turnost'*	99-103, 112, 115, 116
		Kupriianov, Mikhail *See* Kukryniksy	
K		Kurchevskii, Vadim	171
Kaleidoskop	170	Kuritsyn, Anatolii	173
Kamov, Feliks	169n206	Kurliandskii, Aleksandr	169n206
Kandinsky, Vasilii	80, 144	Kustodeev, Boris	174n213
Karaev, Kara	121	Kuz'ma, O.	15
Karanovich, Anatolii	69, 72-73	Kuz'min, Nikolai	174n213
Karlson Returned	170n207	Kuzakov, K.	62
Kashtanka	48n73		
Kayser, Wolfgang	152	**L**	
Keaton, Buster	137	La Fontaine, Jean (de)	123
Keldysh, Iurii	179	laconic language	2, 6, 16, 79, 81-85, 96-97, 105-106, 123, 172
Kelly, Catriona	101, 102n152		
Khachaturian, Aram	53	Lada, Joseph	79
Khait, Arkadii	169n206	laughter	39, 66, 108, 115, 117, 139, 153
Khanzhonkov	6, 14-15	*See also* comic	
Kharms, Daniil	35, 80	Lebedev, Vladimir	22-23, 178
		Lefthander, The	173-174

Index

Legend of the Invisible City of Kitezh and the Maiden Fevroniia, The	179, 179n222
Léger, Fernand	55
Lenfil'm	43
Lengiz	23
Lenica, Jan	164, 165
Lenin (and Leninism)	12, 42, 45, 49n74, 55, 59, 71, 133, 178
See also *Vladimir Il'ich Lenin*; *Lenin and the Revolution*	
Lenin and the Revolution	178
Leningrad	14, 16n32, 17, 22-29, 32, 44, 71, 172
Leskov, Nikolai	173
Let's Bring the Cinema to the Countryside!	20n41
"Letter as Such, The" manifesto	26
Levandovskii, Viacheslav	16n32, 19-20, 43
Life and Suffering of Ivan Semenov, The	171
lightning sketches (chalk talks)	8, 86
limited animation	78-81
See also full animation	
Lissitzky, El	26, 178
Little Bear, The	43
Little Boy and Karlson, who Lives on the Roof, The	170n207
Little Golden Key, The	22
Little Grey Neck, The	46
Little Music Box, The	36-37
Little Scarlet Flower, The	47
Little Time Machine, The	84, 85n
Live Map	8
Lokshina, Khesia	167
Long and Happy Life, The	146
Lotman, Iurii	89, 113, 114n168, 116, 167
Low, Colin	80
lubok	7, 163, 173-174
Lucanus Cervus	5n3
Lunacharskii, Anatolii	17, 17n34
lyric genre	2, 169-172, 179-181

M

MacDonald's Career	10
MacFadyen, David	49-50, 106
Magic Store, The	49n76
Magritte, René	149
Main Star, The	57
Malevich, Kazimir	26, 80, 175, 178-179
Maliutin, Ivan	7
Man in the Frame, The	65, 85, 123-136, 139-141, 125-137
Manezh Gallery Exhibition	54, 147
Marshak, Samuil	23, 25-26, 47
mass songs	70
Master of Daily Life	21
Matches: An Appeal	5
Mayakovsky, Vladimir	7, 26, 30, 36, 53, 57, 69, 177, 178n215
McLaren, Norman	34, 34n52, 80
Mechanics of the Brain	15
Menacing Vavila and Aunt Arina, The	8n10
Merkulov, Iurii	8, 8n10, 11, 16, 20n41
Merry Go Round, The	169-170
Meyerhold, Vsevolod	36, 144
Mezhrabpom-Rus'	11, 11n16, 14-15
Mezhrabpomfil'm	14, 16n32, 36, 41
Mickey Mouse	17, 39
Migunov, Evgenii	44-45, 65n104, 65n105, 69, 72-73
Mikhalkov, Sergei	46n70, 62, 64, 68
Mil'chin, Lev	44
Militant Pages	42
mimesis	105, 149
Mimica, Vatroslav	78
Mimin and Pozharskii	42
minimalist style See laconic language	
Miracle-Maker, The	60-61
Mister Twister	73
Mitten, The	170
Moidodyr	16n32
Moiseev, Igor	87
Moor, Dmitrii	7, 11
Morozov, Pavlik	74
Moscow Olympics	58
Mosfil'm, studio	14, 20, 22, 38, 41, 43, 53
Mountain Master, The	172
Mountain of Dinosaurs, The	123
Mozzhukhin, Ivan	6, 6n6
"Muddle Instead of Music"	35
multiplane camera	40, 79
Murzilka	18, 57
Murzilka and the Giant	57
Murzilka on the Sputnik	57
music and animation	23-24, 29-31, 34-35, 41, 47, 53, 61, 70, 72-73, 80, 87-88, 116-118, 121, 134, 137, 139-140, 144, 148, 156, 163, 169, 171-172, 176, 178-180
My Green Crocodile	171

N

Narkompros See People's Commissariat of Enlightenment	
National Film Board of Canada	80
Nauka i zhizn'	123
Neizvestnyi, Ernst	54
Nekrasov, Viktor	53, 121
NEP See New Economic Policy	
Nesterov, Mikhail	45
New Economic Policy (NEP)	9, 12
New Great Troubles	85n
New Gulliver, The	21-22
Nicholas II (tsar)	5, 37
Night Alarm – Bratishkin In the Barrack	20n41
Night Before Christmas, The	6n6
Nine Days in One Year	57
Noisy voyage, A	41
Nolev-Sobolev, Iurii	54, 147, 150, 157, 163
Norshtein, Iurii	84, 171, 176-180
Novyi Mir	53, 121, 144
Nutcracker	171

O

O'Brien, Willis	5
OBERIU	35
Obraztsov, Sergei	43
Offended Letters, The	17
Okna ROSTA See under poster, propaganda	
Okna TASS See under poster, propaganda	
Okudzhava, Bulat	55

Old Horseman, The	49n74	animated (kinoplakaty)	8n10, 12, 42-44, 58, 63-65
Old Mill, The	40	style	1, 12, 23, 36, 44, 73,
Old Precepts	122		81, 106, 172, 176, 178
Olesha, Iurii	52, 175-176	Okna ROSTA	6-7, 36, 43, 63
On the Forest Stage	46n70	Okna TASS	43, 63
On the Material of Political Caricatures	8n10	Prague Spring	165
One Among Many	12, 13	Pravda	9, 35, 54, 121
One Day in the Life of Ivan Denisovich	54	Presniakov, Aleksander	17
One Hundred Adventures	20n41	Princess-Frog, The	48n73
Operation Y and other Adventures of Shurik	85n	Prokofiev, Sergei	53, 171
Opus I/II/III	27	proletariat See workers, images of	
Ostrovskii, Aleksandr	47	propaganda animated films	1, 6-7, 9-11, 18,
Oswald the Lucky Rabbit	17		20-22, 42-44, 57-67, 73
Othello-67	122	anti-Western	12-13, 43, 55, 69, 72-73, 87-89
Ott in Space	57	function and style	1, 7, 10-11, 13-14, 18, 20,
Our Answer to Chamberlain	8n10		50, 55-67, 73, 88-89
Our Caricatures	8n10	See also heroes; posters; religion; societal ills;	
Out of the Inkwell	18	Scientific-Technological Revolution	
Our Sun	66	Protazanov, Iakov	11, 19
Outpost at the Mountain, The	49n74	Proust, Marcel	80
Overseas Reporter	73	Ptushko, Aleksander	19-20, 20n41, 21-22, 62
		Puck! Puck!	58n91
P		Pudovkin, Vsevolod	15, 29, 42
Pacific 231	28, 30-32, 34	puppet animation See stop-motion animation	
parasitism	21, 60, 60n, 64, 66,	Puppets Have the Word, The	73
	68, 87-89, 97, 127	Pushkin, Aleksandr	34-35, 46-47, 115, 147
Parker, Claire	80	Pyrev, Ivan	53, 83
parody	11, 60, 86, 89-99,		
	112, 122, 136-138	**R**	
Pashchenko, Mstislav	44, 46n70, 49n76, 65n105, 72	Rabelais, François	152
Passions of Spies, The	73	Radio Moscow	70
Pasternak, Boris	53, 121, 144	Raduga	23
Pavlov, Sergei	121	Raffaello Sanzio	151
People's Commissariat of Enlightenment		Raikin, Arkadii	69
(Narkompros)	17	Raspe, Rudolf Erich	17
Perestroika	54	Read and Take a Drive to Paris and China	73
Perets	77	Red Army	9, 66
Perugino (Vannucci, Pietro)	151	Red Cavalry	179
Peter I	42	Red Square	178
Petrov, Anatolii	74	Reed, John	177
Petrov, Vladimir	42	religion	
Petrov-Vodkin, Kuz'ma	177	anti-religious propaganda	10, 59, 146
Petrushevskaia, Liudmila	83	religious works	7, 179
Petrushka	20	zhitie	146
Pfenninger, Rudolf	34	Revolution, October	6, 10-12, 15, 66-67, 176-178
Picasso, Pablo	178	Revolutionary works	7, 36, 175-179
Pickford, Mary	12, 17	See also posters, propaganda	
See also The Kiss of Mary Pickford		Rhythmus 21/23	27
Pil'niak, Boris	80	Richter, Hans	26
Pimenov, Vladimir	178	Rimskii-Korsakov, Nikolai	47, 179, 179n222
Pinocchio	19	rock	72, 87
Pioneer	21, 37, 43, 45, 57n	Romm, Mikhail	57, 83, 147
Plan for Great Works, The	32	Room, Abram	32
Pojar, Břetislav	63	Roshal', Grigorii	21, 147
Poland, insurrection	53	Rossiia Theater	166
Politburo	166	rotoscope (ekler)	23, 47-48
Political Revues	7, 8	Rozhdestvenskii, Robert	53
Political Satirical Journal No.1	42	Rumiantsev, Aleksei	121
Political Satirical Journal No.2	42	Ruttmann, Walter	26-27
Polkovnikov, Vladimir	42-43, 45-47, 49n76, 86	**S**	
pop music	69-70, 140, 169	Saltykov-Shchedrin, Mikhail	37, 174
Post, The	23-31, 35, 24-29	Samarkand	44
poster propaganda	6-7, 11, 88n137,	Samodelkin-sportsman	58n91
	111-112, 176, 178	Samoed Boy, The	16-17

Index

satire 2, 6-7, 55, 65-69, 77, 118-119, 122
  artistic world: *See Film, Film, Film*
  political 7-12, 21, 36-37, 42-44, 67, 73, 123
  of foreign influences 12-13, 73-74, 87-89, 111
  social 20-21, 56, 67-69, 73, 84-85, 89-96, 100, 109-112, 132,139
  See bureaucrats; *Great Troubles*; *Man in the Frame*; *There Once Lived Koziavin*
Sazonov, Anatolii 44, 48
Sazonov, Panteleimon 43-45, 46n70
Schnittke, Alfred 163
School of Fine Arts: Landscape with Junipers 147
science 57-60, 123
  See educational films: scientific films; technological achievements
science fiction, genre 11, 56-58
scientific films *See under* educational films
Scientific Research Cinema and Photographic Institute 32
Scientific-Technological Revolution 57-61
Seasons, The 171
"secret speech" 52, 88, 101
Selected Passages from Correspondence with Friends 147
Sen'ka the African 16
Serebriakov, Nikolai 171, 174
serials (or series) 8-10, 17-20, 42, 57, 67-69, 84, 169-170
Serov, Valentin 45
Shakespeare, William 122
Shapokliak 170n207
SHAR (studio) 24
Shareholders 73
Shchedrin, Rodion 121
shelved, banned works 2, 41, 67, 80, 84, 146, 166-167
  See also censorship
Shiryaev, Aleksandr 5n2
Shklovsky, Viktor (Shklovskian) 96, 116
Shoenberg, Arnold 80
Sholpo, Evgenii 32
Shostakovich, Dmitri 34-36, 53-54, 121, 144, 176, 178
  op. 36 34-35
  Symphony no. 13 55
Shpalikov, Gennadii 54, 146, 163
Shumiatskii, Boris 38, 41
Signature Is Illegible, The 65
Silly Symphonies 40
Silver Rain 20
Siniavskii, Andrei 121, 144
Sinitsyn, A. 62
Skating Rink, The 16, *16*, 19
skaz 173
Skriabin, Aleksandr 171
Smirnov, Viktor 38-39, 41
  Smirnovaia studiia 38-39
Smoktunovskii, Innokentii 167
Snesarev, Arkadii 123
Snezhko-Blotskaia, Aleksandra 47, 66
Snow Paths 58n91

Snow Queen, The 47
Snow White and the Seven Dwarfs 40, 46-47
Snow-Maiden 47
Sober Sparrow: A Tale for Adults 64
socialist realism 1, 36, 38, 49, 53, 101-102, 104, 136, 144, 155, 180
societal ills
  propaganda against 1, 55-56, 61-69, 136
  See also alcoholism; parasitism; absenteeism; bureaucrats
Soiuzdetmul'tfil'm, studio 36, 41
Soiuzkino, studio 14, 21, 38
Soiuzmul'tfil'm 3, 22, 41, 43-44, 61-62, 64, 66-68, 75-77, 80, 82, 84-85, 98, 100, 105, 110, 110n163, 118, 123, 133, 163, 166-167, 167n203, 169-170
Sokol'skii, Gennadii 169
Sokolov, Nikolai *See* Kukryniksy
Sokolova, Marina 173
Solovev-Sedoi, Vasilii *See* "Evenings Outside Moscow"
Solzhenitsyn, Aleksandr 53-54
Song Flies Around the World, The 72
Song of Chapaev, The 66
Song of Friendship 65n105, 72
Song of the Falcon, The 171
Songs of the Inflamed Years 172
"Song of the Motherland" 70
Sooster, Ülo Ilmar 54, 147, 150
Sorokhtin, Igor' 17
sound, experiment with 23-24, 29-34, 34n52, 48
Sovetskoe kino 15
Soviet Hollywood 38
Soviet Toys 9, 20
Sovkino, studio 12, 14-16, 16n32, 17, 20
space flight 56-59
Spies' Passions 122
sport 58-59, 126, 140-141
Sportland 58n91, 59
Sputnik 57
Stalin era 42-46, 49, 51-53, 69, 74, 88, 101-102, 104, 123
  animation during 1, 42-50, 55-56, 87, 148, 173-174
  artistic works of de-Stalinization 38, 45, 61, 71, 51-55
Starevich, Vladislav 5-6, 5n1, 5n2, 5n3
Starr, Fredrerick 88
"Statement of Sound", manifesto 29
Steinberg, Saul 79
Stepantsev, Boris 57, 62, 64, 170n207, 171-172
stiliagi 73-74, 87-89, 88n137, 89, 96
Stites, Richard 66, 70
stop-motion (puppet) animation 5-6, 5n2, 16n32, 18-22, 40, 43, 57, 59, 62, 65, 69, 71, 73, 77, 80, 170-171
Stories About Lenin 49n74
Story of a Crime 71, 82-84, 98-119, *103-117*, 124
Suicide, The 48
Summer Travelers 46n70
Suny, Ronald Grigor 101
Suteev, Vladimir 11, 17, 36, 41, 43-44, 167
Suvorov 42

247

Swift, Jonathan	21	Victorious Destination	42
		Victory Over the Sun	175
T		Vietnam war	179
Tale of Tales, The	84, 180	Villain with a Label, The	62-63
Tale of the Boy-Kibal'chish, The	66	Vintik-Shpintik	16n32
Tale of the Dead Princess and the Seven		Virgin Lands Campaign	64, 74
Bogatyrs, The	47	VKhUTEMAS	11
Tale of the Fisherman and the Fish	48n73	"Vladimir Il'ich Lenin"	177-178, 178n215
Tale of the Pope and his Worker Balda, The	34-36,	Voice of America, broadcast	55, 72
	35n, 33-35	Voinov, Nikolai	32-33
Tale of the Straw Bull-Calf	16n32, 20	Vol'pin, Mikhail	48, 110, 111n166, 118, 167
Tale of the Stupid Little Mouse, The	43	Volga-Volga	48, 111n166
Tale of the Tsar Saltan, The	46-47	Voznesenskii, Andrei	53-54
Tale of the White Bull-Calf, The	36	VUFKU, studio	14, 20
Tale of Tsar Durandai, The	36-37, 46	Vukotić, Dušan	78
tales		Vvedenskii, Aleksandr	35
fables	5, 44-46, 46n70, 49, 64		
fairy-tales and fantastic world	1, 45-49,	**W**	
	55-56, 59-60, 66, 87, 169,171	Wagner, Richard	80
folk-tales	45-46, 49, 56, 60	Walnut Switch, A	47
Tarkovskii, Andrei	167, 169	War, animation and	10-12, 42-44,
Tatlin, Vladimir	178		67, 176-180
Tbilisi	44		
Tchaikovsky, Pyotr	171-172	See also Revolution, October;	
technological achievements	28-29,	propaganda; poster	
	31-32, 39, 52, 56, 58-59	Warrant, The	48
Terrible Vengeance, The	6n6	We Are With You, Cuba!	8n10
There Once Lived Koziavin	65, 123-124,	We'll Be Vigilant	8n10
	139-148, 141-146	Webern, Anton	80
Three Fat Men, The	175, 176-177	Well-Known Pictures	65n104, 69, 73
Three Girlfriends	43	What the 13th Party Congress Said	
Through Fire, Water and ... Brass Pipes	49n74	About Cooperatives	10
Thurber, James	79	When Goebbels Does Not Lie	43
Tip-Top	17n34, 18	When the Fir-Trees Light Up	49n76
Titov, German	58	Who Dreams of What	10
Tiurin, Arkadii	173, 176, 178	widescreen	57
To the Sixth Worldwide	65n105, 72	Wild Swans	175, 175
Today	8	Window, The	171
Toptyzhka	84, 172-173	Winnie the Pooh	84, 170, 170n207
Trauberg, Leonid	49n74	Winnie the Pooh and the Day of Worries	170n207
Trauberg, Vera	167	Winnie the Pooh Goes on a Visit	170n207
Tret'ia Fabrika Sovkino	16, 20	workers, images of	36, 62, 69, 74, 89,
Trnka, Jiří	63, 80, 134, 133-134		110, 127, 128-129, 141, 180
Tsekhanovskii, Mikhail	22-36, 39,	World War I	9-10, 14-15
	43-45, 48, 66, 174	World War II	22, 29, 42-44, 49, 52, 67, 78, 111
Tsvetaeva, Marina	144	Wynne-Penkovsky spy trial	55
Tvardovskii, Aleksandr	144		
Tvardovskii, Vladislav	16n32, 17, 20n41	**Y**	
Twelve Months	47	Yellow Stork, The	47
Twentieth Party Congress	52, 58, 88, 101	Your Health	58n91, 64
Twenty-First Party Congress	101n146	Youth Festival of 1957, Moscow	65, 72
Twenty-Second Party Congress	52, 54, 56n		
		Z	
U		Zagreb school (Yugoslavia)	78-79, 105, 105n156
UPA (United Production of America)	78-80, 105	Zai i Chik	46n70
		Zamiatin, Evgenii	80
V		Zeman, Karel	80
Vail' and Genis	58, 58n90, 59, 66, 170	Zhdanov, Andrei Aleksandrovich	52-53
Val'kov, Mikhail	164-166	Zhdanovshchina (Zhdanovism)	52
variety theatre (estrada)	69-70	Zheliabuzhskii, Iurii	19-20
VDNKh	57	Zhizn' iskusstva	29
Vertov, Dziga	8-10, 20, 59	Zoshchenko, Mikhail	52
VGIK (All-Union State Institute of			
Cinematography)	44, 79, 139, 146-147, 167n203		

www.ingramcontent.com/pod-product-compliance
Lightning Source LLC
Chambersburg PA
CBHW041437300426
44114CB00025B/2910